Andy:

from Dad
with love-
Xmas 1979

MATCH POINT

MATCH POINT

**A Candid View of Life
on the International
Tennis Circuit**

**Marty Riessen
and
Richard Evans**

PRENTICE-HALL, INC., *Englewood Cliffs, New Jersey*

Match Point: A Candid View of Life on the International Tennis Circuit
by Marty Riessen and Richard Evans
Copyright © 1973 by Marty Riessen and Richard Evans
All rights reserved. No part of this book may be
reproduced in any form or by any means, except
for the inclusion of brief quotations in a review,
without permission in writing from the publisher.
Printed in the United States of America
10 9 8 7 6 5 4 3 2
Prentice-Hall International, Inc., London
Prentice-Hall of Australia, Pty. Ltd., North Sydney
Prentice-Hall of Canada, Ltd., Toronto
Prentice-Hall of India Private Ltd., New Delhi
Prentice-Hall of Japan, Inc., Tokyo

Library of Congress Cataloging in Publication Data

Riessen, Marty, date
  Match point.

   1. Riessen, Marty, date   2. Tennis—History.
I. Evans, Richard, date   joint author.   II. Title.
GV994.R53A35   796.34′2′0924 [B]   73–1173
ISBN 0–13–560128–2

To my Parents
  who set me on the road

To my Wife
  who steadies me along the way

To my Opponents
  who make it such a challenging
  and enjoyable journey

CONTENTS

INTRODUCTION

It was Donald Dell's idea. Sometime, somewhere during the summer of 1971 Donald let the thought drop into one of our frequent conversations about whichever current crisis was afflicting tennis.

"Why don't you write a book with Marty Riessen?" he asked. "Marty's got an interesting story to tell, but the book could go beyond that and give an inside view of what life is like on the pro circuit. Think about it."

Then, in his usual whirlwind fashion, Dell—the former U.S. Davis Cup captain who now handles the business interests of more than a dozen of the world's top players from his Washington law office— rushed off to meet one of his clients or business associates.

I did not have to think about it very long. I had known Marty for almost ten years and was, of course, familiar with his career. I felt that few players were better equipped to trace the game's growing pains over the past decade: the struggle to establish itself as a major professional sport through the sixties and the final emergence—battle-scarred but triumphant—as the fastest-growing sport of the seventies.

From the moment he first started playing top-class tennis as a teen-ager in 1958, Riessen's own personal battle to realize his full potential as a leading player had met with the same problems, setbacks, and eventual fulfillment as the game itself. The fortunes of the player and his sport were intertwined, and by 1971 they had come to view each other with mutual respect.

Before Forest Hills came round that year, I told Donald that I was ready to go ahead; he, in turn, spoke to Marty, who was equally enthusiastic. So by the time the three of us met one afternoon underneath the television stand on the Stadium Court there was little left to discuss. It was agreed that I should go wherever Marty went for the remainder of the year. We could work on the early part of the book while at the same time keeping detailed notes on what promised to be a typical segment of the World Championship Tennis tour; it was to begin in Berkeley, California, and wind its way through Europe before returning to Texas for the $100,000 play-off finals.

A tour of Africa followed, and by Christmas we had logged some 25,000 miles and three Atlantic crossings in three months. It provided an excellent exercise in how to write a book on the run.

Armed with typewriter and tape recorder, I met with Marty at odd hours in odd places as we continued to update the book over the next twelve months. We might be found in locker room corners in Berkeley and Bologna; in hotel rooms in Stockholm and Barcelona; sprawled by the pool at the Hotel Ivoire in Abidjan and Caesar's Palace in Las Vegas; talking over the chatter and clatter of the Blue Line Club at the Spectrum in Philadelphia; and against the shrill buzz of crickets on a hot African night at Yaounde in the Cameroons.

These sessions were not always easy to arrange. Marty's first job was, of course, to win tennis matches and this is a more time-consuming pastime than many people realize. Our meetings had to be fitted in among practice sessions, clinics, and actual matches; checking out of hotels and getting to airports; visits to doctors to treat the various aches and pains that are all part of an athlete's life; and talks with agents, businessmen, and journalists, all of whom make demands on a player's time.

In addition I had my own regular working schedule which necessitated filing stories at various times for the London *Evening News, World Tennis* magazine, ABC radio's "World of Sports" in New York, and CBC radio's "Sound of Sports" in Toronto, among several other magazines and radio stations that I work for on a free-lance basis.

Had Marty been anything less than wholly cooperative, the job might have been difficult. But apart from being a genuinely fine person with a great sense of humor, Marty has a professional attitude which is the hallmark of his game and which does not end when he walks off court. He takes pride in living up to his numerous commitments whether they entail catching a plane before dawn to make a personal appearance halfway across the United States or merely pausing for a few seconds to sign an autograph.

A strong sense of integrity forms a fundamental part of his character, and while he is almost totally without jealousy—he begrudges no one success even if it is earned at his own expense—he reacts to cheap tactics and hypocrisy, both on and off court, not so much with anger as with a puritanical indignation that springs from his upbringing.

No book is a one- or two-man operation. Many people helped get this story into print, and on Marty's behalf, I would like to thank Donald Dell's law partner, Frank Craighill, who went out and sold the idea to our publishers; Nick D'Incecco and his assistant Dick Petrella, our editors at Prentice-Hall, for their patience and many helpful suggestions; and Sally Riessen, who acted as a most diligent researcher and memory bank as we threaded our way back through Marty's early career.

Since I took up photography in a somewhat haphazard fashion a couple of years ago, two of the great pros in the art of taking tennis pictures, Russ Adams of Boston and Arthur Cole of the British magazine *Tennis World,* have tolerated a novice in their midst with more patience and kindness than I had a right to expect. I thank them both for their contributions here as well. I am also grateful to Arthur Ashe, Tom Okker, and Frank Froehling who provided pictorial evidence of their ability to handle a camera as well as a racket.

Also I would like to offer a word of thanks to Arthur Ashe for the use of his apartment—an exotic pad on the upper East Side of Manhattan—to which I retired at frequent intervals while the WCT tour moved around the United States in the early months of 1972 to convert tapes and notes into something that hopefully resembles a book.

A word of explanation would be helpful, perhaps, for those readers who are not wholly familiar with the murky and confusing world of tennis politics. The initials ILTF, LTA, and WCT occur frequently in the book, and although I sometimes wonder if they know themselves, I will try to explain what they stand for.

The International Lawn Tennis Federation (ILTF) is the world governing body of the amateur game which has its headquarters at Baron's Court near the famous Queen's Club in London. It has one full-time, paid professional secretary; the rest of the officers are part-time officials, including the president, who currently is a Danish, London-based lawyer named Allan Heyman.

Affiliated with the ILTF are the numerous national Lawn Tennis Associations (LTA) such as the U.S. LTA, the British LTA, the

Swedish LTA. These Associations meet under the banner of the ILTF once a year—one week after Wimbledon—and, in fact, selected officials from the national LTAs furnish the ILTF with its personnel.

World Championship Tennis (WCT) is the pro group formed by Dave Dixon in 1967 and quickly bought out by Texas oil millionaire Lamar Hunt. After a shaky start, it grew to the point where, at the start of 1971, it had 32 of the leading players in the world under exclusive contract and its own schedule of twenty $50,000 tournaments. Fear, resentment, misunderstanding, and personal antagonism created what became known as the "tennis war" midway through 1971, and by January of the following year WCT and its players had been banned from competing in any ILTF-affiliated event—which included Wimbledon, Forest Hills, the French Championships, and any other traditional tournament.

A bemused public later heard that a peace agreement had been worked out at a meeting between Hunt and Heyman in April 1972 and three months later it was ratified by the ILTF in their own sweet time when the Federation met in Helsinki. The ILTF and WCT are now learning to live together and peace reigns. Long may it last.

Long before the game had entered this phase of sophisticated politicking, Martin Clare Riessen, a nice guy from suburban Illinois, had learned to live with the demands and pressures of the expanding international circuit. He had taught himself to be less nice when the chips were down and when pride, prestige, and prize money were on the line.

Echoing what so many leading players have told me, Riessen explains, "It's a question of getting tougher on the big points. There is so little difference in technical ability between the top ten or twenty players in the world now that a single point won or lost at a crucial moment can decide the match. Break point down on your serve at 2-all in the second set may not seem too vital, but in fact it can be as important as match point because you may never get that service break back again if you lose it. Really, all those points are like match points, and in tennis, winning match point is what it is all about."

Marty has learned to handle the crisis of match point, and his record of steady improvement over the past few years proves it. In 1971 he was ranked in the world's top ten by both *World Tennis* magazine and that much respected assessor of world form, Lance Tingay of the London *Daily Telegraph*. He finished seventh in the WCT points standings for 1971; fifth—higher than any other American on the tour—at the end of the 1971–72 segment of the tour; and fifth again during the final six months of 1972 when another twelve-tournament tour was completed.

This kind of consistency on a tour that requires one to meet and beat the likes of Laver, Rosewall, Ashe, Newcombe, Okker, Drysdale, and Emerson week after week has earned Marty the respect of his colleagues and admiration of his fans. Having worked with him so closely for so long, I know that both sentiments have been justly earned.

                                                                R.I.E.
                                                                Paris

MATCH POINT

PART ONE

PART
ONE

1

"SHAMATEURISM"

"Would you come this way, please?"

He was speaking in Portuguese, but even without the beckoning nod from Edison "Bananas" Mandarino, we would have gotten the message. Obediently, we followed him, threading our way through little groups of elegantly attired club members. Long, manicured fingernails were curled around cocktail glasses; long, supple palms swayed gently overhead as the evening's first cooling breeze came up off the ocean. A vast Olympic-size swimming pool shimmered darkly in the dusk until someone, somewhere, threw a switch, piercing the blue water with yellow shafts of light.

Like many similar establishments in Brazil, the Nautico Tennis Club at Fortaleza was heavy with opulence. It was Palm Beach with a Latin beat. Inside the clubhouse the club president led us on up a broad, winding staircase, perspiring slightly under his Panama hat. We were taken, not to an office as we had expected, but into an adjoining salon that obviously served as a card room. With a wave of his cigar the president motioned us to be seated at a green baize-topped table; he lowered his bulky frame into a chair and glanced briefly at the expectant faces around him: Tom Okker, my close friend and doubles partner from Haarlem in Holland; Edison Mandarino and Tom Koch, the two stars of the Brazilian Davis Cup team; and myself, the son of a tennis teacher from the quiet Chicago suburb of Evanston, Illinois. "Amateurs" all. Then, delving into his pocket with stubby fingers,

3

he drew out a fat wad of those enormous Brazilian notes and began to deal.

It was payoff time.

With less ceremony, perhaps, similar scenes were being enacted in tennis clubs all over the world in those absurd, chaotic days of 1967. The following year the All-England Club used its power and prestige to bring an end to shamateurism by opening up Wimbledon to the contract pros—thereby forcing everyone to recognize the reality of Open tennis. But in October 1967 those of us who were attempting to make a living out of the game were still obliged to wheel and deal our way around the globe, airing our talents in the sunshine and accepting our rewards in some dark, secret place. A muttered conversation in a corner of a clubhouse; a price mentioned; a deal made and then sealed with nothing more than a promise to turn up in two or three weeks, racket in hand, at a club somewhere on the other side of the world. And then, win or lose, the public applause and the private, note-filled handshake before dashing for another plane for yet another place. It was a chaotic way to do business—a crazy way to earn a living.

We were forced into doing some crazy things, too, like carrying around huge sums of money. There was no alternative because, of necessity, everyone was paid in hard cash. How do you explain away a check for $3,000 made out to an "amateur" tennis player? Mandarino for instance, had as much as $14,000 in his bag at one stage; on another occasion Ray Ruffels, the Australian Davis Cup player, arrived in Tehran with $4,000 and lost the lot to a thief. Ray made such a fuss that the Shah of Iran eventually heard of it and made him a present of $2,000 as compensation. Lucky for Ray that the Shah was a fervent tennis fan.

Not long after the Brazilian tour I won a tournament in Caracas and collected my $400 in five and ten dollar bills. By the time I had come to be paid, all the larger bills had been used up. Determined not to part company with my loot, I stuffed the bills into my shoes and trod my way daintily through Caracas Airport, feeling like some lucky Western gambler in high-heeled boots making his getaway from Dodge City.

It was hard work being a "shamateur"—lugging all that booty around. Television sets and recorders were additional prizes from the sponsors, Philips, when I won a round robin tournament at Tennispark Buitenveldert near Amsterdam in 1968. Tom Koch (center), Edison Mandarino (left), Tom Okker (not pictured), and I were all guaranteed $600 for three days' play. As the winner—Koch came second—I got the smallest TV set but, I was hastily assured, the most expensive one. *Credit: Sally Riessen*

But in that upstairs room at the Nautico Tennis Club in Fortaleza it quickly became apparent that Tom Okker and I were not on the winning end of this particular deal. A few days before in Rio we had arranged to play a week of exhibition matches with Mandarino and Koch in various cities for $700 each or $100 a night. In those days it seemed like a good price and we never thought to inquire what our Brazilian colleagues were getting. We just assumed they were getting the same. We assumed wrong. That much became evident as the club president began the payout. The pile of notes in front of the Brazilians was growing twice as fast as our own. I glanced up and Mandarino's wicked, toothy grin confirmed my worst suspicions. We never did find out exactly what he and Koch got for that tour but I suspect it was very nearly double the sum we had accepted in all our trusting innocence.

But in fact I was not overly worried about the money side of it. For those days, our cut was fair enough and if the Brazilians were getting more, good luck to them. It was their country. More than the financial angle, it was the type of tour we were on that really disturbed me. It necessitated a life-style I had no wish to pursue. One-night stands; exhibition matches; long, exhausting hours of travel, often by car as well as plane—it frayed one's mental and physical condition and consequently did nothing to improve one's game.

This was the way Rosewall, Gonzales, and Laver had kept the pro game alive during those desperate days in the early sixties. I think they won the respect and admiration of all of us who had followed a similar course on a few brief occasions. It was a way of life that required dedication, a tough constitution, and a strong faith in one's own ability to pull through. I was not entirely lacking in some of those qualities, but even so I vowed never to turn pro until the professional game was at least heading in the direction of a standardized program of proper tournaments.

That did not mean, however, that I was content with my lot in the amateur ranks. Far from it. In the previous couple of years my whole personality and attitude had gone through some pretty radical changes—mostly as a result of the disillusionment that had set in over my continued lack of recognition in the Davis Cup and my general distaste for the way in which the amateur game was run. Yes, I had changed, all right. Marty Riessen, the good guy—the amenable Joe who was always the model sportsman on court and the perfect gentleman off—had tarnished his image and he had done so with a certain amount of cold deliberation. I had been the happy water boy of the Davis Cup team long enough and it was time, I felt, to assert myself. No longer was I going to stand shyly in the shadows. I had come to the conclusion that there was some truth to the old saying that nice guys finish last.

I had been on the Davis Cup squad seven straight years and yet a succession of captains had entrusted me with the singles berth on only two occasions and a doubles place just five times. It was not until 1967 that I finally became a regular first-choice doubles player, and by then everyone else had been tried. Most of them had lost, too, for the middle sixties was a bleak period for the United States in the Davis Cup, with defeats in successive years at the hands of Spain, Brazil, and Ecuador. I was an active member of the team by the time we lost to Ecuador because, hell, I could lose too. Until then, though, no one had even thought it worthwhile to give me the opportunity.

So I'd had enough of handing out the towels and going through the sad little "Bad luck, Dennis," "Bad luck, Cliff" routine whenever another of my colleagues trudged, weary and defeated, off some glutinous clay court in some foreign land. It was not that I considered myself a better player than Arthur Ashe, Dennis Ralston, Clark Graebner, Cliff Richey, or Frank Froehling. It was simply that my record and experience entitled me to a chance once in a while and nobody had shown enough confidence in my ability to give me one.

So I started to pay less attention to some of the finer virtues my parents had instilled in me and began thinking less of "the team" and more of Number One—me, Martin Clare Riessen, tennis player. Tennis is an individualistic sport anyway, and if you don't look after yourself, you're dead. Once this lesson sank home, I concentrated more on becoming a tougher, meaner tour-

nament player. If I couldn't end up Number One in the world
then at least I was going to bust myself trying. I had come to
realize that if you don't aim for the stars, you never get off the
ground. And if that meant shedding my angel's wings and shaking
the heavens a little in the process, so be it.

Whether that exhausting week in Brazil was helping me
achieve my aims was another matter. However, we soldiered on,
leaving Fortaleza for Bahia and then going up to Recife before
heading back south again to Bauru. All were large, sprawling
towns where the majority lived in squalor and the minority in
luxurious opulence—standard for South America. To get to
Bauru we had to fly to São Paulo where a local tennis official
picked us up and drove us for five hours to the Bauru Tennis
Club. After the matches it was back to the car for the five hour
return journey to São Paulo Airport. Tom was going on down to
Rio to pick up a connection to Amsterdam so I had no alternative but to wait for my Pan Am flight to Chicago which was due
in at 9:00 A.M. It was sometime around four in the morning
when they deposited me at the airport. There was not a soul in
sight. It was raining lightly and through the drizzle I could dimly
make out the silhouettes of two cargo planes on the tarmac. The
large empty arrival hall echoed with my footsteps as I searched
for a place to rest.

Easy chairs were not very much in evidence at São Paulo Airport at the time, and all I could find was a long wooden bench.
I lay down on it, listening to the quiet murmur of the rain amid
all that emptiness and thinking of my career, of where it was
leading me and of all the strange situations it landed me in. But
soon dreams overcame conscious thoughts, for after a week
charging around Brazil, sleeping on a wooden bench is no hard-
ship at all.

2

SHORT-TERM MANAGER

I suppose the change in attitude I spoke of first revealed itself, ironically enough, shortly after I had been given a rare reward for what I could laughingly describe as my long and selfless service to the cause of American tennis. I had been appointed manager of the team that was to play throughout the South Pacific and New Zealand in preparation for the Australian circuit in the winter of 1965–66. It was not an appointment that lasted long. By the end of the Australian tour I was dishonorably discharged, having somewhat shattered my image by calling Bill Bowrey a cheat in the middle of our match at Sidney's famous White City Stadium. That wasn't the old Riessen. Not good old Marty at all. When I compounded the crime by refusing to apologize, my spell as team manager ended in a suitably climactic row. Thus it ended roughly as it had begun, for things had started to go wrong from the moment we landed at Auckland from Fiji at 5:00 A.M. one Sunday morning several weeks before.

The only contact I had been given was John Gunn, a New Zealand LTA official whom I knew from his frequent visits to Wimbledon. So I phoned him. With enormous alacrity for a man who had obviously been roused from a deep sleep, he drove straight out to the airport to pick us up. He seemed very insistent that we make an early start on a sight-seeing trip he had organized for us to Maori country at Rotarua, where there are sulphur springs, mineral baths, caves with bugs that light up and all manner of things that you don't get to see in Evanston.

9

Arthur Ashe, Clark Graebner and his wife Carole, Herbie Fitzgibbon, and Jim McManus—the other guys on the team—all
thought it was a great idea, and I—big team manager—couldn't
see any objection either. But my wife Sally could. For a start
she was tired, which was reasonable, and also she wanted to go
to church which, it being Sunday, was also reasonable. However,
she was eventually talked into making the trip when John Gunn
promised to take her to church in Rotarua.

But that end of the deal never transpired and it was not long
after we arrived there that Sally began to feel ill and started to
cry. Sulphur springs and mineral baths obviously weren't going
to help, so I insisted that we start off on the three-hour homeward
journey immediately while the others went on to see the bugs
light up in the caves. That proved to be a near fatal decision, for
halfway back to Auckland we burst a tire, swerved across the
road, and missed an oncoming car by the width of a baseline.
It was getting to be one of those days.

As it turned out, however, our troubles were just beginning.
When we woke next morning after a long refreshing sleep we
were hit between the eyes by newspaper headlines which demanded, "Where is the missing American Davis Cup team?"
Missing? We didn't think we were missing. As far as I knew, my
team was all present. I could even hear McManus snoring down
the passageway. Everything had to be all right. But on reading
the article I discovered that we had been scheduled to appear
the previous day at a televised press conference, organized by
the New Zealand Lawn Tennis Association in order to publicize
our arrival. This was a fact that John Gunn had somehow omit-
ted to mention. Later we found out why. Gunn, unknown to us,
was involved in a feud with his LTA colleagues and had whisked
us off to Rotarua in a highly successful attempt to sabotage the
press conference. We had, in fact, been used as pawns in an in-
ternal battle between warring factions of the New Zealand LTA.

I had no way of knowing any of this because Gunn was the
only name given me by U.S. Davis Cup captain George MacCall
before our departure, and as far as I knew Gunn *was* the New
Zealand LTA. Consequently it was difficult to see how I could

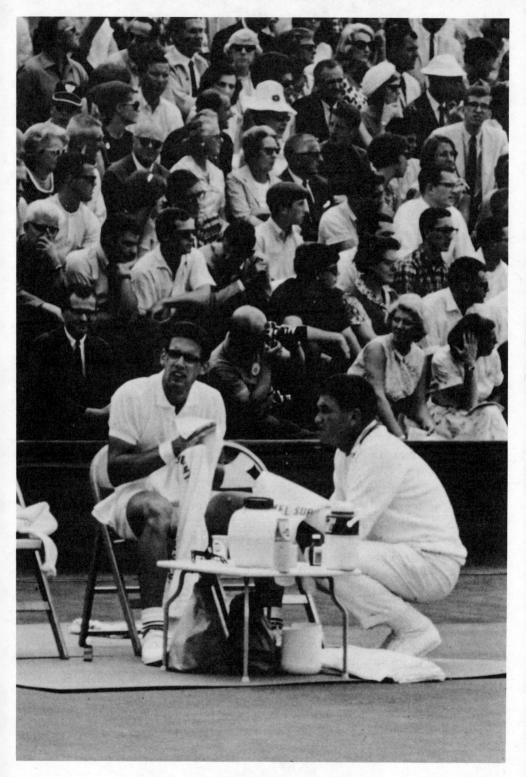

Clark Graebner and captain George MacCall discuss strategy during a Davis Cup tie in Cleveland. *Credit: Marty Riessen*

have avoided being sucked into the surprisingly nasty world of
tennis politics. But it was a lesson learned and I resolved to take
greater care in the future before accepting any invitations to visit
luminous bugs. Sally's instinct was right. We should have gone to
church.

So it was hardly an auspicious start to my career as a touring
team manager and things didn't get any better when we trouped
down to Wellington and lost most of our matches to New Zealand players who were not supposed to be in our league. It was
with a certain feeling of relief that we flew off to Australia.

The arrival of George MacCall obviously lessened my respon-
sibilities and apart from one incident in Tasmania when I left
the Hobart tournament a day early to fly back to Sydney—thus
earning myself a suitable rebuke from George—I had no more
problems until the Bowrey incident.

Had I been a little more careful with my choice of words, it
might have been a very small incident indeed. But uttering the
word "cheat" was as good as handing the sensation-hungry Australian press a headline on a plate—especially as Clark Graebner
had served them up a very appetizing hors d'oeuvres a couple
of days before by using all kinds of unprintable language during
his match against the Australian Alan Lane. So by the time I
played Bill Bowrey in the round of sixteen in the Australian
Championships at the White City, the Sydney papers were ready
to tear at the main course like a pack of wolves. Foul-mouthed
American tennis players were the diet and they made a meal of it.

The incident occurred midway through the second set of our
match when I banged a first serve straight down the center line.
Bowrey moved to reach it, realized he was beaten, and instead
of acknowledging the ace, pretended it was out by moving back
in anticipation of receiving the second ball. There are very few
ways one can actually cheat on a tennis court, but there are many
sly actions and gestures by which one can influence the linesman's
thinking in your favor. This was one of them. Maybe I was wrong
—maybe Bill really did think the ball was fractionally out. But
I had seen him pull the same stunt against Ken Fletcher a couple
of weeks before and Ken had become so furious that he even-

tually lost the match—just as I was to do now. This was one factor that triggered my untypical reaction. The other stemmed from the frustration of having my game hampered by a nagging muscle injury which was beginning to fray my temper as well as my form. So for the first time in my career I really blew my cool on a tennis court and, in a clearly audible voice, called out, "You're cheating on those, Bill."

The reaction was instantaneous. The crowd started to whistle; Bowrey looked startled and George MacCall who, by some strange twist of fate, was on court calling a line—although not the one in question—was up off his chair, shouting at me to pack it in and get on with the game.

The game continued all right but I lost it, and when match point arrived and went in Bowrey's favor only the play was terminated—not the arguments. Predictably, the press smeared the word "cheat" all over the papers the next day despite the fact that Bowrey, to give him his due, had been very restrained in his comments afterwards. "Tex," as he is known to us all on the circuit, is basically a very pleasant and popular guy who has no reputation whatsoever for dubious tactics and I am glad to say the incident has not impaired our friendly relationship.

He simply told the press that I had obviously said it in the heat of the moment and that I probably didn't mean it. But the fact was that I did mean it, purely because I was convinced I was right. It was for this reason that I refused to apologize when George MacCall asked me to. For the first time in my life I was going to stand my ground and stick up for myself in the face of authority. A new me emerged from that otherwise trivial flare-up and, on reflection, I think it was probably a turning point. Maybe it wasn't the best moment to make an issue out of something, but I had had six years of being gently and politely pushed around by officials who thought they could get me to sit up and beg at the flick of their fingers and I just wasn't going to take it any more.

Two days later MacCall was still trying to get me to apologize publicly when he waylaid me underneath the White City grandstand. But the more he insisted, the more adamant I became and pretty soon the conversation turned into a flaming row, with our raised voices carrying like a jet stream straight up the adjacent staircase to where the reporters were seated in the press box. Their well-tuned ears obviously caught every word. Afterward George went up and somehow talked them into ignoring this spicy feud between the U.S. Davis Cup captain and his team manager. It was a diplomatic coup of considerable proportions. He must have been very persuasive, knowing the Australian press. But then MacCall has never lacked charm, nor, indeed, many other fine human qualities, and even through my anger and obstinacy I could appreciate his position. But there was nothing he could do to make me change my mind. Even dark hints that I would be sent home did not deter me. Although I was anxious to go on the State Department tour of Southeast Asia that was to form the next portion of our around-the-world tour, I was almost beyond caring at that point. Somewhere along the line I had changed and, as the U.S. LTA was to find out to its dismay in the coming months and years, this was only the beginning.

3

UNSCHEDULED VACATION

A tiring but unforgettable month in Southeast Asia followed before my next brush with authority. George MacCall returned to the United States as scheduled; the Bowrey affair was finally forgotten, and with Jim McManus—the quiet, conscientious Californian from Berkeley—replacing me as team manager, we set off to investigate the mysteries of the Orient—courtesy of the State Department.

The trip was described as a goodwill tour and I think we created enough of it to justify the title. We took an entertaining brand of tennis to Manila, Singapore, Kuala Lumpur, Ipoh, Penang, Vientiane, Bangkok, Rangoon, and Mandalay—places that rarely have the chance to see top-class players in action. But the real beneficiaries were probably ourselves, for we gathered a host of memories and learned more of that fascinating subcontinent than we could ever have done from a college course in Oriental history. We met Prince Souvanna Phouma, Prime Minister of Laos and an ardent tennis fan, when he came to watch the exhibition we played in the dusty, spy-ridden little capital of Vientiane on the banks of the Mekong River; afterward we had string tied around our wrists in the traditional Laotian friendship ceremony, and Sally overcame the fears of the wary Laotian children to the extent that one of them would not leave our side for the rest of the afternoon and eventually had to be carried back to her parents. We gazed at Buddhist temples and shrines, mostly on foot, and once, in Burma, from an eight-seater aircraft which

15

Sally with her new friend at a village outside Vientiane, Laos, during our tour of Southeast Asia in 1966. *Credit: Marty Riessen*

Hot but happy—that was the way I felt after I beat Prem Lall in four sets in Bombay in 1963. As we had already clinched a winning lead over India in this Davis Cup Interzone final, I was allowed to play my first Davis Cup singles for the United States in the fifth rubber. *Credit: Frank Froehling*

was flown down a valley, alternately and precariously, by Herb Fitzgibbon, Clark Graebner, and myself as we clambered in and out of the co-pilot's seat with Sally sitting petrified in the back.

Of all the places we visited, Burma was the most inaccessible and therefore, in many ways, the most interesting. We were allowed in that very private nation only because a Soviet soccer team had been there a few weeks before us, and even in its sporting relations with the outside world, Burma's nonaligned government was anxious to balance East and West.

After a few days in New Delhi, it was time to join the circuit again in Egypt. I seem to remember that it was during the Nations Cup in Cairo that I first met Ilie Nastase and Ion Tiriac, that celebrated Rumanian pair who were later to make such an impact on the game.

A week in Alexandria was cold but personally rewarding, for I won the tournament, beating an apparition called Torben Ulrich, who came on court for the final in seven sweaters and an army jacket with the hood pulled up to protect him from the March winds. Contrary to the image presented by all those World War Two desert movies, there are moments of the year when *Ice Cold in Alex* does not necessarily refer to the beer.

But as I was to discover when we returned to Cairo for two days of exhibitions, there were still colder winds blowing in my direction from across the Atlantic in the form of a cable Jim McManus received from MacCall. It contained two thoroughly unwelcome items of news. The first concerned us all, for it stated that anyone who was not happy with the $20 a day allowance we were getting from the U.S. LTA and who therefore wished to make their own financial deals with tournaments, could count themselves out of the Davis Cup squad for the rest of the year.

The second item affected me more directly, for it revealed MacCall's decision to have Dennis Ralston play with Graebner in the forthcoming Italian Championships in Rome and to continue the partnership for the remainder of the European tour. It was a nasty jolt to my hopes and my pride. Clark and I had played together for six years at college and tournament level with no little success but never had we been allowed to test that partnership in competition for the United States. In all my years on the squad I had been given the doubles berth only twice, once with Ralston against Venezuela in 1963 and once with Chuck McKinley against Canada in 1965. Just seven months prior to receiving this cable—in the autumn of 1965—the Graebner-Ralston partnership had been tried during the debacle in Barcelona and they had lost to Manuel Santana and Luis Arilla. It was logical to assume that Clark and I, the most experienced *pair* MacCall had at his disposal, would now be given the opportunity to show what we could do. But once again it seemed that I was being passed over. Once again the man in charge was indicating that he had no confidence in my ability. When McManus handed me the cable in our Cairo hotel, my immediate reaction was one of anger and acute disappointment. We were due to leave for Uganda two days later to play some more exhibitions, but on the spur of the moment I said to McManus, "I'm not going to Uganda, Jim. My arm hurts."

As a matter of fact my arm had been giving me some trouble but Jim knew damn well that it was my pride and patience that had been rubbed sore to the point of rebellion. Just as in Sydney two months before, I was past caring what the U.S. LTA did to me in retaliation. My attitude was not the result of quick temper and petulance. It was from the accumulation of six years' well-stoked but previously well-controlled resentment that had, I suppose, reached bursting point a year before when the United States played Mexico in Dallas.

That was the year—1965—that McKinley and I were the doubles pair for the previous round against Canada. We had won easily enough and although McKinley was not available for Dallas, I had every reason to suppose that I would make up half the doubles team again. Silly me. Plucked from yesteryear, riding back through the mists of time like some half-forgotten but ever-loved Western hero came Ham Richardson. To my amazement Richardson and Ralston were selected for the doubles and to my lesser surprise they were thrashed in straight sets by Rafe Osuna and Antonio Palafox—thus suffering America's only reverse in our 4-1 defeat of Mexico that year.

In April 1966, Jim McManus and I won the doubles at Catania, Italy. Jim, who was player-manager of the American team on that tour, recently was made secretary of the newly formed Association of Tennis Professionals. *Credit: Sally Riessen*

There was no doubt that Ham had been one of America's greatest ever David Cup competitors in his time. His incredible 17-0 record in Davis Cup singles rubbers was testimony to that. But he had not played Davis Cup since 1958 and seven years is a long time out of the firing line for a man who had not been a regular member of the International circuit for most of that period. Why, then, was he chosen? Could it have had anything to do with the fact that Ham not only was a Dallas boy and a great crowd-pulling local favorite but was also in charge of the organization for the Davis Cup matches? Would it be too terribly cynical to suggest that this had something to do with his selection? I think not. I have no doubt that MacCall was under all sorts of pressure from U.S. LTA bosses to play Ham ("It would be really appreciated by the local community, George, and you know how much we need a good second-day crowd"—I'm sure MacCall had to suffer all that and more) but for me the net result was that I got to carry the water again.

I started to have terrible visions of this going on forever, with me applauding like an imbecile from the sidelines as they wheeled on Billy Talbert and Gar Mulloy for the 1975 Challenge Round against Australia. But still I kept my disappointment to myself and played the good team man. My reward was to be told that I had been dropped from the team that was to play Spain in the Interzone final in Barcelona but that, as I was such a good fellow, I could travel with the squad as a nonplaying reserve and practice partner. Looking back, I can't think why I accepted except that I suppose I wanted to see Spain and keep close to the scene of action in case everyone got food poisoning or something. (In fact that was pretty unlikely because the U.S. team mortally offended their Spanish hosts by taking their own specially prepared food with them.) But as it turned out, that was about the last time I was to mutter, "Yes, sir; no, sir; anything you say, sir."

It wasn't simply a question of Ralston's being chosen to play with Graebner for the European tour the next year that caused my explosive reaction to MacCall's cable in Cairo, either. We were all hacked off by George's refusal to let us make our own financial deals with tournaments. In 1966, European players were just beginning to command healthy sums of money for tournament and exhibition matches. But the U.S. LTA, in a not wholly unworthy attempt to keep their players free of the taint of shamateurism, had put the Davis Cup team on an "expenses only" basis. In some respects it was not a bad deal because we were paid $28 a day in the United States when we were actually playing, $20 a day in the States when we were not playing, and $20 a day abroad. The best part was being able to return to school—as I did that winter—and still receive $140 a week. The worst part was trying to exist on twenty bucks a day while traveling around the world with one's wife. This money was supposed to cover everything—meals, hotel bills, and incidental expenses— all but the air fares. I know Europe used to be done on $5 a day but not by athletes competing against the best in their field. If you spend an average of five hours each day on court playing the kind of tennis we play, two things become imperative if you are to survive or at least win any matches—good food and good sleep, and plenty of both. That means at least one big steak every day and, in hot climates, a room that is air-conditioned. Getting that for two people on $20 a day—even in 1966—was not easy. Sure it was possible but it didn't leave much change in your pocket.

So it was pretty galling to see average European and South American players being offered $300 or $400 a week by tournaments and then collect another $100 for an exhibition in a nearby town if they lost in an early round. Consequently we had written to MacCall asking permission to make our own financial arrangements while we were abroad, knowing—just as he knew—that we could double or triple our income and save the U.S. LTA some money in the bargain. But now he had cabled us saying, in effect, that we could not have our cake and eat it—that we had to either accept the U.S. LTA's terms and instructions or get off the team.

Okay, I thought, if that's the way they want it, they can have me long-term but they can do without me short-term. My sore arm was the perfect excuse and I intended to make the most of it. "I'm sorry," I told a protesting McManus, "but my arm really does hurt and I'm taking a week off. I'll take Sally to Athens for a vacation and meet you all in Monte Carlo."

And that's what I did. We had a great time, Sally and I. We were broke but happy. We found a little pension in the shadow of the Acropolis for $6 a night and saved every penny we had for those incredibly delicious pastries you can find in Greece. For lunch we would buy some wine, cheese, and bread and feast off that staple diet as we sat in one of the squares watching the teeming life of that lovely, ancient city. We spent hours up on the Acropolis and visited every museum we could find. I had taken an art history course at Northwestern and now everything suddenly came alive. It was good to be reminded how much pleasure can be derived from the simple fact of knowing, of having learned. Museums often bore me stiff, as did many class-room lectures; yet when the subject matter of both coincide and one's memory is jogged into remembrance, a whole new world opens up. For Sally, too, it was a great experience, for she had majored in interior design, a subject that required a lot of art study.

So for us Athens was romantic, educational, and fun, and I was in a much better frame of mind when I arrived in Monte Carlo. There we had an education of another kind—at the Casino. I am not a gambler by nature and it really kills me to lose as much as $25. That night in Monaco we put $2.50—that was the mini-mum, I think—on a number on roulette, lost it and left. But, of course, we had gone more to have a look at the famous establish-ment than to gamble. It is quite a sight. It has an aura of slightly faded opulence now with the cigar smoke curling up to the huge chandeliers but it was not difficult to envisage those zany days between the wars when bejeweled ladies and top-hatted gentle-men won and squandered fortunes without flickering an eyelid. Some, having lost more than they could afford, felt obliged to shoot themselves on the imposing marble steps leading down to the square. It was considered the honorable thing to do in those days.

Ken Fletcher, whose talent for living life to the full exceeded even his skill on a tennis court—which was considerable enough, for he was seeded Number Three at Wimbledon one year—was not the type to become suicidally morose if luck ran against him. That night he gave me my first glimpse of how money can be thrown around with gay abandon. They say all Aussies are born gamblers and Fletch has done his best to give credence to the legend. On this particular occasion we found him strutting between the roulette tables with that urgent little swagger of his, throwing 100-franc chips about as if they were confetti. "Well, I'll be buggered," Ken would mutter as 24 came up seconds after he'd staked his life on 25. Then off he'd hustle to see how his chips were doing on table Number 2. Sometimes he would win, of course, but that night he must have lost close to $500. I admired his buccaneering spirit but it wasn't my style. Ruing the fate of our two and a half bucks, Sally and I climbed up the hill to a little restaurant from where you could see the lights on the millionaire's yachts twinkling in the harbor behind the Casino. It all seemed just as beautiful from that distance—and a lot safer.

Then it was south again to begin a slow, week by week progression up the boot of Italy from Sicily—Catania, Reggio di Calabria, Naples—hot, Latin towns full of broad-hipped, full-lipped women and aggressive, cocky teen-agers who would never tire of making adolescent passes at Sally—or any other attractive fair-haired girl, for that matter. But they were harmless enough and it was good to be back in Italy again. I have always found it easier to communicate with the Italians than with any other European people. There is a warmth and charm about them that strikes an immediate chord in me, and I respond. If you were to mold all the more attractive characteristics of the Italian female into one human being—especially those one finds around Naples and further south—I suppose you would come up with someone bearing a striking resemblance to Sophia Loren.

But my love of the Italians did not prevent me from getting involved in another on-court row when we got to Rome for the Italian Championships. I had played well the previous three weeks—so well, in fact, that I was somewhat surprisingly seeded Number Eight in Rome, a seeding I managed to justify by reaching the quarterfinals where Roy Emerson beat me in four sets. On the way, however, I had precipitated an incident during my match with the Russian Tomas Lejus over a line call. It was not in itself of anything but passing importance and I cannot even recall the details too clearly now save for the fact that I refused to give in over a doubtful line call on my serve and called for the tournament referee to adjudicate. If I remember correctly, he ruled against me and I lost my serve only to win it back immediately by hitting four outright winners off Lejus's serve in the next game. For once a little controlled anger paid off. The only significance of the incident was a personal one in that it provided another example of my changing attitude. A year before I would not have called the referee and would probably have generously conceded the point.

I want to emphasize that I had not made a conscious decision to become difficult, nasty, and belligerent on court. I had merely promised myself that I was going to become tougher in standing up for my rights whenever I felt I had a fair case to argue about. The Bowrey and Lejus incidents were merely manifestations of that promise. I think I only really became aware of what effect this change was having on my reputation when I got home several weeks later and read the *World Tennis* account of the Italian Championships by David Gray, the much respected tennis correspondent of *The London Guardian*. In referring to my match with Lejus, David had made some mention of "the temperamental American." After years of reading about good old well-behaved Marty, the All-American boy, it came as a bit of a shock and I admit it hurt. But I quickly realized that this was the sort of press I was going to get if I followed through with my determination not to allow a gentlemanly upbringing interfere with my chances of winning tennis matches.

So I learned to live with my press notices and they no longer bother me. In every aspect but one I tend to agree with the theory that any press, within reason, is good press. After all, we are in the business of trying to persuade people to part with their money to see us perform and they are not about to part with anything to watch a bunch of nonentities. The old Hollywood movie stars were not far wrong when they said, "I don't care what you say about me—just make sure you spell my name right." That dictum comes unstuck only when you try to manufacture a phoney image solely for the sake of publicity. I was far from being guilty of that. In fact, there was reason to believe that this was the real Riessen that was beginning to emerge at the ripe old age of 24 and that the meek and mild Marty of previous years had, to some extent, been the manufactured one.

From one point of view, however, I was concerned about the amount of publicity my rows with Bowrey and Lejus had received—especially back home. I was thinking of what effect it might have on the kids who were just taking up the game. Teenagers with stars in their eyes can be very impressionable and I dread the fact that they might think, after reading of our antics, "Well, maybe that's what you're supposed to do." Well, it isn't necessarily what you are supposed to do at all. What you are *supposed* to do is ride with the rough and the smooth—to meet, as Kipling said, with triumph and disaster and treat those two imposters just the same. That's what I tried to do and I found myself getting trodden on. But that was my personal problem. There is no reason why it should happen to everyone. Arthur Ashe has maintained his impeccable image of the ultimate "Mr. Cool" through innumerable crises and yet no one has trodden on him. That is great, if your temperament allows you to behave like that. But before you decide that your nature is too explosive and volatile to play it the Ashe way, remember that a truculent, loud-mouthed, unappealing personality on court makes life a lot tougher for you in the long run, quite apart from presenting a bad image for your sport and whatever country you represent.

Some players have suffered for this type of behavior. Dennis Ralston and Cliff Richey both have hot tempers but their reputation is five times as bad as it might otherwise be simply because they do not project a sunny disposition on court. Although I don't think I look as mean and glum as Dennis or Cliff, I know that there is very little I can get away with before the crowd is on my back. If I slam a ball into the stop netting, everybody whistles. If Tom Okker, my happy little doubles partner, does it, everybody laughs, "Ho, ho, isn't he sweet." If only they could hear what little angelface was saying under his breath. . . .

4

MEXICO CITY

During the next eighteen months I made steady progress, gaining confidence in myself as a person and in my ability as a tennis player.

After returning to graduate school at Northwestern in September, I spent much of the winter living in fear of the draft call which never came. I was classified 1A, but being married helped, I suppose, and somehow my number never came up. So I emerged in 1967 from the wintry little backwater of Evanston to find that MacCall was finally prepared to give me a chance to show my worth in the Davis Cup—at least in the doubles.

Another disastrous defeat the previous fall, this time at the hands of Brazil, had given him an unwelcome excuse to try something different, and since graduate school had prevented me from even being on the squad that traveled to its doom in Pôrto Alegre, I was untarnished by the stigma of that particular defeat. Having played only four Davis Cup rubbers in my life up to that point, I qualified as something different although hardly something new. Six years' peripheral service to the team made me feel somewhat like an old sweater that had been lying around in a drawer for years without being worn. When you feel the draft, you take it out, slightly surprised to find it still there, and discover it wasn't such a bad buy after all. That, at least, was what I hoped to prove to MacCall, and at first this was not difficult.

When Clark Graebner and I walked out on court at the Tranquility Square Tennis Club, Port of Spain, Trinidad, Charlie

27

Pasarell—who was to finish the year as America's top-ranked player—and Cliff Richey had given us a comfortable 2-0 lead over the British West Indies. One more rubber was needed to make the tie safe in the best of five Davis Cup format, and Clark and I quickly obliged by defeating Richard Russell and Lance Lumsden 6-4, 6-2, 6-2.

By the time we moved on to Mexico City for the next round, I had had one of my best tournaments ever on clay by beating Ashe and Richey to win Atlanta. As a result I thought I might have an outside chance of selection for the singles against Mexico. The fact that Dennis Ralston had turned pro with the National Tennis League by that time obviously helped my chances, but when the team was chosen, I was still in a doubles-only role.

The pressure was greater here for not only were the Mexicans considered more dangerous opponents, but they proceeded to prove it when Rafe Osuña, who was to die so tragically in a plane crash two years later, defeated Richey in the opening singles. Before his own wildly partisan crowd, Rafe was at his electric best, using his catlike agility and razor-sharp reflexes to demolish Cliff in the final two sets after the Texan had led by two sets to one.

Ashe quickly disposed of Marcel Lara to level the tie at one rubber each, and on the second day it was up to Clark and me to see that we did not fall behind again. This is when you really start to feel the pressure of Davis Cup play—in a tie that is poised in temporary equality against opponents who are fighting with all the inspired aggression of underdogs in front of a crowd that is screaming for your downfall. You have to grit your teeth, ignore the butterflies in your stomach, block out the wailing wall of noise that rises all around you, and get stuck in. Happily this was just what Clark and I managed to do. We never allowed Osuña and his talented little partner Joaquin Loyo-Mayo to get into the match; we beat them in straight sets. Arthur powered his way past Osuña in the first of the reverse singles the following day to give us a 3-1 lead and we were safely over a difficult hurdle. In the warm afterglow of victory, confidence was beginning to seep back into the team following the disasters of the previous two years, and George MacCall was wearing his happy smile again. Poor George. Little did we know then that another debacle was awaiting us later that summer which effectively was to put an end to MacCall's career as Davis Cup captain and, coincidentally, to mine as a Davis Cup player.

It was just prior to this tie in Mexico City that the sporting public was allowed its first behind-the-scenes peek into the world of tennis shamateurism. At that time, under-the-counter payments to top players were an open secret to anyone inside the tennis fraternity, but they had been only obliquely hinted at in the press and precise figures had never been published. So it came as something of a shock to pick up the Mexican papers one morning and find huge pictures of Manuel Santana, Roy Emerson, John Newcombe, and Tony Roche over captions reading, "$1,000 a week—$800 a week—$750 a week."

It transpired that Pat Hughes, the former British Davis Cup player who had worked in player liaison and promotion for Dunlops ever since the war, had just retired and, as a parting shot, had divulged a few facts and figures of tennis life to the press. My name was there, too, quoted along with Graebner's at $400 a week, while Okker was listed at $500. It was all fairly accurate but it made startling reading in those days.

It seems strange to think of it now, but I had been playing top-class tennis for several years before I even considered the possibility of making a living out of it. Throughout my college days I was working steadily toward a Master's degree in education, and I envisaged quitting the International circuit within a year or two and settling down to a steady job. It was not until September 1963, just after the United States had defeated Britain in an Interzone Davis Cup final at Bournemouth, that my eyes were opened to the possibility of actually making money out of the game.

The team was to make its way to India for the next Davis Cup tie via Paris, Rome, and Tehran, where we were scheduled to play small tournaments and exhibitions. Palermo was added to that itinerary when tournament officials there offered several hundred dollars as an inducement.

According to U.S. LTA rules we should not have accepted the offer, but Bob Kelleher, who was Davis Cup captain at the time, decided that this was an appropriate moment to turn a blind eye. The money was equally distributed among Chuck McKinley, Dennis Ralston, Frank Froehling, and myself, and although it did not amount to much more than $100 each, it served as a good boost to team morale and this, of course, was just what Kelleher intended. Apart from being a man of great personal charm, Kelleher stood head and shoulders above most U.S. LTA officials as an administrator with sensitivity and common sense. Unfortunately that did not prevent him from becoming something of an establishment figure in later years when he was elected President of the U.S. LTA, and I was always sorry that we found ourselves disagreeing on so many fundamental issues.

However it was Kelleher's generosity in Palermo that first started me thinking about a professional career in the game, and although I could not call myself a pro in name for another five years, it was only a matter of months before I was accepting under-the-counter payments as a routine and necessary way of life.

5

ECUADORIAN DISASTER

I have this fortunate ability to put really bad memories out of my mind—or at least shove them so far back into the dark recesses of my brain that a lot of excavation is needed before they can be brought into sharp and painful focus.

For instance, if someone mentions the name "Ecuador," I do not immediately break out in a cold sweat—which is surprising, for I cannot pretend to be unaware of what Ecuador means in terms of American tennis. But by refusing to dig around back there in my memory bank, I will probably manage to get through the conversation with a minimum of discomfort.

It is only when some sadist says, "Go on, Marty, tell us what really happened down there," that the whole desperate episode surfaces like a half-forgotten nightmare.

Okay, this is what happened in Ecuador. Four guys named Arthur Ashe, Clark Graebner, Cliff Richey, and Marty Riessen took a bunch of shovels and spades instead of tennis rackets down to a place called Guayaquil on Ecuador's Pacific coast in June 1967, dug themselves a big grave, and fell into it. A gutsy and not untalented Ecuadorian team offered an accommodating nudge to help them on their way, and a frenzied, fanatical crowd went wild with delight when they hit the bottom. Amen.

You want more? Well, when I really start to think about it I suppose the story of the next Davis Cup round following our encouraging victory in Mexico was even more extraordinary in detail than it appears from that grisly synopsis. So I will give

31

myself a pain-killer, dig around a bit, and see what I come up with. But I warn you that unless you happen to be Ecuadorian or a particular fan of the country of Pancho Segura—who wasn't playing, thank God—you won't find the tale particularly gratifying.

The memories are especially bad for me because this was finally to have been the year of my Big Chance and there could be no more excuses. I wasn't at graduate school as I had been when the United States was beaten by Brazil in Pôrto Alegre the previous year. Nor was I sitting on the sidelines as I had been when we lost to Spain in Barcelona in 1965. I was a full-fledged member of the team and as such I have to take my full share of the blame for what must go down as one of the darkest moments in U.S. Davis Cup history. I helped dig that grave all right; perhaps only Cliff Richey, who won both his singles, came through with his reputation unscathed.

And it was all going to be relatively easy. Of course, I don't think anyone expected a string of love, love, and love victories, for we were well aware what a great leveler slow clay courts and hysterical crowds can be for American players. But we had overcome a far stronger team in Mexico City just a few weeks before and even if we had lost to Brazil and Spain in the previous two years, so what? Ecuador was simply not in the same class.

We were going to have to work hard—there are no shortcuts to success on clay—but we were going to win, that was for sure. Pancho Gonzales, the team coach, thought so. He was so sure of it, in fact, that he didn't even come. I can't remember the exact reasons for his absence but no one felt it very important for him to be there at the time—at least not in the beginning. Midway through the second day's play we began to have second thoughts about that. But initially everyone considered that George MacCall, the nonplaying captain, and a four-man team were quite sufficient to take care of the Ecuadorians. Pancho shared that opinion and, with his long experience with South America, he probably felt that Guayaquil was a good place to miss anyway.

We realized why as soon as we stepped off the plane. The

whole town was stewing silently in that humid, suffocating heat which drains the body and the mind of all energy and purpose. We were saturated within three minutes of stepping onto the practice court, but fortunately we had given ourselves a good ten days to get used to the conditions and we practiced hard. For hours on end each day we would try to hit balls into boxes placed at the corner of the base and sidelines to improve our accuracy and consistency. Displaying unwarranted confidence, Clark Graebner and I even practiced rushing the net so that we would be in good shape for the fast grass courts at Wimbledon a couple of weeks later. Yes, we were already thinking ahead too far and too fast.

Precisely what that parrot perched in a palm tree overlooking the practice courts was thinking about, we never discovered. But the darn bird had an awful lot to say for itself. There had been a parrot lurking about during our practice sessions in Trinidad as well, but the one in Guayaquil seemed to have a particularly malicious wit. Cliff Richey was certain it cackled with glee every time one of us missed a volley and chortled throaty obscenities in Spanish just as we would throw the ball up to serve. Cliff would often fix it with that glowering, drop-dead stare of his, but the parrot's yellow and blue plumage must have been armor plated. It didn't even wobble on its branch.

Richey didn't wobble either when the tie finally got under way, for he battled Pancho Guzman in the opening singles with discipline and determination and beat him in four tough sets to give us a 1-0 lead. But from that moment on the great American Davis Cup team got the shakes, and the harder we tried to correct it, the worse it became.

In the second singles Arthur Ashe went out and collapsed in disarray, 4-6, 6-4, 6-4, 6-2, in the face of Miguel Olvera's clever but relatively inoffensive clay-court game. That Ashe should lose to the little-known Ecuadorian was, on paper, almost unthinkable. But the fact was that Arthur had little idea of how to combat sound clay-court strategy in those days. It is no use trying to serve and volley your way out of trouble on that stuff unless you are getting a perfect feel of the ball, moving exceptionally well, and generally playing at the peak of your form. Arthur wasn't. He looked stiff and nervous and played that way.

When Olvera hit the winning shot at match point, the crowd went berserk and the Ecuadorian captain, Danny Carrera, took a flying leap at the net in what was supposed to be a victory jump. But he never made it. Catching his foot on the tape, he fell flat on his face and broke his leg. He spent the rest of the tie at courtside in a wheelchair. It was getting to be one of those occasions when one didn't know whether to cry or collapse in hysterical laughter.

For precisely the opposite reason, George MacCall also inflicted personal injury on himself when the proceedings maintained their standard of high farce the following day. George is a charming, soft-spoken, thoroughly delightful guy with a great sense of humor and a lopsided grin, who just happens to get very emotional about things that matter to him. At that time winning Davis Cup ties mattered to him more than just about anything, and when Clark and I managed to lose our doubles to Guzman and Olvera, George heaved his fist into the nearest cabinet door in the locker room. Ion Tiriac, the wire-haired Rumanian, once did that after losing a match at Stade Roland Garros in Paris. But Tiri, who I have long suspected of being one of the great actors of the circuit, was careful to choose a cabinet with a plywood door. His fist went straight through it, thus creating precisely the required effect. The door George elected to use as a punching bag for a few bone-crunching seconds was made of steel. I don't know whether he actually broke any bones in his hand, but it certainly looked like an awful mess by the time he was through working off his frustration.

I suppose he should really have been aiming his blows at Clark and me. We had really made a hash of the doubles. At the start it looked so easy. We won the first set 6-0 and were leading 5-2 in the second. Guzman had been pushing over his soft little serve and we had been killing it. But suddenly he started to get more pace on his delivery and held on to it to pull back to 5-3. At that point Clark got a little nervous and served two double faults to drop serve for 5-4. Olvera served out for 5-all and the pressure started to mount.

The crowd, led by a little man who kept on jumping up to orchestrate the rhythmical chant, kept screaming, "Ec—wa—dor, Ec—wa—dor." We were losing our cool and pretty soon we had lost the second set as well, 9-7. Inspired by this turnaround, Guzman and Olvera took the third 6-3, and we retired to the locker room to try to pull ourselves together. The break evidently did some good, for we leveled the match by winning the fourth 6-4. But then, as the fifth began to develop into a long, tense struggle, I started to crack. There was one game when we must have had at least half a dozen break points on their serve, mostly as a result of Clark running around onto his forehand and cracking away fine winners. But each time, I blew the next vital service return through a desperate and very basic inability to get the ball over the net. I connected with the shots pretty well but nearly every one caught the tape. There was perhaps an inch of it—an inch that served as a barometer of the state of my nerves. I eventually lost my serve when Olvera put away a forehand winner and we were beaten. At two rubbers to one down, overall defeat suddenly loomed as a very distinct possibility.

On the evidence of their form up to that point, the Ecuadorians were quite capable of winning one of the remaining two singles, and that was all they needed. The next day they did it at the first try when Guzman beat Ashe by the strange score of 0-6, 6-4, 7-5, 0-6, 6-3.

The scene in the locker room when Arthur came in for the break two sets to one down was unbelievable. We haven't talked about it much between ourselves since, but I doubt if any of the five of us involved will ever forget it. The problem really centered around George MacCall, who was near breaking point by this stage. Poor George had had a rough ride as Davis Cup captain and the specter of yet another defeat looming before him proved too much. Seized by a fit of emotional desperation, he started yelling at Arthur: "Just play tennis. Get back out there and just play tennis."

What he meant was for Arthur to play his natural game; and under normal circumstances this is not bad advice. But these were far from normal circumstances and in any case Arthur's normal game is serve, charge into the net, and volley. Against a confident clay-court player on his own surface, that is suicide —a fact of which we had been all too painfully reminded during the previous two sets. Once Guzman had weathered Ashe's initial first-set onslaught, Pancho had found no difficulty in passing his net-rushing opponent at will.

Obviously Arthur needed some much calmer and more thoughtful advice than what George was offering, and he needed it fast. There was only one thing to do. Separate Ashe and MacCall—physically if necessary. Unfortunately it was necessary. George was beyond listening to reason, so Clark and I grabbed hold of him, bundled him backward across the locker room to the far wall, and quieted him there while Cliff knelt down in front of Arthur, who was sitting stiff and scared in his chair. Speaking quietly and earnestly, Richey tried to drum into his colleague the need to stay back and rally, to wait for the openings, to restrain and restrict his natural instincts of all-out aggression.

Ashe just nodded. When he's really nervous, Arthur literally scares himself rigid. People who don't know him think his appearance of outward cool means he doesn't care. Actually it means just the opposite. He cares so much that his limbs stiffen up to the point where he can barely move. His voice goes an octave higher and he can hardly talk. He all but goes into a trance of fear.

Knowing this, Richey wasn't looking for any "Gee, wow, thanks a million" type of response as he tried to guide Ashe to victory during that traumatic locker room interlude. He just hoped his advice was sinking in. Over by the wall, so did Clark and I. George was calmer by then, and after the ten-minute break was up, we all trooped back out into the cauldron of heat and emotion that awaited Arthur in the arena.

For a time it seemed that Richey's words had indeed sunk in. Staying back a bit more and showing a little more patience before unleashing his superior power, Ashe completely dominated Guzman for a while—long enough, at least, to take another love set. But it was still not long enough. With the crowd screaming in his ears and Guzman pressing hard at the start of the fifth set, Ashe instinctively reverted to his more natural style and began rushing his strokes in the process. A lifetime habit is tough to resist when you are nervous and in trouble, and so Arthur quit the unfamiliar base line for the very familiar net. It was a position from which there was no retreat and it was fatal. Guzman started dissecting the space between Ashe and the sidelines to his left and right with the expertise available to any good clay-courter on a surface that gives him time to measure his shots. Pancho snatched the vital service break and clung resolutely to his own to take that fifth and final set 6-4. Ecuador had beaten the United States and the crowd's joy was earsplitting, overpowering, frightening. . . .

Carrera was hugging Guzman from his wheelchair and looking as if he would like to have another try at jumping the net, plastered leg and all. And somewhere up in a palm tree that bloody parrot was no doubt cackling away in merry contentment.

But the drama was not finished. Officials were so concerned by the behavior of the spectators that when Richey began the final rubber against Olvera, armed guards were posted along the tops of the concrete walls surrounding the center court. As Ecuador had already secured its winning 3-1 margin, the match was meaningless; but the crowd was thirsting for more American blood, and if they failed to get it in the sporting sense—Richey beat Olvera—they nearly got it literally when some people outside the arena started lobbing rocks over the walls. When one narrowly missed Richey, Cliff yelled at the referee, "If you don't stop those savages, I'm going to quit this match right now."

That ultimatum did nothing to soothe emotions, but the match continued and toward the end Clark Graebner turned to me and said, "When Cliff gets to match point we'd better get ready to make a bolt for the locker room or we'll never get out of here alive."

It may sound like a hackneyed line from a bad TV script now, but at the time I can assure you it seemed like the best advice I'd ever heard. We bolted all right—only to discover that the locker room was anything but a sanctuary of peace and serenity. A few minutes after Richey fought his way through the delirious crowds, the door flew open and there was a white-faced Danny Carrera furiously wheeling himself into our presence. He hadn't come to offer condolences, either.

"How dare you call my people savages," he screamed at Richey. That was enough for Cliff. He had a pretty short temper in those days and after the trauma we had all been through, he just blew his fuse. Ignoring the fact that his target was confined to a wheelchair, he made a lunge for Carrera and this time it was MacCall who stepped in and dragged the young Texan away before any blows were struck.

The whole day had turned into a rather brutal scene and under the circumstances I felt we made quite a generous diplomatic move in putting in an appearance at the victory celebration party that was held at the club that evening. Needless to say, we didn't stay long, and as we left, ugly-looking crowds swarmed around our car, thumping it with their fists and rocking it. I think we all got a quick and frightening insight into what it must feel like to be an unpopular politician in South America.

There was an early-morning KLM flight to London the next day and we were on it. I have never been so glad to get out of a place in my life. It was a long flight and I had plenty of time for reflection. I remember wondering what on earth we were going to tell the tennis community that would be waiting to greet and grill us at Wimbledon. They would never believe we had lost to Ecuador. On a more personal note I could not believe Clark and I had lost the doubles. In between fits of sleep across the Atlantic I crowded my mind with all sorts of painful questions and self-doubts. I asked myself whether I had the temperament that is required to play well under the tremendous pressures imposed by a Davis Cup tie. Maybe it was all too late for me. Maybe I had been kept hanging around too close to the scene for too long. Continual rehearsal without ever getting to play the part does nothing to help a case of stage fright.

I felt I should have been blooded much earlier in my career before the buildup of expectancy and hope over six long years began to breed a tension of its own. But suddenly I felt all that was in the past. It just didn't seem to matter so much any more. Maybe I was subconsciously erecting a protective shield, or maybe I had reached the point of emotional exhaustion over the whole rally-round-the-flag, play-for-your-country routine. At any rate something told me I had finished with the Davis Cup. At about that time, in fact, some people were suggesting that I was finished with top-class tennis. In the darker moments of that flight to London I was inclined to agree with them. But it was only a passing fit of depression and I knew in my heart that I was now beginning to play much better, both in singles and in doubles.

Doubles, of course, had always been a specialty of mine, but I had never enjoyed it as much as I was now beginning to. Tom Okker was the reason for that. It was during that tour of Australia in 1965–66 that we first played together. As with so many good things in life, it happened by accident really, for we both arrived in Perth for the Western Australia Championships without a doubles partner. Clark Graebner was injured, and I forget who Tom was supposed to be playing with. So we teamed up and won the title, beating Wimbledon champions Newcombe and Roche. We were already good, if casual, friends off court and it became quickly obvious from that brief experiment that our styles jelled nicely on court as well. I reverted to playing with Clark, of course, for the remainder of the Australian tour; but as soon as our tournament schedules permitted it a few months later Tom and I teamed up again, and I think the experience has been fruitful for us both. Certainly playing and traveling with a foreign player broadened my outlook and I became anxious to play more tournaments in Europe. The more familiar the European life style became, the more I started to understand and enjoy it. In addition, Tom was much better known around Europe than he was in America at that time, so it was easier for us to get good deals from tournaments.

There was also the thought that by playing in Europe, I was putting as big a distance as possible between myself and the nagging interference of the U.S. LTA. Nothing had gone particularly well between the Association and myself—especially since

I had ceased to be its pet houseboy by actually daring to question the wisdom of some of its decisions. But although one startling solution did occur to me some months later, I knew that finishing with the Davis Cup and trying to play more often abroad would not be enough. The only way to make a clean break from their stifling parental control was to turn pro, and as we arrived at London's Heathrow Airport for Wimbledon 1967, that did not seem a very feasible alternative for a player of my standing. But then we had no way of predicting the revolution that was just around the corner.

6

THE END OF MY AMATEUR CAREER

I think anyone who has the remotest interest in tennis knows what Wimbledon stands for. It is quite simply the best tournament in the world. But apart from the drama that continues for two long weeks on court, it also serves as the great gathering point and marketplace for everyone involved in the sport— players, agents, tournament directors, representatives of sporting goods companies, and International Lawn Tennis Federation officials from all over the world. They meet formally in committee rooms and informally over tea in the players' tearoom or, for those who have access, in the well-guarded locker rooms. It is during Wimbledon that players make their deals and fix their schedules for the rest of the year. It's barter and bargain time. Less so in recent years, perhaps, because the pros under contract to Lamar Hunt have a fixed schedule that is arranged for us by Mike Davies and the staff of the World Championship Tennis organization. Even the ILTF circuit is becoming more carefully planned ahead of time now that the Grand Prix format has given it some sort of cohesion and unity. But in 1967 it was different. That was the year shamateurism reached its peak with tournaments openly flouting the "amateur" rules in their desperate scramble to secure the best players. Competition is particularly hot in the weeks immediately following Wimbledon, for there are tournaments all over Europe in places like Gstaad, Baastad, Newport (Wales), Dublin, Aix-en-Provence, and Kitzbühel, as well as in the American clay-court circuit in the Mid-

41

My mother and father on a sight-seeing trip to Windsor Castle after coming to see me play at Wimbledon in 1970. *Credit: Marty Riessen*

Rod Laver displays perfect balance and the bulging muscles of that massive left arm during play on Wimbledon's No. 1 Court in 1969. Rocket was on his way to his fourth Wimbledon crown that year. *Credit: Arthur Cole, Tennis World*

west. It was up to each individual player to squeeze the best possible deal out of the tournament directors who were grappling for their services.

Speaking English—the language of the circuit—in a variety of accents, tournament directors would make their bids, quoting dollars—the currency of the circuit. If one tournament was offering a $400 guarantee plus full hospitality—i.e., a place to stay and all meals—then another would offer air fare as well, or maybe up the price to $500. "And how about my wife? Any chance of an air fare for her as well?" "Ah, so you have a wife this year, do you? Ah, so. . . ."

And the poor harassed tournament director would retire into a corner with another of those sticky Wimbledon buns and the inevitable cup of tea to do his sums and ponder whether the player who had just asked for two air fares, full hospitality, and $500 win or lose was really worth it. What was his recent record? Was he really that much of a crowd-puller? Hadn't he gotten drunk and made a pass at the Club president's wife the previous year? Well, presumably his own wife would eliminate that problem this time. . . . During these considerations, of course, nothing was more likely to influence his decision in the player's favor than a couple of good wins right then and there, at Wimbledon. Everybody wants to do well at Wimbledon because of the atmosphere, the prestige, and the sheer thrill of succeeding in the world's biggest tournament. But every player knows, too, that if he is lucky enough to knock out a seed and make it through to the quarterfinals or beyond, his bargaining power with that man from Gstaad or Kitzbühel will skyrocket. And these, of course, are his bread and butter tournaments, the ones that will enable him to make a living for the rest of the year.

The living was just starting to get good. Pat Hughes' estimation of what Manuel Santana was receiving that year was, if anything, on the modest side. There were occasions when Manolo would be paid $1,500—big money in those days—and to my mind he was worth it. If a player with the popular Spaniard's unique talent and crowd appeal could pull 4,000 people through the gate at $3 each, it did not seem unreasonable that he should be paid handsomely for doing so. Certainly, if I were a tournament director, I would much rather pay $1,500 for one Santana than $250 each for six lesser players.

The fact that payments at that particular time in tennis history were considered illegal did not worry me in the least. Sure, I felt the system was bad, but until the ILTF caught up with the times there was nothing one could do about it. To play tennis at the top, one had to make a living out of it and we owed it to our families and ourselves to make as good a living as was humanly possible. Apart from being a tough tennis player, one also had to be a tough businessman. In the bargaining arena I was never tough enough. I was too inclined to say, "Yes, that seems reasonable," and accept whatever the tournament was offering. In this day and age "reasonable" isn't good enough. No one knows that better than Donald Dell, which is why I am very happy to have him today as my agent and lawyer. Donald, who was later to take over from MacCall as Davis Cup captain for a spell, looks after the business interests of most of the top American players like Ashe, Smith, Lutz, Ralston, and Pasarell, as well as several European stars. Sometimes Donald pushes too far and scares someone off, but that's okay with me. I'd rather miss a few deals than continually undersell myself.

Many of us were guilty of underselling in the old days, but not Santana—nor indeed, Roy Emerson and Fred Stolle. In 1966—the year after they had met each other in their second consecutive Wimbledon final—these two immensely popular Aussies extracted out of the U.S. LTA, $1,000 a week each for five weeks to play the Eastern Grass Court circuit. Although it has never bothered me if other players get more than I do in an open market—after all you have no one to blame but yourself if you do not win enough matches or push for a good enough deal—I did take exception to the inconsistency of the U.S. LTA's position. How could they justify keeping their Davis Cup players on $28 a day and threaten us with dismissal if we tried to make a deal on the side while they themselves were handing out $1,000 a week to a couple of top Australians? The hypocrisy of it made me sick, and before the end of the year I was making the first

For three years, from 1963-1965, Fred Stolle was the perennial brides-maid at Wimbledon, losing in the final to Chuck McKinley one time and to Roy Emerson twice. Here, in the 1964 final against Emerson, Fred reaches for a forehand volley on the famous Centre Court. *Credit: Arthur Cole, Tennis World*

exploratory moves to get out from under their jurisdiction.

By that time, of course, the All-England Club, acting on the initiative of its chairman, Herman David, had decided that the hypocrisy that was rampant throughout the game had indeed gone far enough and, to their eternal credit, set about the problem in a brave and revolutionary manner. Herman David simply announced that, whether the rest of the world liked it or not, in 1968 Wimbledon would be open to amateurs, quasi-amateurs, and professionals alike. The rest of the world, in the form of the ILTF, huffed and puffed for a few weeks and even managed to have the British LTA, which was backing Wimbledon, expelled from the International body. That move backfired rather badly, however, when it was revealed in the London *Evening News* that the man who had pressed vociferously for Britain's banishment in the most high-handed moralistic tones—ILTF President Georgio di Stefani—had been responsible six year earlier for paying Italy's top player, Nikki Pietrangeli, several thousand dollars to stay "amateur." Pietrangeli confirmed that he had been paid a sum of money by his Association as an inducement to break a preliminary agreement he had signed with Tony Trabert, who was then heading the former Jack Kramer professional troupe. Orlando Sirola also confirmed that he and Pietrangeli had been paid a monthly "salary" whenever they had been on duty for Italy in the Davis Cup.

Italy was far from being the only country guilty of this practice, but Di Stefani was one of the few officials who had the barefaced effrontery to cast stones at the British for trying to put the situation to rights and inject a little honesty into the game. More and more I wondered about the sort of people who were running tennis.

Fortunately, Di Stefani and his reactionary cronies on the ILTF were outvoted when a special meeting was called to debate the crisis. The majority of the delegates capitulated in the face of the All-England Club's power and prestige, and Open tennis was born.

The first serious contact I had with the professional side of the game came in the winter of 1967 when all this furor was

taking place. I had just returned from the Brazilian tour when
a guy named Dave Dixon phoned and asked me to fly down
to New Orleans to see him. Dixon was a New Orleans sports
promotor who decided that pro tennis was the most under-
developed, underpublicized sport in the world and set about
trying to do something about it. Although his original idea of
broadening pro tennis's appeal with show biz gimmickry ended
in disaster—and an eventual sellout to Lamar Hunt—let no one
underestimate the beneficial effect of Dixon's sudden and short-
lived involvement with tennis. It was his raid on the amateur
ranks to secure the signatures of John Newcombe, Tony Roche,
Cliff Drysdale, Roger Taylor, and Nikki Pilic that made the
ILTF realize the futility of opposing Wimbledon's move for
Open tennis. It was the biggest mass defection that the amateur
game had ever suffered, for even in the heyday of the Kramer
tour, Jack usually contented himself with signing one or two top
amateurs at a time.

When I flew down to talk to Dixon, he was still in the process
of forming the group that was to gain brief notoriety as "The
Handsome Eight." He told me that he would be interested in my
joining his tour, provided that he did not take either Butch
Buchholz or Pierre Barthes from the other pro group in existence
at the time, the National Tennis League. Ken Rosewall, Rod
Laver, and Pancho Gonzales were the stars of that tour, which
was run by none other than my old friend George MacCall. As it
turned out, both Buchholz and Barthes did join Dixon, along
with Dennis Ralston, so there was no room for me. Initially, of
course, I was disappointed, for apart from everything else, I
enjoyed the company of Newcombe, Roche, and the other guys
on the tour. They were good friends and good opponents. One
cannot ask for more.

But once the tour got under way—starting, ominously enough,
on a court laid over an ice rink in a freezing stadium down
among the slaughterhouse yards of Kansas City, Missouri—I
began to think I was well out of it. By the time they reached
Orlando, Florida, the crowds were down to about 27—attendance
one night was definitely under 30—and poor Dave Dixon was

beginning to think that perhaps tennis and the more obvious gimmicks of show business promotion didn't mix after all.

In retrospect, it was probably better from all points of view that my entry into the pro ranks was delayed, for I had a highly successful run on the amateur circuit in the first six months of 1968. I made two journeys to South Africa in the space of three months, once for the Sugar Circuit and later for the South African National Championships, where I battled my way through to the final before losing to Tom Okker. In between I played the Caribbean circuit, winning Caracas and Curaçao, losing to Okker in the final of Barranquilla, and, with Tom, cleaning up all three doubles titles.

By the time I left Johannesburg after the South African Nationals and headed for Italy to begin the 1968 European season, Open tennis was a reality and the game had entered a new and supposedly enlightened age. But, as in the wake of any revolution, the new regime was faced with some initial confusion as it laid down and then tried to enforce an appropriate set of rules. It should have been quite simple. Open tennis had recognized and, to a limited extent, welcomed the existence of the professionals within the structure of the old amateur game, and had also to some extent acknowledged the fact that some "amateurs" were nothing of the kind.

In truth 90 percent of all players who were appearing regularly on the International circuit were professionals in that they earned the bulk of their money from playing tennis. If the International Federation had faced up to this fact and created two straightforward categories—professionals and amateurs—a great deal of confusion would have been avoided. Instead they dreamed up a third category called a "registered player." This strange specimen was to be neither professional nor amateur, although his Association could "register" him as a player who would be allowed to accept prize money. To any rational mind this in effect made him a pro, but the word still stuck in the throats of a lot of crusty old colonels at the Queen's Club and other tradition-bound institutions around the world. I have often thought that they couldn't help associating the word with "prostitute," which, in their eyes, was someone one made use of for a fee but didn't talk about in polite company. So while Basil Reay, the full-time secretary, and his part-time cronies on the ILTF tried to hide from the facts of life by inventing absurd names for perfectly straightforward occupations, the confusion set in.

It was compounded in my case by the fact that Tom Okker had been made a registered player by the Dutch Association—a progressive body which was at least allowing Tom to act like a pro even if it couldn't call him one—while the U.S. LTA was still floundering around in the Dark Ages and calling their players "amateurs."

Amateurs, hell. We were all accepting ever-increasing sums of money and they knew it. Most of the time one could afford to laugh at their determination to live a lie, but on a few occasions it hurt. The ultimate travesty of justice occurred at Forest Hills that year when Arthur Ashe beat Tom Okker in the final. The first prize was $14,000—the biggest in tennis in those days. But Arthur as an "amateur" was not allowed to accept it; Tom, as a registered player, was. So while Okker, who had lost, walked off with fourteen grand, Ashe, who had won, got a cup, a pat on the back, and a big handshake. Luckily for Arthur, Donald Dell was waiting in the wings ready to make sure that, as the first black man to win Forest Hills and the first American to win it in thirteen years, Ashe got the recognition he deserved in the form of publicity, contracts, and endorsements.

Endorsements of various pieces of sporting equipment now form a sizable part of most top professionals' incomes. I make in the region of $40,000 a year in off-court activities directly connected to tennis, and Ashe, largely as a result of the impetus that his Forest Hills victory gave his career, earns more than twice as much.

The most obvious piece of equipment a player can endorse, of course, is his racket. And 1968 proved to be a significant year for both Arthur and me in that respect. I had been playing with a Wilson racket for eighteen years and Arthur for fifteen by the time our agreement with the company came to an end that year. The "agreement" did not include any payment—simply the free supply of rackets and various other items of Wilson equipment. In return I would do clinics and publicity appearances for them as well as use their rackets exclusively throughout the world.

But when I asked Donald Dell, who had just become my business manager, to renegotiate a contract with Wilson in more realistic financial terms, the company would not offer what both Donald and I felt I was worth. They were quite honest and straightforward about it. They said that they did not regard me as a good investment for the future; that my career had gone just about as far as it was going to go and that Stan Smith and Cliff Richey both seemed to be better prospects. From a strictly business point of view I could not blame them, but after playing with one racket since the age of eight, it still hurt a little to be told that you weren't worth more than a pittance in dollars and cents.

In fact Donald was asking a great deal more than a pittance for both Ashe and myself, and Art recalled the incident when we were talking about endorsements recently.

"I remember the scene perfectly," he said with a great grin spreading across his face. "We were sitting by the pool at the Beverly Hills Hotel and when Donald told Gene Buick, the Wilson guy, what he thought I was worth, Gene spilled his coffee right into his lap!"

Head, the ski people, were less shocked by Donald's demands and Arthur soon signed up with them, helping to develop the fiber glass "rug-beater" he now uses.

When Wilson turned me down, I told Donald that I wanted a deal with a top-class wood company. Metal, aluminum, and fiber glass were becoming all the rage just then but I was determined to stick with a frame that best suited my style of play, namely wood. So when Dunlop came through with a fine offer, I was elated. It meant that I would be able to endorse a racket I really felt happy with, and in fact I do not consider it a coincidence that certain aspects of my game have improved since I switched to Dunlop. The fact that it is a lighter racket has helped me get the racket head through faster on my fore-hand—a stroke that has improved appreciably—and my service has picked up, too. Although I have absolutely no hard feelings against Wilson, I must say it gave me a certain amount of satisfaction when Dunlop decided to come out with a Marty Riessen model at the end of 1972.

One of the best things about Dell's advice as a business manager is that he never even suggests that one of his players should endorse a piece of equipment they do not personally like using. Having watched some leading players switch rackets from continent to continent as they moved out of one company's area and into another's, frantically trying to pretend they could play with one racket as easily as another, I became determined long ago never to endorse anything I would not be absolutely content to use myself. I think most players have by now concluded that it is better to win and feel happy with your game than collect a few thousand extra dollars for using equipment that, however good it may be, does not suit your particular requirements.

"VS" gut is another example of a vital piece of equipment that I am happy to endorse. I think "VS"—a French company that is one of the last still using lamb gut instead of the beef gut that is most commonly used today—has also helped my game. I particularly like the thin "VS" gut for indoor play, and as the thin type pulls up tighter, I string it a little looser than the normal gut.

I like to do my own stringing on dad's "Sorano" stringing machine at home. For play on fast surfaces I like a tension of about 60 pounds, as that gives less play and greater control on the volley. For clay, when the ball fluffs up more, I string at 58. As I do not use an excessive amount of top spin, I am fairly light on wear and tear and a Dunlop racket will last me between two and three months before too much stringing makes it weak in the head.

Most players like a tension between 58 and 60 pounds, although John Alexander pulls his up to 63 or 64, which is incredibly tight. Frankly, I think he is headed for trouble if he keeps his strings that tight, as every shot has to jar his arm with that kind of tension. I doubt if any arm can take so much constant pounding over several years.

The little Italian wizard Beppe Merlo was famous for going to the other extreme. His strings were so loose they were like a fish net. If one broke during a match he could repair it right there at courtside just by pulling it through with his hands. There was no sound when Beppe hit a tennis ball—just the faint whoosh of the ball through the air. It was uncanny.

Pancho Gonzales has begun to use much looser strings in recent years—only about 50 pounds tension—and he is now learning to play with the trampoline effect which takes the pressure off your muscles and lets the racket do the work.

Adidas, another European company, has become a big name on the tennis circuit in recent years and, like many players, I endorse their tennis shoes. They have various designs to suit various surfaces. On clay I use the Robert Haillet model, which has a very thick, hard sole and although it is a little inflexible, it prevents you from spraining an ankle. Indoors and on grass I use the much lighter Bungert or Wimbledon model. Normally I wear out the sole of my shoes in about two to three weeks, but I usually have about three pairs, breaking them in on the practice court and then wearing them in rotation as I don't like to wear a new pair in matches.

Outside of endorsing equipment, there are deals that can have a lasting effect on one's future career. Donald's partner, Frank Craighill, finalized one for me during Forest Hills in 1972 that I am particularly excited about. It entails my becoming the touring pro at Amelia Island Plantation, a new residential resort community situated 32 miles northeast of Jacksonville, Florida. When the 1,800-acre plantation area is completed in 1976, it promises to offer one of the finest tennis centers in North America with 30 courts—including a center court constructed to seat 2,500 spectators—a pro shop and a racket club with swimming pool and playground. Eight courts were due to be completed by the spring of 1973 and I expect to be holding two tennis camps there each year. As it is also an ideal spot for Sally and me to go and relax for the occasional week between tournaments, I have bought a two-bedroom condominium on Amelia Island and I am looking forward to a long and happy association with the Plantation community.

The development is owned by the Sea Pines Plantation Company of Hilton Head Island, South Carolina, and its president, Charles Fraser, has been meticulous in preserving the natural beauty of Sea Pines. There are no neon signs or other trappings of honky-tonk commercialism on Hilton Head, nor will there be at Amelia. Stan Smith is the touring pro at Sea Pines and Charlie Pasarell has taken a similar post at Palmas del Mar, an enormous tennis resort now under construction in Puerto Rico. Maybe a few years from now you will find Stan, Charlie, and me leading our respective plantation teams in an annual battle for the Fraser Cup!

7

"RELAX, EVERYTHING'S OKAY.
YOU'RE A CONTRACT PRO"

However, back in early 1968, before Arthur had won Forest Hills or I had turned pro, contracts as lucrative and fulfilling as those I have since signed with Dunlop, Adidas, and Amelia seemed like a faraway dream. I knew that, first of all, I had to sign a piece of paper that would satisfy an ambition I had harbored—perhaps even subconsciously—for a very long time. I wanted to become what I already was in everything but name: a fully declared, authentic professional tennis player. In the spring of 1968 I was not at all sure how I was going to achieve this. In truth I was too preoccupied with trying to earn a living on the "amateur" circuit to give it a great deal of thought.

But when I was in Naples at the beginning of the European tour, I received a cable from Tom Okker that set in motion a whole series of events which finally led to the achievement of that ambition three hectic, trouble-strewn months later.

The cable from Tom contained the terms for Berlin—a tournament that traditionally conflicted with the French Championships in Paris. I had taken the precaution of getting permission from the U.S. LTA to miss the more prestigious French Championships because Tom and I had been thinking of going to West Berlin, partially because they were liable to offer considerably more money and partially because I was anxious to see the city.

Tom's cable confirmed that the Germans were offering $600 a week and that the deal included two additional weeks in

55

Helsinki and Stockholm immediately afterwards—a good package. I cabled back to Tom, who was at home in Holland at the time, to accept which he did on our behalf. While seeking permission to play Berlin, I had also asked the U.S. LTA to let me stay in Europe after Wimbledon instead of returning home to play the U.S. Clay and Grass Court circuits in July and August. Naturally, the Association requires most of its players to support their own tournaments, but from time to time they give one or two players the opportunity of gaining foreign experience by allowing them to remain in Europe. It was the first time I had made the request and Bill Clothier, the official who is responsible for securing players for the American summer circuits, readily agreed. So everything seemed set for an interesting summer. Tom and I were planning on a tour through West Germany, northern Italy, and Eastern Europe—a part of the world that I have still not managed to see to this day. The places would be fascinating, the company congenial, and the competition tough. All the tournaments would be on clay, which would do my game an immense amount of good, for European clay is slower and much more demanding than the type found in the United States. Only by continuous match play against the real experts like Manolo Santana and the ageless Hungarian Istvan Gulyas can you gain the experience and confidence to improve.

It was a nice dream but it was quickly shattered. We made it to Berlin only to discover that Donald Dell, who was the new U.S. Davis Cup captain by this time, had entered me, along with other prospective members of the team, for the French Championships. I was unaware of this and consequently had made no attempt to tell them I wasn't coming. That went down rather badly with the French, especially as they had seeded me Number Eight.

Donald was furious. Oblivious to the fact that I had received permission to play Berlin, the French Federation reported me to the U.S. LTA, which promptly withdrew my permission to stay in Europe after Wimbledon and demanded to see my expenses. Although the $20 a day expense allowance still held, the Association was beginning to realize that it was powerless to stop players from making their own deals abroad, and for the most part it turned a blind eye. However if it wanted to get nasty it could suddenly demand to check a player's expense account and if the expenditures were far in excess of $20 a day it could suspend him. This was a convenient way of maintaining arbitrary control over players who did not always see the benefit of dancing to its tune. The U.S. LTA could have followed the example of most modern-minded associations like Britain and Holland and allowed their top men to become registered players. But that sniffed too heavily of professionalism, which of course it was. The whole game was becoming professionalized one way or the other—either honestly or dishonestly.

Anyway it was obvious that I was in for a tough time, and when I heard that I was no longer going to be able to remain in Europe, the fury and frustration built up to bursting point. Every contact I had with members of the U.S. LTA made me more determined than ever to get away from their control. The deceit and hypocrisy of their actions appalled me, but there were moments of pure farce that one could not help laughing at. One occurred after I had joined Tom in Holland just prior to our departure for Berlin. We were having supper at the home of a Dutch LTA official when a call came through for Tom from Clothier in the United States. We were in the living room, eating informally with our plates on our knees, so Tom took the call right there. Totally unaware that I was sitting only a few feet away, Clothier proceeded to offer Okker $700 a week to play the American summer circuit. When Tom refused on the grounds that he was already committed to playing European tournaments, Clothier upped the bid to $750.

"I'm sorry, Bill," Tom replied, throwing me an amused glance across the room, "no matter how much you offer, I can't accept. I'm already committed."

After Tom hung up, everybody had a good laugh about the irony of the situation. But it became a little more than ironic a few weeks later when the same Bill Clothier, acting on the instructions of his Association, banned me from playing in Europe and started interrogating me because I had been spending more than

$20 a day. That was the final straw as far as I was concerned. I was at the point where I wanted a showdown with the U.S. LTA. I was going to open up my expense sheets down to the last nickel and dime and challenge them to do something about it. In a perverse sort of a way I wanted them to suspend me. I wanted them to show some guts for a change and stand by whatever set of irrational rules they thought they were trying to uphold. But of course they wouldn't go that far. All they did was to order me home after Wimbledon to play their tournaments. This came out during a dinner Sally and I had with Bill Clothier at a suitably staid and Victorian hotel called Brown's in London, where he was staying during the Queen's Club tournament the week before Wimbledon. There were no harsh words between us because Bill and I have always gotten along reasonably well and he has maintained a better working relationship with the players than most of his colleagues on the U.S. LTA. However, while sympathizing to some extent with my position, he made it clear that the Association was going to punish me by insisting that I return to the United States.

It was then that I tried my most drastic ploy. I tried to defect. It was Tom who put the idea into my head when he asked: "Why don't you come and play with me in Holland under the jurisdiction of the Dutch LTA? They'll make you a registered player and you won't have to put up with any more of this nonsense."

It was a fairly startling suggestion but, as there seemed no chance right at that moment of turning pro, it seemed to be the only possible way out. There had been precedents of a sort, for several disgruntled Australians had left their Association once it became obvious that they were never going to get the chance to play Davis Cup as long as Emerson, Stolle, Newcombe, and Roche were around. Martin Mulligan, for instance, had moved to Italy and eventually represented his adopted country in the Davis Cup. Bob Hewitt went to South Africa, Ken Fletcher to Hong Kong, and Bob Carmichael to Paris where he played under the auspices of the French LTA before turning pro. But as far as I knew no current member of the U.S. Davis Cup team had ever tried to seek shelter under another nation's umbrella. I talked it over with Tom and finally decided to try the British LTA first. There were many reasons for this. Apart from knowing a few British LTA officials like Derek Hardwick and Derek Penman quite well, I also knew that they were very much in favor of the registered player category. They had, after all, been party to the whole Open tennis revolution and seemed to be taking quite the most realistic attitude toward the modernization of the game. In addition, England was already very familiar to me and, like many tennis players from the English-speaking world, I had long considered it something of a home away from home.

So I decided to call Derek Hardwick and put the suggestion to him. I did so, needless to say, with a certain apprehension, for I had little idea of exactly what a change of national affiliation would entail. I knew that I would not be able to play Davis Cup for Britain, as I had already represented the United States, but I was not at all sure what other demands an adopted country would make on me. Would I have to live in England? Would I have to commit myself to playing a certain number of British tournaments, including, perhaps, County Week—a sort of Inter-state doubles championships held every year at Eastbourne? How would I be received when I did return to play some tournaments in America? All these questions were buzzing through my head as I made my way through the throng of people in the members' tearoom at the Queen's Club. I was heading for the row of three public phone booths situated in the narrow corridor between the tearoom and the bar. If there are other telephones at Queen's I have never discovered them, so although I would have appreciated some privacy there seemed to be no alternative. I waited in line with players and players' mothers and uncles and friends as press men and officials pushed past, peering through the glass doorway to see if the bar was open. My thoughts were racing. I knew that this one phone call could set in motion a whole series of events that could change my life in a rather dramatic manner, and I was a little surprised at my own determination to go through with it.

Eventually a booth became free and I leaned forward into the supposedly soundproof canopy in an attempt to keep the conversation as private as possible. In fact it would have been pretty easy for anyone to have overheard, and it was one of the more amazing aspects of the whole affair that the alert British tennis writers never got wind of this potentially explosive story.

Well, this is it, I thought to myself, as I heard Derek's voice on the line. Following the back-to-front instructions of how to operate British coin boxes—you put the money in after the number answers—I shoved my threepenny bit firmly into the slot.

"Derek, this is Marty Riessen," I began hesitantly and then, taking courage, blurted out, "I want to talk to you about the possibility of my playing under the jurisdiction of the British LTA."

With typical British aplomb, Hardwick sounded only mildly surprised at my unusual request. But he did sound interested and we agreed to meet and talk about the matter in detail at Wimbledon the following week.

When we did get together Hardwick confirmed that the British LTA would be only too happy to take me under its wing, but there was one snag. It would have to obtain the permission of the U.S. LTA first. As soon as Hardwick made that stipulation I knew it was hopeless. They weren't going to lose face by letting one of their leading players walk out on them. We did go through the motions of speaking to my Association, but of course they refused. The British were revolutionary minded, but only up to a point. They weren't going to risk a confrontation with a fellow member of the ILTF over one disgruntled tennis player, and I understood their position. I did speak to Dutch officials a little while later, but I found them equally reluctant to risk being accused of poaching players without the parent Association's permission. So even in the genteel little world of tennis, defection was not that easy.

The barriers erected to prevent a man from making that dash for personal freedom were invisible but real, and they were erected in the name of tradition, protocol, and social behavior. In some ways they were almost as hard to crack as that wall I had stared at in horror in Berlin just a few weeks before. At least with bricks and mortar you know what you are up against. I am exaggerating, of course, but there is nothing more frustrating than being fenced in and told how to lead your life by people you don't respect—even if it is a very nice life like playing tennis.

And at that point it did seem as if I had fenced myself right into a lonely little corner, for apart from rather obviously alienating the U.S. LTA, I appeared to have ruled myself out of the Davis Cup reckoning as well. A few days earlier Donald Dell and I had finally aired our differences at the Queen's Club. Donald had just taken over as Davis Cup captain and, true to form, he was throwing himself into the job with all his incredible zest and energy. He has been nicknamed "Deal"; "Zeal" would be almost as appropriate. Donald is a 100 percenter. He gives it and he demands it. He wants 100 percent effort, 100 percent dedication, 100 percent loyalty from anyone associated with him in any project. As far as the Davis Cup was concerned he wanted 100 percent and then some. That was where he lost me, because I don't believe in half measures either. If I feel that I cannot do a job properly then I don't want to do it at all, and deep down I knew that after seven frustrating years I was through giving 100 percent to the Davis Cup. First of all, I was not prepared to give up my partnership with Tom Okker, which by now meant more to me than representing my country.

Donald had insisted that I renew my partnership with Clark Graebner, but for me that was past history, and in any case I had no particular wish to play with Clark any more. Stories had filtered back to me over the years about how Clark used to put the blame on me after we had lost. I think Clark has matured a great deal since we played together regularly, but even if one can forgive things like that it is difficult to forget them, and there is no way a doubles partnership can flourish without the vital ingredients of mutual confidence and respect. There was no way I was going to break up my association with Tom to go back to something I had lost my appetite for, and I had cabled Donald to this effect a few weeks earlier. As a result he was pretty mad when he cornered me at Queen's, because he was under the impression that I was trying to have things all my own way—to continue playing with Tom and still be on the team.

A verbal confrontation with Donald is somewhat similar to
going ten rounds with Joe Frazier. You need to have the resilience
of Marciano and the mental footwork of Muhammad Ali to with-
stand the verbal barrage. It's not that he gets angry. Donald is
too much of a professional in the art of persuasian-by-bombard-
ment for that. He just leans forward and gives it to you straight
between the eyes.

"I don't want anyone on my team who is not prepared to give
100 percent" he said vehemently. "And if that means giving up
your partnership with Okker then that's what you'll have to do."

"Look, Donald," I said, cutting in quickly before he got into
his stride, "you don't seem to understand. I don't want to play
Davis Cup any more. It would be a mistake for you to even name
me to the team. I would be doing the United States a disservice
if I played. I'm at the stage where I don't feel I could play a good
match for America. I'm sorry, Donald, but I've had the Davis
Cup up to here and I just don't want to be a water boy any
longer."

My attitude amazed him. He tried to tell me that I shouldn't
think that way . . . that he really wanted me on the team as a
playing member . . . that I should reconsider. But basically
Donald understands straight talk and I think he realized that I was
simply being honest with him. At any rate, the point seemed to
get home and although I was very nearly proved wrong a few
weeks later, I reckoned I had effectively finished my Davis Cup
career then and there. Ironically, however, my relationship with
Donald Dell, far from coming to an abrupt end as one might
expect, was just beginning.

But before I saw him again, I was to become involved in another bizarre incident to which the U.S. LTA took the gravest
exception. The Dutch Association had asked Tom if he and I
would play an exhibition match with John Newcombe and Tony
Roche at Scheveningen in Holland on the Sunday immediately
following finals day at Wimbledon. Now there should have been
no problem about this. What could possibly be wrong with four
professional tennis players putting on an exhibition match for a
set fee? If tennis had been run with any honesty or logic, the

answer could only have been, "Nothing." As it was there was plenty wrong. This particular quartet included all the various labels the ILTF had devised. As members of "The Handsome Eight," Newcombe and Roche were contract pros, while Okker was a registered player and I was an "amateur." John and Tony could play together. Tom and I could play together. But according to the rules, the four of us could not step onto the same court outside the half dozen or so ILTF-sanctioned Open tournaments that were being held in that first revolutionary year of 1968.

Knowing this, I went to Bob Kelleher, then president of the U.S. LTA, and asked if he would grant special permission, since it was only for a Sunday afternoon exhibition match and we would be coming straight from Wimbledon where we had all been competing together anyway. But Kelleher said "No." He gave permission for me to play with Tom on the same day and on the same court as Newcombe and Roche—as long as we did not actually occupy that court at the same time. It seemed absurd, but I said okay and told Tom that I could accept on that basis.

However, when we arrived in Holland, the Dutch LTA president whisked us off to his house for lunch and became very persuasive. What the people really wanted to see, he explained, was a doubles between Tom and myself and the two Australians who, just 48 hours before, had won the Wimbledon doubles title. He understood our problem, he assured us, but we were not to worry because he would take full responsibility and arrange everything so as to break as few of the rules as possible.

What he did, in fact, was to announce to the crowd after the singles that the exhibition was over but that as all four of us felt like a little extra practice, Tom and I would team up to play against Newcombe and Roche. "It will be just a practice match, you understand," he explained over the loudspeaker, "but of course if any of you want to stay and watch, you will be most welcome." It must have been the only practice match ever played with a full complement of linesmen and ball boys in front of a crowd of 3,000 people! They got their money's worth, too, because Tom, the local boy, and I beat the Wimbledon champions.

I didn't give it much more thought the following week, which

I spent at home in Evanston before driving up to Milwaukee for the U.S. National Clay Courts. Sure we had bent the rules a little, but it all seemed so harmless that I became lulled into thinking that the Dutch Association would be able to smooth over any objections that might emerge from the ILTF hierarchy in London.

It takes a special type of bureaucratic mind to see the harm in entertaining a large number of people on a lovely summer's afternoon and getting well paid for your efforts. I know there are well-intentioned men on the ILTF who had thought up all these rules to protect what they considered to be vital bastions of amateurism, but they were still refusing to face up to the facts of life. The public wanted to see the best, and to be the best you had to play tennis full time. As the average tennis player doesn't have an oil well in his back yard, that means he has to be a professional. Even in 1968 that much seemed pretty obvious. I knew that I had been a professional at heart for years, but I was reaping none of the benefits from what I considered to be a perfectly healthy attitude. Like most other registered players and "amateurs," I was continually being hounded by unrealistic officials with their never-ending list of petty restrictions and directives.

My patience was wearing thin, but there seemed to be no way out until, quite unexpectedly, Bob Briner arrived in Milwaukee. Briner was the executive director of "The Handsome Eight," which was already becoming known by the more serious title of World Championship Tennis. To my surprise Briner had come for the sole purpose of obtaining my signature. With enormous relief I realized that a door had opened. Anytime I wanted I could walk through it and into another world.

I was flattered that Briner wanted me, of course, but I had learned enough about the art of bargaining not to swoon with gratitude at the suitor's feet like some desperate spinster. I didn't consider myself to be on the shelf. The affair in Holland seemed to have been forgotten, and despite what I told him at the Queen's Club, Donald Dell, who was also in Milwaukee, was still trying to persuade me to change my mind and make myself available for the Davis Cup team. I talked things over with my parents and Olen Parks, the representative of the Wilson Sporting Goods

Company, whose long association with the game dated back to the earliest days of the pro tour. My mom and dad, who were even more sensitive than I was over the way I had been treated by the U.S. LTA, were inclined to favor my turning pro, and Parks also suggested that this might be a propitious moment to begin a new career.

Certainly it seemed the obvious thing to do, and I was all set to start discussing details of the contract with Briner when I received a phone call a few days later. It was from a local Milwaukee newsman asking if I had seen the wire-service story from London.

"What story?" I asked guardedly.

"The story quoting the ILTF as saying that they have asked the U.S. LTA to suspend you for playing an exhibition in Holland with Newcombe and Roche," said the voice on the other end of the line. "They're asking the Dutch LTA to suspend Okker as well."

"I don't know anything about it," I replied, and added hurriedly that I didn't want to discuss it either.

So they hadn't forgotten. Their pettiness angered me, but I must admit the suspension threat scared me a little. It cut my options, and although I could have gone straight back to Briner and signed the first piece of paper he handed me, something told me that that was too easy a way out. For some reason the voice I listened to most was Donald's. He still wanted me back on the team and he suggested that I join the other members of the Davis Cup squad in Philadelphia the following week and play in the Merion tournament.

"In the meantime I'll fight off the suspension," he said. "Come back for a week and see how you feel and tell Briner to hold off for a while."

From anyone else that would have been so much talk, but as I have said, Donald is a most persuasive guy, and not for the last time, I decided to take his advice. At least this would give me a little longer to think before committing myself.

Donald didn't finalize arrangements for me to play at Merion until the following Monday morning—the day the tournament

was due to begin. So I had to make a dash for an early plane
to Philadelphia, leaving Sally to pack some extra gear and follow
by car. Although I didn't know it at the time, this was just the
start of a whirlwind ten days that was to change the course of
my life and necessitate some pretty hectic traveling, even by the
standards of the jet-age tennis player.

Sally eventually arrived at Merion two days later, having survived a hazardous journey through the rain-swept mountain
passes of western Pennsylvania. We immediately sat down for a
final discussion to decide my future. After weighing all the various
factors involved, I realized that I couldn't go backward. It had
been fun being with Arthur Ashe and other members of the
Davis Cup squad again for a few days, but I still couldn't work
up any renewed enthusiasm for that particular aspect of the game.
Donald had once said that Davis Cup requires a lot of dedication, a lot of giving. And I had nothing left to give. Like in a
floundering marriage, the spark had gone, and I realized then
that there was only one thing to do. Get a divorce. Get out.
Turn pro.

The patient Bob Briner turned up again on Friday, contract in
hand, and the following day I told him I was ready to negotiate.
It was a relief, I think, for everyone concerned, but for me in
particular it was the end of a long hassle—the end of a weari-
some, troubling period of perpetual bickering and arguing with
the U.S. LTA. The thought of no longer being answerable to
them for my every move was probably the most attractive aspect
of the whole affair. I was sick to death of the wheeling and
dealing, of having to sell myself week by week around the circuit,
of never knowing quite what I was going to do or where I was
going to play from one week to the next. As a pro, I would have
my schedule worked out for me. I would be free to concentrate
on playing tennis, pure and simple. If I played well, I would do
well financially. If I didn't, there would be no one to blame but
myself. No longer would I be able to say, "But they didn't give
me the chance." It would be up to me—and that's the way I
wanted it.

There remained one final and rather important detail to be
completed—the negotiation of the deal with World Champion-

ship Tennis. I needed someone to help me—someone who not only was capable of understanding the legal implications of the fine print on the contract, but who also had an intimate knowledge of my market value as a tennis player at the time. There was, of course, just such a person right there at the Merion Cricket Club. His name was Donald Dell.

A conflict of interests is nothing new to Donald. He is one of the few people I know who seems to thrive on it. His background as a Washington lawyer deeply involved in politics no doubt helps. For a man who was only 29, his experience even then in the legal, political, and sporting worlds was considerable. He had served as a top aide to Sargent Shriver at the Office of Economic Opportunity and later had worked as an advance man for Robert Kennedy during the Senator's tragically brief 1968 campaign. Donald's tennis credentials were equally impressive. In 1961, the year after he graduated from Yale, he was ranked Number Four in the United States and was a member of the Davis Cup squad. He had traveled the world circuit extensively during the sixties, and toward the end of his playing career had slipped naturally and comfortably into the role of advocate and agent for Arthur Ashe, Charlie Pasarell, and other top American players.

Once it became obvious to him that it was in my personal interests to turn pro, he put his own interests as far as the Davis Cup was concerned to one side and readily agreed to help me negotiate my contract with Briner. I had never set eyes on a contract before in my life, but fortunately there was nothing very complicated about this one. Briner, whom I always found to be a most reasonable and understanding man, was not pressing any hard bargain. World Championship Tennis was not in a position to do so at that time anyway, as Tony Roche was injured and they were badly in need of a new player to fill in. The terms Briner had mentioned seemed reasonable to me; just before I walked out on court to play Ashe in the final on Sunday afternoon, I had no qualms about telling Donald: "Work it out for me. If you think its fair within the framework of what we've discussed, go ahead and finalize it. I'll sign when I get off court."

So I left the two of them huddled together in the clubhouse as

I began what would normally have been a big match for me. But it was a little hard to concentrate knowing that my future was being decided out of earshot just a few yards away.

I had already lost the first set to Arthur by the time Sally left a note for me by the umpire's chair. I picked it up and read the scribbled words while changing ends midway through the second set. It read: "Relax, everything's okay. You're a contract pro."

I walked back to receive serve with my thoughts anywhere but on the thunderbolt Ashe was about to unleash at me. But even the most meticulous concentration would not have helped, for Arthur was in the middle of his great winning streak that brought him thirty consecutive victories and culminated in his winning the U.S. Open title at Forest Hills a month later. He crushed me in straight sets. But somehow it seemed not to matter too much. For me it was the end of a long road and the beginning of a new adventure.

As soon as the match was over I went upstairs to the clubhouse press room and signed the contract Briner handed me. Donald had assured me it was a good deal and he was right. WCT was to pay me a guaranteed $16,000 for the remainder of 1968, and a further guarantee of $32,500 for 35 weeks' play each of the two years thereafter. Any prize money that I won in excess of that sum would be mine also. I am happy to say that it has never cost WCT a cent from that day to this to have me on a guaranteed contract. I have always won far more than they agreed to pay me.

From the moment I shook hands with Bob Briner, things moved fast. I had 48 hours to get back to Chicago, repack, and catch a plane to the south of France where WCT was due to play an eight-man tournament the following week. While Sally threw things back into a suitcase, I phoned Hal and Kay Semars at South Orange, N.J., traditional site of the Eastern Grass Court Championships. I had been expecting to go there directly from Merion and stay with the Semars as I had done every summer for the past eight years. For one week every August I had become almost part of the family—at least Hal and Kay had made me feel that way—and as I spoke to them on the phone I got the first pang of nostalgia for a passing way of life. They wished me luck in my new venture and as I hung up I realized just how different things were going to be. There is not too much that South Orange, New Jersey, has in common with Cannes on the Côte d'Azur.

Racing back down the same highways that Sally had traveled only a few days before, we made Chicago in one day's drive and a few hours later I was on a TWA flight for Paris with a connection to Nice. Best-selling author Harold Robbins was on the plane and we got to talking over a drink in the transit lounge of Orly Airport during the stopover. He was returning to his home and his yacht on the Riviera and made a fascinating traveling companion. Somehow, chatting to the man who had written *The Adventurers* and all those other fast-moving tales of glamor and intrigue seemed to heighten my own sense of adventure.

Marc Brissac, the French teaching professional who became the coordinator for pro events in France during the early days of the Kramer tours, met me at Nice Airport and drove me to the hotel in Cannes. I discovered that Mal Anderson, the veteran Australian pro who was making a comeback to the circuit that year, was the only other player to have arrived. I had never met Mal, who won Forest Hills in 1957—a year before I first played there. But he soon made me feel right at home by entertaining me half the night with stories about the rough old times on the Kramer tour. Hoad, Rosewall, Gonzales, Sedgman, Hartwig, Trabert—names I had idolized since I had watched them play once when they passed through Hinsdale during my school days. Mal, of course, had played with them all, and by the time the tournament got under way I had a better understanding of what it was like to live and survive on the pro circuit. It was a challenge I relished and proceeded to prove I could handle. I beat Mal to reach the final, where I lost to John Newcombe, and then teamed with Mal to win the doubles title.

I knew then that I had made the right decision—that I had finally arrived at the destination I had been heading for ever since I first toddled onto a tennis court in my father's shadow more than twenty years before.

8

LOOKING BACK

The celebration of my birth was brief. Three days later the Japanese attacked Pearl Harbor.

Not that the war ever got very close to Hinsdale, the quiet, middle-class suburb of Chicago where I was born and brought up. It was a normal enough childhood, if one takes "normal" to mean the average sports-minded American kid from the average white suburban family of the forties. But looking around my contemporaries today on the World Championship Tennis tour, I realize, of course, that there is no such thing as "normal" or "average" for a group such as ours. Certainly there was very little similar about our childhoods. Tom Okker, the man who was to become my best friend, was a little Dutch boy living under Nazi occupation in Amsterdam—just a mile or two from where Anne Frank was hiding in her attic. Tom was luckier than she—he, too, is Jewish. In Yugoslavia, where partisans fought the Germans and then the Allies in a struggle that spilled over into the so-called peacetime years, there was a young kid called Nikki Pilic growing up in the seaside town of Split. In Blackbutt, Queensland, Roy Emerson was learning how to hunt kangaroos; and not far away on a farm near Rockhampton a scrawny kid called Rod Laver was peeking enviously through the wire netting that surrounded his father's courts while his elder brothers got all the tennis lessons. And in Sheffield, England, Mrs. Taylor, a steelworker's wife, discovered a way to give her son Roger some alternative to playing soccer on the streets of that grimy industrial

70

city. She took him down to the public park and taught him tennis.

So what did we have in common? Not much except the ability to hit tennis balls better than most kids. And, of course, the very necessary opportunity of doing so. I was luckier than most in this respect, for not only was my father a teaching professional, but when I was four or five we moved to a house right across the street from the public courts where Dad used to teach. Almost as soon as I could walk, I would automatically follow him across the road, clutching my junior-size Cardinal racket and hanging around until he had finished his lesson. Then he would give me a hit.

He was, and still is, a fine teacher, my dad. A strict one, too, and a glutton for hard work. His ancestry probably accounts for that, for while my mother has a half-German, half-English background, my father is of 100 percent German stock. He was raised in a little farming community called Osmond in northeast Nebraska and later attended the University of Illinois in Champaign. It was there that he met my mother, Mildred, whose father, Samuel Ludlow, had at one time been county judge and mayor of the nearby town of Paxton. They met in the University library; I have always thought it an amazing coincidence that I met my wife Sally in the University library at Northwestern. After their marriage my parents moved out West to Yuma, Arizona, where Dad took a teaching job which carried them through the depression years with a minimum of discomfort. Shortly after my sister Susan was born, they moved back to Illinois and took up residence in Hinsdale, where my father taught history and physical education at the local high school.

Just as he did with me soon afterwards, my father tried to turn Susan into a champion tennis player. But she rebelled. I thought that was great. She was always far more independent and ready to challenge Dad's authority than I was and I admired the stand she took against tennis. Susan is married now, with two kids, and lives in Des Moines, Iowa. She plays tennis for fun and gets much more enjoyment from it than she would have as a reluctant tournament player.

I never rebelled for the simple reason that I never wanted to.

I loved the game right from the start, and there was only one crisis as far as I can remember in the slow and methodical development of Marty Riessen, tennis player. I must have been about eleven at the time. I was due to play a tournament one afternoon and that morning I broke a cardinal rule by going up to the lakes in southern Wisconsin for a swim. These lakes are only about an hour from Hinsdale. Swimming is about the worst possible preparation for tennis, because it loosens your muscles, and sure enough I suffered a bad loss in the tournament. Understandably Dad got mad, and for about 24 hours eleven-year-old Riessen was marching around in an equally black mood thinking about how he was going to quit. "That's it," I told myself, "I'll just chuck it in and then I'll be able to go swimming exactly when I want."

A day later I made a sheepish return to the practice court and, in spirit as well as in body—or so it seems—I have been there ever since. Even when college basketball took five months out of the tennis year, I never seriously considered giving up the game that has become my life.

Crises, in fact, were few and far between during my childhood. I remember getting hit by a car as I came roller skating out of the park, without any particularly drastic result. I remember raising the seat on my sister's bicycle and going straight over the handlebars when I tried to ride it. And possibly one of the very first things I remember was setting fire to some leaves in the park and getting caught by the police. I must have been barely five at the time and I was really scared. They took my name and I cried a whole lot because I was quite sure they were going to put me in jail. But my sentence turned out to be nothing more serious than a gentle lecture from my mom and dad; and apart from the occasional desire to burn my racket after missing a volley on match point, I have never felt any subsequent inclinations to pursue a career as an arsonist.

I suppose I was, in fact, a singularly law-abiding child. There is no doubt in my mind that the Victorian austerity of my father's powerful personality was the cause of this. In recent years I've discovered that I have much more of his character in my own makeup than I had believed and now, looking back, I see that it was probably supressed at a very early age as a result of ultra-strict parental tutorage. My father's lessons on personal discipline, 100 percent effort at whatever task one undertook, impeccable manners and tight-lipped control of the emotions in difficult situations were all taken to heart by his awe-struck son. So much so in fact that Dad occasionally would be worried at my reluctance to speak up for myself in an argument. He knew precisely how to deal with my sister's spirited outbursts against the rules and regulations he imposed, but when I confronted him with silence, he was at a loss to know what to do. Inevitably this side of my personality carried over into my sporting activities, with the result that I gained the desired reputation of being a model sportsman in both tennis and basketball. It was a nice reputation to have, but it also led to charges that I lacked sufficient aggression to make it really big in either sport. As I already related, it required a deliberate effort on my part to rid myself of this image in tennis and I have no doubt that the passive attitude I adopted early in my career retarded my progress to the top.

Bringing up kids—something Sally and I have yet to do—has to be one of the most difficult jobs in the world, and the so-called generation gap that has engulfed society in the last decade has not made it any easier. Obviously my parents were doing what they thought best, and I respect them for it. But my own ideas and values have changed dramatically in the last few years and I have no doubt that I will be a good deal more liberal with my own children.

But like so many of us who grew up in the unquestioning fifties, I find it impossible to reject completely all the values our parents' society instilled in us. I cannot go along with the extreme radicalism of some young people, blacks, and other minority groups, even though my exposure to the ghettos of America and other poverty-stricken areas of the world has enabled me to develop a better understanding of their initial despair and resulting militancy. Sally, who is less conservative than I am, and Arthur Ashe, who has asked me to help him with ghetto clinics on several occasions, have given me more insight into the complex problems of the underprivileged—problems that one never imagined existed in the affluent all-white neighborhood of Hinsdale. When I eventually retire from competitive tennis, I intend to work closely with various sports programs in the Chicago area. Grant Golden, the former U.S. Davis Cup player, is already doing great work with Youth Action programs, as is Helen Shockley of the Chicago Tennis District. Much can be done to alleviate boredom and to give youngsters some purpose in life if enough people show concern. But I am still sufficiently square to believe that it should be done within the system. That is my legacy of a strict and conservative upbringing.

And even my own battles with the tennis establishment, which stamped me as something of a rebel by the time I turned pro, have done nothing to change my opinion on that score. I was not rebelling against the establishment as such, but only against the establishment as represented by an association that preached one set of rules and practiced another.

However, all these problems were still a long way off as I progressed through Monroe grade school, Hinsdale Junior High, and then Hinsdale Township High School. I had played my first tournament, a local village affair for elevens and under, at the age of seven and began in suitable style by winning it. My father entered me for tournaments on a regular basis after that, and by the time I was fourteen I was beginning to make a breakthrough on the national scene. That year I partnered a short, stocky guy with a bouncy, aggressive style; his name was Chuck McKinley and together we carried off the National Junior Doubles title at Kalamazoo, Michigan, by beating Mike Neely and Don Caton 6-1, 6-2 in the final. The singles title was won by a seventeen-year-old left-handed Australian with copper colored hair and a mass of freckles. I had never heard of him before, but I soon realized Rod Laver was a name I was never going to forget.

Throughout these early years my mother was helping my development as a player and a person in her own unobtrusive fashion. She was always meticulously careful to keep me from stuffing myself with the kind of trashy foods that kids hanker after, and much of her time was devoted to driving me to tournaments and watching my matches. She was never the kind of mom who felt it necessary to interfere to the extent of shouting words of encouragement or giving hand signals from the sideline—something for which I was very grateful. Just having her there was a source of comfort.

I think I was about ten years old when Mom piled my sister and me and two childhood tennis-playing friends, Don and Belinda Thorne, into our old silver-gray Chevy Impala for my first long-distance tennis journey. We were headed for Rochester, Minnesota, which was about a day's drive from Hinsdale, and of course it was a big adventure. I sometimes think about that trip as I hop casually on a jet for Sydney or Rome. The distances were shorter in those early days but our old Chevy didn't go quite as fast as a Boeing and Mom seemed to log as many hours behind the wheel driving me all over the eastern half of the United States as some of the jet pilots who have flown me around the world.

Another sport soon began to play a big part in my life—basketball. At fourteen, I was already 6'1", so I was well equipped for a game that was to give me just as much enjoyment as tennis over the next five or six years. However by the time I was in my junior year at high school, height was the least of my assets, for I had ceased to grow and 6'1" is tantamount to being a pygmy in basketball. I had to rely on other physical assets to maintain my position as guard on the team. It was no coincidence that most of those assets are precisely the same qualities that go to make a good tennis player, for the sports have much in common in this respect: short, quick sprints; rapid stops and changes of direction; anticipation; jumping; fast hands; and of course aiming a ball for a specific target. It was this physical similarity between basketball and tennis that enabled me to forget my racket for as long as four or five months during the year—as I did at college—and then pick it up again with a minimum amount of difficulty.

As a result of my success in two sports, I was lucky enough to have a number of universities offering me scholarships by the time I was seventeen. Some wanted me for tennis, and after I had been named to all-state teams by the newspapers in both junior

and senior high-school years, others were after me as a prospective basketball player. I eventually chose Northwestern, not only
because of the geographical advantages—the university town of
Evanston is less than an hour's drive from Hinsdale—but also
because they were offering a basketball scholarship. This meant
that my father, who had switched jobs to become head tennis
coach at Northwestern a year before I went there, did not have
to use up one of his tennis scholarships on his son.

So in September 1960 I enrolled at Northwestern and thus
began four hectic years of sporting and academic activity, during
which time I became one of the few college athletes of recent
years to participate at the highest level of two sports. It was the
following year that I was named to the Davis Cup squad for the
first time. I managed to confine the two games to their allotted
seasons with not great problems of overlap until 1963. That was
the year America reached the Davis Cup Challenge Round
scheduled in Adelaide, Australia, and with the opportunity of a
trip like that coming my way, basketball had to take a back seat
for a time.

Even then, assisted by jet-age travel, I cut my absence from
Northwestern's basketball team to a minimum by pulling such a
fast switch from Davis Cup reserve to basketball guard that I left
myself dizzy. Just four days after practicing with Dennis Ralston
and Chuck McKinley—who won the cup for us that year—on a
back court at the Memorial Drive Stadium in Adelaide, I was
appearing at Yost Field House in Ann Arbor for Northwestern in
the Big Ten Conference match against the University of Michigan
—a little matter of 10,000 miles and 24 hours of travel away.
We lost but I think I can honestly say that it wasn't because of
any lack of preparedness on my part. I had been filled in on the
plays by my teammates as soon as I stepped off the plane, and
once I got the travel stiffness out of my legs I was in great shape
physically after weeks of hard training with the Davis Cup squad.
Even in Adelaide I hadn't been neglecting basketball altogether.
I found a gym near the courts and, having bought myself a ball,
I used to follow up five hours of tennis with an hour of shooting
practice at the net. Both Ralston and McKinley had played bas-

Roy Emerson (foreground left) and Neale Fraser look downcast as Chuck McKinley's racket sails into the air at Memorial Drive, Adelaide. Chuck and Dennis Ralston had just given the U.S. a 2-1 lead over Australia in the 1963 Davis Cup Challenge Round in 1963—the year we regained the Cup. *Credit: Marty Riessen*

ketball in high school, but I couldn't persuade either of them to join me in my lonely workouts. I think they thought I was slightly mad.

But the effort seemed to be appreciated back home. Chicago newspaper columnist Bob Casterline was kind enough to write:

> Though he was still shaking the "down under" dust off his shoes, [Riessen] already is proving to be a most important man in the Wildcat basketball lineup and is helping make the Cats a tougher team than they were before Christmas.
>
> Though Marty may not make All-American, and may never score more than 15 points in a single game, he's a guy who makes the Cats go. His sharp passing and floor leadership are sparking a difference between an ordinary team and one that shows flashes of brilliance.

And in the Chicago *Sun-Times* Jack Clarke wrote:

> The injection into Northwestern's bloodstream of Marty Riessen has acted as a stabilizing influence, tranquilizing the jitters and inducing dreams of grandeur. Riessen spent the fall months gadding about the globe as a member of the United States Davis Cup team.
>
> Just off the plane from Australia, equipped with a deep tan and a beatnik haircut, he accompanied the Wildcats to Ann Arbor last Saturday where his expert ball handling, shrewd resourceful tactics and nine points enabled his side to make a presentable showing despite an 85-73 rebuff.

I never thought that I would make a better basketball player than tennis player, but I did become a fairly decent performer with the big ball and I started every game in my junior and senior years at Northwestern. Although I had been known principally as a scorer in high school, I switched to playmaker and leader of the team at Northwestern largely because the other guard, Rich Falk, was a top-rate shooter. Also, the reader will

The Northwestern University basketball team in 1964. *Credit: Northwestern University*

Flanked by my Wildcat colleagues Rich Falk (left) and Phil Keely at McGaw Hall, I display a replica of the Davis Cup after my return from Australia in 1963. *Credit: Chicago Tribune Photo*

not be surprised to hear, Falk was considered a more aggressive personality. At that stage I was still a long way from shedding my Mr. Nice Guy image.

Northwestern was never a great team during my three years, but we were quite respectable and I am sure that only the lack of a really tall and talented center kept us at arm's length from greater success.

The year after graduation I played in a local industrial league with a few of my old college cronies and it was a lot of fun. But I had decided to make a serious, full-time assault on the tennis circuit by then, and I quickly realized that basketball would have to go. Apart from the fact that I had suffered a small but nagging wrist injury, I was wary of further accidents while playing with guys who were only partially fit. It is always twice as easy to receive or inflict injuries with poorly tuned muscles, for the obvious reason that you have less control over them. In the casual, slaphappy atmosphere of the industrial league, I was always getting kneed in the groin or trodden on—simply because many of the other players were not fit enough to have proper control over their limbs.

So with many regrets but a host of happy memories, I put my basketball career behind me. Even now I get a big kick out of realizing that I played against many of today's big pro stars— players like Cazzie Russell of the San Francisco Warriors, John Havlicek and Don Nelson of the Boston Celtics, Jerry Lucas of the New York Knicks, and Gail Goodrich of the Los Angeles Lakers, and the Van Arsdale twins.

I never had the opportunity of playing against Bill Bradley, but I did get to meet him when we were recruiting for future Northwestern teams. We weren't too successful in persuading the Rhodes Scholar to join us. I remember taking him down to Chicago to see the movie "Exodus" after showing him around the University, and the next day he exited from the Northwestern picture. Still, it was fun meeting him.

My only regrets about my basketball career began after I had finished with the sport. The press, who have only just begun to realize that tennis deserves proper coverage in its own right,

were always harping on my basketball achievements when they
were writing about me as a tennis player. Each article seemed to
get a little more exaggerated than the last until, through hearsay
and journalistic license, they were portraying me as a much better player than I ever was. I found it embarrassing—especially
when a couple of writers had me down as an All-American. Let
me put the record straight: I *was* a college basketball star for
three years, but I was *never* an All-American.

But it was basketball that had the mass appeal; tennis players
just had to live with that fact back in the early sixties. A column
by Bill Gleason, then writing in the *Chicago Herald American,*
underlined the identity problem tennis had (at any rate the topic
provides a good excuse for reprinting what was a very pleasantly
complimentary article):

> When Marty Riessen plays his final tennis match for
> Northwestern, the school ought to dispense with the mono-
> gram act. Instead of giving the guy a felt letter, Stu Hol-
> comb and his associates should put up a plaque in Riessen's
> honor.
>
> This plaque, as I visualize it, would make no references to
> the fact that Riessen has been one of the most accomplished
> and versatile athletes since the tale of the Wildcats began
> twitching.
>
> The plaque would be somewhere between the new ten-
> nis courts and McGaw Hall and it would merely say: "A
> nice guy shuttled this way."
>
> With arrows in both directions.
>
> Because tennis is a better kept international secret than
> the personal letters from United States Presidents to USSR
> Chairmen, there are probably no more than 93 persons in
> the Chicago area who are aware that Riessen is one of
> America's better tennis players. And 91 of those 93 learned
> about Marty's other pastime while they were watching the
> telecast of a Big Ten basketball game.
>
> Riessen undoubtedly has had 100 times the publicity as
> an associate of Rick Lopossa and Rich Falk than he has
> had as a teammate of Chuck McKinley and Dennis Ralston.
>
> The way other athletes feel about Riessen was expressed

last winter by Lapossa, Northwestern's elastic basketball forward, when he said: "If any athlete has earned a right to be cocky it would be Marty. He's been around the world twice and has played with and against the best tennis players in the world. Most guys in his position wouldn't even bother with college basketball. But he came back here after the Davis Cup and sacrificed himself for the continuity of the team. Marty could average 20 points a game if he were hungry, but he'll pass up 12-foot jump shots to pass up to another guy."

Lapossa summed up the thing that sets Riessen apart in our time.

The day of the versatile university athlete has virtually ended because most collegians can't or won't take the pressure of more than one sport and maintain good grades.

Riessen plays tennis and basketball and has a B-minus scholastic average.

When he explains why he competes in two sports, Marty uses exactly the same words that are used by other youths to explain why one game is all they can handle.

"To play only one sport is too tough," Marty said just before he departed to play in the Big Ten Tennis Championships Saturday in Champaign. "By playing basketball and tennis I get a mental rest. I couldn't play tennis twelve months a year."

Of course I play tennis about ten months in the year now, but in those days I think basketball did keep me fresh for tennis and vice versa. And although the name of Riessen was always spoken of in the same breath as Falk and Lapossa around town, I started to form another athletic partnership at that time—one that was to gain as much, if not greater prominence abroad than it ever did with the mass of the American sporting public. For Clark Graebner had arrived at Northwestern a year after I did and had quickly revealed himself as a tennis player of above-average ability. Strong, tall, bespectacled and crew-cut, Clark strode about the courts like some Marine master sergeant, and often his language and actions fitted the image, too.

So, as can be imagined, there was nothing very similar about our personalities. But we managed to get along pretty well and soon turned ourselves into a formidable doubles team. We carried Northwestern to the Big Ten Conference Championship in 1963, and although we couldn't repeat the success as a team the following year, Clark and I still won all our matches. In fact I became the first player in Big Ten history to go unbeaten in both singles and doubles for three straight years.

Clark and I managed to put Northwestern's name to the fore in the NCAA Championships during that period as well. In both 1963 and 1964 we finished third behind the West Coast giants UCLA and Southern Cal, who just happened to have a few players like Arthur Ashe, Charlie Pasarell, Dennis Ralston, and the late Rafe Osuña around at the time.

My personal record was consistent but frustrating. I reached the NCAA singles final three years in succession and lost each time—once to Osuña and twice to Ralston. But with Clark's help I had still given Northwestern something of a reputation in tennis circles in those days, though, and as far as sports fans back in Chicago were concerned I was Marty Riessen, the Wildcat basketball guard.

9

MIXED DOUBLES

Northwestern has a reputation more for its academic than its sporting achievements. Adlai Stevenson, Arthur Goldberg, and George Ball all graduated from the University in the thirties, worked as lawyers in Chicago during the immediate pre-war years, and then, by an amazing coincidence, were successive U.S. ambassadors to the United Nations in the sixties.

But the school has another reputation of which I took greater advantage. It is known for the beauty of its female undergraduates. There were so many of them around the campus, in fact, that I wasn't knocked out of my chair when Bill Leary, my roommate and a fraternity brother, brought his date down to the library where I was studying one Saturday night. His date was a cute-looking girl all right, but since there were so many of them around, my eyes didn't exactly pop out of my head. I don't want to sound blasé about this because the very fact that I was working alone in the library on a Saturday evening suggests that I wasn't exactly overrun with dates. Which was true. During the whole year I had spent at Northwestern up to that time, I had had only one steady girl friend, and I lost her by spending too much time on Davis Cup duty in India and Italy. Some girls might have been impressed by their boy friend's representing the United States in such exotic places, but not this one. She was obviously not the waiting kind. When I returned, suitably armed with a nice-looking sweater as a present, I found that she had something else to keep her warm.

So I won't pretend that I wasn't interested when Bill walked into the library that night with this pretty blonde on his arm. They were on their way out for the evening and Bill, who knew I was working there, had just dropped by to give me a message.

"Marty, I'd like you to meet Sally," he said.

"Hi," I said by way of an original reply.

After telling me whatever it was he had come to say, Bill left with Sally, leaving me to agree with Frank Sinatra that Saturday night was the loneliest night of the week. And that was how I met my wife.

A couple of days later Sally and I passed each other on the way to class and I said "Hi" again. I really used to come on strong in those days. Not that I had to, if you believe Sally's end of the story. She insists that she had already made up her mind to get me even before we met. I don't know about all that bull, but it is true that she probably knew who I was because she came from Milwaukee and I had been playing tournaments up there for several years. Apparently she saw a large picture of me in the local paper saying that I was at Northwestern. As Sally was due to go there a few months later, she apparently promised herself then and there that one day we would meet. She is a pretty headstrong girl and she certainly got her way on that one. After eight years of marriage I must say I am very happy that she did.

Our relationship took a little time to develop, however. We continued to pass each other on the way to class almost every day for several weeks and gradually got past the stage of monosyllabic greetings. After a month or two we started dating. Happily, Bill Leary's relationship with Sally had petered out of its own accord, so there was no conflict there. To cut a love story short we decided to get married in December 1964.

The wedding was set for December 19 at Wauwatosa, the Milwaukee suburb where Sally was brought up. Heavens, what an awful day that was. I'm not big on ceremonial occasions at the best of times, and I found this one more traumatic than most. The whole affair got off to a bad start because Sally was still in school and had been taking exams right up to the 17th. The following day there was a rehearsal dinner with members of both families present. The problem was that for a while it seemed as if the one absentee would be the bride. Although she's improved a bit now, Sally was notorious at the time for being late, and with the exams offering a fairly genuine excuse she turned up an hour behind schedule, having driven up from Evanston in a state of near exhaustion. My father was furious and everybody was on edge.

After going through the ceremony with the minister of the First Congregational Church who was to marry us the following day, I fled to my uncle's cottage on Lake Geneva where some friends had arranged a traditional bachelor party. We sat up half the night playing poker and, after a few hours' sleep, woke next morning to be confronted by a snow storm. The weather was so bad that many of the guests who were due to come in from Chicago couldn't make it, and even my parents had a tough time getting there over the icy roads from Evanston.

But I managed to make it to the church on time, and more amazingly, so did Sally. I was so relieved to see her coming up the aisle that I relaxed to the point where I didn't listen very carefully to what the minister was saying. After the previous day's rehearsal, I thought I knew what I was supposed to repeat; but suddenly I realized that he was adding a lot more and I hadn't heard what he'd said. So I started mumbling frantically in a low and barely audible stream of gibberish in the hope that I'd be able to pick up the thread again. By this time my best man, Dennis Hansen, a basketball teammate from Northwestern, was struggling to control his laughter and I had broken out in a cold sweat. But at least Dennis didn't drop the ring, and somehow we managed to get through the whole performance.

Sally's parents, Mr. and Mrs. Joseph Lybek, are of Polish, French, and German ancestry, and they laid on a sumptuous feast with music and dancing and mounds to eat. Some of my more hilarious friends pulled off my shirt and wrote all the obvious directions for matrimonial bliss over my body in lipstick and then sprayed the car with shaving cream, and everyone was saying what a great time they were having. I'm glad they did, but it only confirmed my belief that weddings are for everyone but the two people getting married.

But at least we made up for it on our honeymoon. Roy Etnyre, an old fraternity brother of my dad's, had kindly offered us the use of his cottage at Estes Park, which is a little town in Rocky Mountain National Park, Colorado. He gave us the keys when we left the reception, and after spending the night totally exhausted in a nearby hotel, we flew to Denver and eventually arrived at what turned out to be an idyllic hideaway. The cottage was one of a group situated in a gulley with towering mountains stretching up on either side. There was a creek at the end of the gulley and the mountainsides were dotted with pines and aspen. A few hundred feet above us snow glistened on the branches in the winter sun, and at night we could hear the wind whistling softly through the pine needles. At that time of year all the other cottages were deserted, except for one which was occupied by an aged couple. They asked us in one night to play Parcheesi; but the rest of the week we were there, Sally and I had entirely to ourselves. We went climbing up the mountainside to cut our own Christmas tree and survived a brush with disaster carrying it back down, when Sally slipped into a crevice. We decided to roll the tree after that. On Christmas night we went into town to try to find a restaurant, but everything was closed so we returned to the cottage and feasted on bean soup and other leftovers. We didn't really miss the turkey. Somehow it was quite a romantic Christmas dinner.

The second week of our honeymoon was spent in New Orleans, which was great, too, except for the fact that I made a rather embarrassing attempt to play tennis. We had gone down there because I was due to play in the Sugar Bowl, but as soon as I stepped on court I realized I was in no condition to do so. I was so weak that the first time I tried to serve, the momentum of the swing carried me straight through and pitched me flat on my face. Needless to say, that act brought the house down because everyone knew I was on my honeymoon. It was so embarrassing. The result of the match was even more so because I was ranked fifth in the country that year and I proceeded to lose in straight sets to a guy called Jim Beste, who was ranked a formidable 56th. New Orleans is a good place to put little horror shows like that out of your mind, and we managed to enjoy the rest of the week pretty successfully, breakfasting at Brennan's, searching out some great seafood restaurants, and living it up a little along Bourbon Street. Then it was back to Evanston, where Sally still had a term of college to complete while I was due to begin graduate school.

10

"IT ONLY HURTS WHEN I PLAY"

Every athlete must pamper his body. He must inspect it, nurse it, exercise it, protect it, and generally spend more time contemplating its aches, pains, and idiosyncracies than anyone in any other walk of life. Physical fitness becomes a matter of pride as well as of necessity. That is why I was doubly embarrassed by my performance in New Orleans. Honeymoon or not, it wasn't very professional to go on court so totally out of condition. And even if I was almost a genuine amateur in those days, it made no difference. You don't have to get paid to develop professional pride. A kid of ten can have it and he'll be a better player if he does.

So I learned to look after my body from an early age. Of course I had an ideal tutor in my father. Such was Dad's reputation that I was often asked by schoolmates at Hinsdale Junior High if the Riessen family was ejected from their beds in the morning by father's whistle with orders to do twenty push-ups and deep knee bends. It was never like that, but strenuous exercise was a routine part of every day. As a result I grew up strong but, for some reason, faintly crooked. I am round-shouldered to a limited extent and I have a definite bow in my left leg. The whole effect gives me a rolling but mobile walk. Both the round shoulders and the bow leg seemed to have derived from "hanging loose" on the baseball mound at a very early age, but neither supposed defect has given me any problem. I do have a slight weakness in the left ankle, but generally I have a great feeling of fluidity of

motion when I am in top physical condition. The speed and
fluency come from the top half of my body, the strength from
the stomach and the legs.

Several people have been kind enough to tell me they like to
watch the way I move on the court. But none of them put it with
quite such delightful candor as one young lady from Yugoslavia
at Forest Hills in 1971. I had just lost to Stan Smith and was
standing chatting with some friends on the clubhouse terrace.
Suddenly this person whom I had never set eyes on before
walked up to me and said in the sexiest foreign accent you ever
heard, "Excuse me, but I want to tell you that I love your body."
While I was staring at her speechlessly, she went on, "The way
you move—the movement, it is so great." By this time I had
burst out laughing and she realized her remarks were being mis-
construed. "No, no I don't mean it that way," she said, suddenly
embarrassed. She obviously didn't know tennis players very well.
They have enough good opening lines of their own without being
presented with "come-ons" like that—intentional or otherwise.

At any rate, whether or not my body gives esthetic pleasure
on a tennis court, it has served me more than adequately over
the years and I have managed to remain remarkably free of
serious injury. I have been forced to pull out of a tournament on
only two or three occasions—once because of tennis elbow when
I was about fourteen and once in the French Championships in
1966 when I sprained an ankle. The twinges of tennis elbow and
other minor muscle ailments in the arm that have cropped up
from time to time have been painful occasionally, but it has
always been a pain that I could live with. Freezing the elbow
in a basin of ice after play or taking some Bufferin usually does
the trick. I have never yet had to resort to cortisone injections
like so many players. Usually the pain just comes in short, sharp
jabs when you actually hit the ball. So it becomes a mental
hurdle that you can clear by telling yourself, "Okay, it's going
to hurt, but as soon as you've hit the ball it will stop."

Some players maintain that the mental concentration required to overcome a limited pain barrier helps them play better.
I have never really subscribed to this theory, although the fact

that one of my greatest tournament victories was achieved while I was suffering from quite a painful injury suggests that they might have a point. It happened in March 1970 when tennis was first brought into the august, Victorian setting of the Royal Albert Hall in London.

Gilt-edged boxes stacked in tiers high to the ceiling, seats with plush red upholstery, chandeliers and carpeted floors, champagne glasses clinked by waitresses in apron and cap—this was a new image for tennis, just as tennis was something of a new image for the old nineteenth-century concert hall. With the aid of some typically excellent promotional work from the tobacco sponsors, Rothmans, the event quickly became popular with both players and the public, not merely because of its warm and somewhat regal atmosphere, but also because of its geographical location. The Albert Hall, which faces Hyde Park between Knightsbridge and Kensington High Street is a whole lot easier to get to than Wembley's Empire Pool, the traditional site of indoor tournaments on the northern outskirts of the city.

But frankly for the way I played that week, I would have been happy to play on the moon. In retrospect it was amazing that I did win, for the sixteen-man field was a tough one, lacking only Gonzales, Emerson, and Roche of the top contract pros, and in addition my arm really was rather bad. The damaged muscles in the shoulder and upper part of the arm were so tight that only by continual exercise and treatment could I manage to keep playing. I didn't realize quite how bad it had been until I arrived in Indonesia the next week to find that I could barely swing a racket after three days of inactivity.

But if continual exercise was indeed the best remedy, I had plenty of it at the Albert Hall. Those were the days before the tie-break had become an automatic part of the pro tour, and I needed 294 games to win the singles and doubles titles. It would have been more, but the singles final had been reduced from five to three sets because BBC-TV wanted us to play the doubles final before the singles so they could show it live on their afternoon sportscast; the doubles which Tom Okker and I eventually won over Rod Laver and Owen Davidson 6-3, 13-11, 9-11, 2-6,

7-5 was more than a little exhausting, so the referee, Captain Mike Gibson, decided to take pity on me by restricting the possible length of the singles final that evening. But in fact I was so full of confidence by that time that I think I could have played all night, bad arm and all. As it turned out, I beat Ken Rosewall pretty quickly 6-4, 6-2.

In her account in *World Tennis*, Linda Timms wrote:

> The key to Riessen's game was always his own first serve; when it was going in he was full of assurance and dash and his volleying in particular was so powerful and deep that it gave Rosewall little scope to pull off his best passing shot. . . . But Riessen won not by overhead power alone but by all-court enterprise. His two most memorable shots were a couple of brilliant backhand passes to break for the second time in the second set to lead 4-1. His whole performance was a revelation in its versatility and confidence.

I must admit it was a bit of a revelation to me, too. I had never strung together such a succession of topnotch victories. In the twenty months since I had turned pro I had been making steady improvement, but this success constituted a major breakthrough. I had proved that by sheer hard work and relentless concentration I could battle my way through one of the strongest fields tennis had to offer. The scores of my matches on the fast carpet court proved that. I beat John Newcombe 3-6, 14-12, 6-3; Mark Cox in an incredible marathon 25-27, 8-6, 7-5 after surviving one match point, and then Tom Okker in the semifinals 9-7, 6-3. After that and the doubles victory I was going like an express train and there was nothing Rosewall could throw across the tracks to stop me. I think I won my spurs that week. From that moment on I felt I had the right to call myself a professional.

Maybe, in a strange way the arm injury did help. Maybe, subconsciously, it made me all the more determined—all the more aware of the need not to let up and to battle for every point. But even if that is true I must confess that I prefer playing tennis when I am completely free from pain and discomfort. I reckon I'm just not a masochist.

In between my matches at the Albert Hall I had been paying regular visits to Dr. Sohickish, whose office was just a few houses down the road from the entrance to the Queen's Club at Baron's Court. Dr. Sohickish has been tending the walking wounded of the International circuit for many years; the public, who see only a fit and spritely looking tennis player walk on court, would not believe the number of sore muscles, pulled tendons, damaged ligaments, chafed and bleeding blisters, and tennis elbows that he has nursed back to health or merely kept in operational order while some major title is being won. Generally tennis players tend not to publicize their injuries. The idea is to get through the match without your opponent ever realizing that all he has to do is make you bend on your backhand side. If you tell the whole locker room that you have a pulled stomach muscle that sends a pain like a white hot needle through your guts every time you bend to your left, you'll find yourself getting nothing but low chips to the backhand when you get out on the court.

The Aussies in particular are past masters at keeping their ailments secret. I was amazed to discover that Rod Laver had been playing for years with a bad back and a bad wrist and all sorts of other semi-crippling complaints. Although he has become a little less reticent about these problems in the last year or two, "Rocket" certainly never let on when he was at the peak of his powers in the late sixties. John Newcombe won Wimbledon in 1970 on a diet that was liberally but secretly supplemented by pain-killing pills for a bad arm. And in 1965 Roy Emerson disappeared from sight for three or four days before Forest Hills; with everyone practicing in little groups at various clubs in the New York area during that period, it is easy not to notice that someone is missing, and so Emmo was able to recover from a severe attack of flu without anyone ever knowing that he had just spent 72 hours in a hospital bed. Emmo was so strong physically in those days that you could have run him over with a beer barrel and then drowned him in the contents without making any noticeable effect on his ability to play razor-sharp tennis. That was the year of the much-publicized water shortage crisis in New York. What the public never got to hear about was the beer shortage on the Eastern Grass Court circuit after Emmo and Fred Stolle passed through, drinking the cellars dry on their merry way. They seemed to thrive on about four hours' sleep a night and still find time for a few rounds of golf in between winning every tennis title in sight. They were incredible.

The Aussies' philosophy, which is shared by many other leading players who adopt the proper professional attitude, is that if you are healthy enough to walk on court, then you are healthy enough to take a beating without complaint. If you have an injury that is so bad that you cannot possibly play with it and win, then there is a simple solution. Don't play. You are only abusing yourself, cheating the public, and embarrassing your opponents if you do. I know John Newcombe fell into that trap once and regretted it afterwards. It was during the U.S. Professional Championships in Boston in 1970 when he was seeded Number One. He was suffering from a back problem that hopelessly restricted his mobility, and he lost to Clark Graebner in the first round. It was so obvious that there was something wrong with him that the press found out about it and played it up in the papers next day. Newcombe realized then that it would have been much fairer to everyone if he had scratched and given Clark a walk-over.

Newcombe's doubles partner Tony Roche has probably been the most injury-prone of any of us, and for a time it seemed that his elbow and shoulder problems were threatening to put an end to his brilliant career. Tony realized the futility of playing with a persistent and ever-worsening injury, and he quit the circuit for six months midway through 1971. After an operation at the end of that year, to remove the troublesome nerve, he rejoined the tour the following January. And it was several painful months later before he was back at his best. But, unhappily, not for long. A second operation was necessary in the fall of 1972. One wonders how long Tony can continue the battle.

As I say, I have been lucky in avoiding anything that serious so far. The only really scary thing that has happened to me as far as physical disability is concerned occurred during a practice match I had with Ray Moore, the South African independent pro who played with WCT for a while. Without any warning, my vision started going in one eye. It was like an eclipse. Everything began going black as if something was slowly covering up half the pupil. I went on playing for a set but eventually had to stop. Apart from a rather obvious problem in trying to sight the ball, I was beginning to get rather worried. But it cleared up just as suddenly as it came and has never recurred. A bow leg and round shoulders I can live with; but my eyesight has always been slightly better than 20-20 and the way the guys are hitting the ball these days, it would be nice if it stayed that way.

11

ON THE TOUR

There are many extraordinary things about the nomadic band of athletes who roam the world under the banner of World Championship Tennis. But to my mind there is nothing more remarkable than the fact we all get along so well. Sounds corny, doesn't it? But when you stop to think about it, the chances of everyone being on speaking terms with everyone else in such a diverse and varied group as ours are pretty remote. Consider for a moment. As the group was comprised in 1971, there were players from ten different nations on four continents, ranging in age from Alexander at 20 to Rosewall at 37, all battling head to head for prize money that could either make them super rich like Laver with his $290,000 for the year or relatively hard up like Barth who won only $14,000. There were the free-thinking hippy-orientated left-wingers like Ulrich and Borowiak, and middle-of-the-road conservatives like Laver, Rosewall, and Ralston. There was an Egyptian, El Shafei, and a Jew, Okker. There was a Cambridge graduate, Cox, and Taylor, a steelworker's son. There was Ashe, who was black, and then of course there was Drysdale, a South African who called Pilic "Commie Bastard," and Pilic, a Yugoslav who called Drysdale "racist pig." They played doubles together.

There is enough ammunition there to start World War Three on six different fronts at once. Judging by the standard of behavior in many other sports, one would expect to wade through blood to get to the locker room. But the facts are these. On-

97

court arguments which flare up occasionally are very, very seldom carried back to the dressing room and it is commonplace for two players to be seen dining and drinking together a couple of hours after one has knocked the hell out of the other on court and deprived him of five thousand bucks in the process. I cannot stress too strongly that this does *not* mean we do not care if we win or lose. It simply means that we are professionals and we know precisely whom we have to blame for a defeat. Ourselves. We may rant and rave for a bit about bad line calls, poor backdrop, invisible lighting, and courts with holes in them. But we know deep down that it was the same for the other guy and we also know that on the WCT tour conditions are rarely so bad that they can be legitimately accused of having affected one's play. "Amateur nights" are over for us. A pro loses because his opponent was better. Period. If it doesn't always sound like that in the papers, that is because we are human and because, let's be honest, a few spicy quotes make for more interesting reading next morning.

But even if a player harbors no ill feeling against the man who beat him, that does not mean he is not mad at himself. For as I have said, we hate to lose. The cynics who think otherwise should have witnessed a couple of small dressing room scenes that occurred on the tour recently.

One, in Cologne, involved Tom Okker, who had just lost his match against Bob Lutz—not a bad loss for Tom, because Lutz was ranked ninth in the points table and is quite capable of beating anyone, as he proved that week by going on to win the title. But Okker also knew that, had he played well enough, he could have won. The anger that was evident in his face as he sat in the locker room immediately afterwards was directed entirely toward himself, but it was no less real for that. Suddenly the door opened and someone none of us knew—presumably just an unsuspecting fan—walked in and asked Tom for his autograph. Of course the man shouldn't have come into the dressing room without an invitation in the first place, but normally Tom would have pointed this out to him gently and given the autograph. Instead he looked up, white in the face, and said bitingly:

"This is the *players'* dressing room. You've no right to be here. Kindly get out."

It wasn't very polite, but then Tom wasn't in a very polite mood. He had just lost a tennis match and was entitled to a fifteen-minute recuperation period to let the wound heal.

The other incident concerned John Newcombe early in 1972 after he had suffered a whole string of disappointing defeats. Nothing, in fact, had gone right for Newk since he had injured his knee while winning the Forest Hills doubles title with Roger Taylor the previous September. The injury had cleared up but he had never really trained himself back to the peak physical condition that is vital to his robust game. By the time he arrived in Chicago for the Kemper International—the fourteenth leg of the 1971–72 WCT tour—he hadn't gotten as far as the final round since winning the Canadian Open in Toronto eight months before. At that time he had been at the top of the WCT points list; now he was ninth and slipping. He badly needed a string of victories to restore his confidence, but in the second round he ran into Okker and lost.

Other players who witnessed the incident at De Paul's Alumni Hall say they have never seen Newk so angry. He stormed off court and let fly in the dressing room with the greatest racket-throwing, table-thumping display of sheer uncontrolled frustration they had ever seen. Newcombe wasn't mad at Tom. He was wild with anger at himself because he knew he could play better than that and he knew that all it really required was lots and lots of hard work on the practice court. It wasn't the loss of potential prize money that was getting at him. Newk is never going to starve. It was something closer to a professional athlete's soul: it was pride. John Newcombe was then the Wimbledon Champion, a title that he treasured for all that it meant in the world of tennis, and he knew in his heart that he was abusing it by playing below his best. We all knew how Newk felt, and although it was to our benefit to have a man of his caliber losing matches rather than winning them, I think most of us sympathized with his position.

But sympathy has its limits and basically we are all too

wrapped up in our own problems to worry much about the other guy. Despite our basic liking for each other, we are not a bunch of saints and I don't think anyone breaks the cardinal rule that, first and foremost, you look after yourself. Tennis is too individualistic a sport to do otherwise. It's you against the rest of them and from the moment you step on court you are on your own.

But of course special friendships develop, often between doubles partners because the human need for moral support is very real. Those lonely moments before a big match or just after a bad defeat are the times when you really need a friend. It *can* be lonely—strangely lonely for such a gregarious, fast-moving way of life. It is often too gregarious for me and frequently I seek solitude to enjoy some time to myself. So, too, does Arthur Ashe, among others. But you can still become too introspective. Brooding in hotel bedrooms about your last defeat is no way to break a losing streak, and that is why I think most of the guys enjoy the camaraderie of the doubles—especially those of us who have a regular partner with whom we are at ease on and off the court.

In a sport like tennis there is sometimes a need to inject a little team spirit into the week-by-week tournament grind, and most often this happens automatically. The Aussies tend to pull for each other—except, of course, when they meet across the net—and so do the Americans. There is a definite bond, too, between those of us who are associated with that energetic Washington law firm, Dell, Craighill & Fentress. That's Donald's outfit and along with his partners, Frank Craighill and Lee Fentress, he burns the midnight oil on our behalf with unflagging enthusiasm. The way Donald tells it, more work gets done in that office than at the White House just down the road. At any rate, it is not unusual to find the whole office staff, including secretaries, still at it at 10:30 P.M. That kind of dedication tends to breed a team spirit of its own. Not all the players whose business interests are handled by Dell and his colleagues are American, nor were all of them with WCT. Stan Smith, Tom Gorman, and Erik Van Dillen were Independents; Jan Kodes is Czech, Zeljko

Franulovic is Yugoslav; and Tom Okker, of course, is Dutch.

But even though the temporary ban on WCT erected artificial barriers between us for a time, we continued to help each other out as much as possible by stepping in to take over a clinic or make a personal appearance for a player who was involved in a particular long match or was delayed by airline connections somewhere on another continent. This team spirit still exists, and although we all moan and groan when Donald schedules us for a tennis camp appearance at some remote backwoods resort, we all have too much fun kidding him about it to complain for long.

Sometimes Dell's scheduling defies credibility even in this era of jet-age travel. Harassed players calling Donald's Washington office for last-minute instructions are often a source of great amusement among those of us who don't happen to be involved on that particular day. It could be Bob Lutz, for instance, perspiring gently in a telephone booth at some airport while a bundle of rackets and a dreamy-eyed beauty wait outside. The conversation is familiar.

"Now where is it I'm supposed to be going, Donald? Bear where? . . . Bear Lake. What state's that in, Donald? . . . No, I'm not in Sacramento, I'm at L.A. Airport and I'm certain there aren't any planes to Bear wherever it is tonight. . . . Yes, I did win, thanks. Managed to scrape through 7-5 in the fifth and I have this blister. I also have someone who wants to cook me dinner tonight and . . . What's that? There's a flight out of here in half an hour? Why's your office so efficient, Donald? . . . Yeah, yeah, okay. Just remember it's Charlie's turn next, okay?"

The hangdog expression of gloom on Lutz's face as he emerges from the booth is enough to double us up with laughter, and the fact that the laugh could be on one of us the following week makes no difference. We do these extra chores because we want to, and in the long run it is all good for the morale.

So there are cliques within cliques and bonds that are sometimes tied with financial string, by ethnic background, or by just plain friendship. Of the 34 players who competed on the WCT tour during 1971 and 1972, I obviously knew some a great deal better than others. But in all honesty I am able to say this: There was not one whose table I would avoid on walking into a hotel dining room, no one with whom I would be unhappy about sharing a long car or plane ride—no one, in other words, who I genuinely disliked as a person. For a group like ours I think that is rather remarkable.

12

THE PLAYERS

Here are my personal appraisals of 44 remarkable guys as they appear to me both off the court as a colleague, which is one thing, and on it as an opponent, which in our tight, tough little world of WCT, is quite another.

So that agents, lawyers, and friends will not get upset about the billing, I give you first—in alphabetical order—

John Alexander: The press likes to call him the baby of the tour. Some baby. A powerfully built six footer with long, silky blond hair, J.A. is the youngest member of the group—he was nineteen when he joined WCT in 1971—but he is already threatening his elders and betters. Until Jeff Borowiak equaled the feat late in the year, he was the only player outside the top eight to reach a WCT final—losing to me in Tehran—and he finished a creditable twelfth in the WCT points table at the end of the 1971 season with a prize money total of $29,000.

I first met him on the Italian circuit when he was traveling with his doubles partner Phil Dent and the two Aussie girls Kerry Harris and Lesley Hunt. He was sixteen then and under the care of Harry Hopman, the legendary Australian coach who was responsible for instilling the champion's streak into the incredible dynasty of Australian stars beginning with Sedgman and continuing through Hoad, Rosewall, Cooper, Fraser, Anderson, Laver, Emerson, Stolle, Newcombe, and Roche.

I didn't think he would make it then. Now I am not so sure.

He may yet break through to become another Newcombe, whom he resembles in style. But at the outset I don't think he had enough of Hop. The great disciplinarian quit the Australian tennis scene when J.A. was still in his formative years, and Alexander's extrovert, fun-loving personality needed Hop's stern influence to keep him in line. But some improvement in his over-all play has been evident recently. He has improved his service return, especially on clay which, untypically for a big serving Aussie, may now be his best surface. He has also scored wins over Rosewall, Laver, Emerson, and Stolle; this is a good sign, for the younger Aussies are often intimidated by the stars they hero-worshipped as a kid.

Off court John has a strong, attractive personality and has a passion for fast cars.

Arthur Ashe: I consider Arthur to be one of my best friends. I don't even know whether in Arthur's mind I am or not, because he's a very difficult person to get really close to. But I just accept that I am and leave it at that. I have spent a great deal of time with him on and off over the years, and on the few occasions we have played doubles together it has been a most enjoyable ex-perience—never more so than when we teamed to win the French title in Paris in 1971. Tom Okker wasn't entered that year so I was only too happy to have Arthur as a partner, especially when I discovered that he was really keen to win. One accepts that everyone wants to win a major title, but one night over dinner, just after we had reached the quarterfinals, he said, "You know, I'd really love to win this tournament." That made me feel great because Arthur rarely expresses himself that way and it re-minded me once again of just how keyed up he can be under that cool exterior. After that I wasn't fooled by his relaxed, seem-ingly casual attitude on court. Despite his ability to crack jokes in between points and stroll about twiddling his racket, I knew that he was really giving everything he had.

In singles he can be one of the most devastatingly aggressive players the game has ever known, but there is no doubt that outside pressures have prevented him from realizing his full potential. From the moment he became the first black man ever to win the U.S. title at Forest Hills in 1968, he was public property. Everyone wanted a piece of Arthur, especially the blacks, and despite his quiet, introverted personality he became a leader of his people in sports, by virtue of his intellect and his sincerity as well as his color. All top players have commitments to make personal appearances for companies whose products they endorse, but no one is in such continual demand as Ashe. He rarely refuses either. He is always giving of himself—far too often and far too generously for the good of his tennis. Although many of these commitments are financially rewarding to him, money is far from being the motivating factor. His visits to college campuses and to black ghettos in Harlem, Boston, and elsewhere, and the tours he has started making every year to Africa are born of a very real feeling of responsibility and concern. I have great respect for him, as do most of us who know him well.

When he is relaxed and among friends, he is delightful company, a mixture of engaging naiveté and sharp intelligence. Girls, of course, find him irresistible and he had had a succession of the most super girl friends you ever saw.

Roy Barth: Somehow Roy seems to keep cheerful, which says a lot for his spirit and determination, for he had a depressing start to his career as a contract pro. It can be no fun at all losing in the first round week after week, and one wonders whether he really has a big enough game to survive on a circuit as tough as this. The little sandy-haired Californian is a consistent percentage player but he has no shot that can hurt you, and although he practices hard, he never gets enough match play to improve.

Jeff Borowiak: This happy, hippy health-food nut from Berkeley spent much of his first WCT tournament in Cologne, alternating between playing good enough tennis to reach the final and practicing his flute in the hotel elevator. The elevator, Jeff explained, was the only place he could find with acoustics to his liking. Borowiak is a highly intelligent, likable personality who is going to become a big name, not merely because of the unorthodox image he presents but also because he will develop into a fine tennis player. He is big and strong and will learn quickly now that he is playing regularly against the best players in the world. He was 22 when he joined WCT in October 1971 and beat Andres Gimeno and Cliff Drysdale on his way to that Cologne final. He followed up that win with a brilliant victory over John Newcombe in Philadelphia the following February.

Bill Bowrey: Bill has quit the tour now to take up a teaching job in Texas. It is probably a good move for him, for he seemed to lose his appetite for the competitive game toward the end of his playing career. He was anxious to settle down to a family life with his wife, the former Lesley Turner, who was one of the top three or four women players in the world in the sixties, and their child.

A quiet-spoken Aussie who enjoys a beer with the boys, Bill, to his credit, has never allowed our famous row in Sydney, when I called him a cheat, to impair our friendship and there has never been any bad blood between us since then. For some reason I always found him one of the most difficult players to beat. He hit his backhand very well against me and I never seemed able to take advantage of his apparent slowness about court.

Bob Carmichael: "Nails" gets his nickname because he started life as a Melbourne carpenter, but it might equally apply to the fact that he is as tough as nails on court. Here is the classic example of a self-made tennis player who should serve as an inspiration to all those hackers who think they can never make it because they do not possess the God-given talent of a Laver or a Rosewall.

Nails is not even a natural athlete, let alone a natural tennis player, and yet he is now capable of beating the best in the world. Outside the top dozen there is no one in our group that I would less like to meet in the first round than Carmichael, and most of the leading players feel the same way—especially Rosewall. Nails is one of the few players on the tour who fancies his chances against Ken. He always gives the little Maestro a really tough fight and he beat him at South Orange in 1970, the year that Bob reached the quarterfinals at Wimbledon—a year, in fact, that saw a decade of relentless determination and hard work finally pay off. He was in his late twenties then and he had been a long time coming, but his achievements that year established him as a tough, feared competitor. He fights, he's strong, he's always prepared. He takes his defeats hard. He even takes the loss of a point hard, shaking his copper-colored head and mumbling dark oaths in that deep, baritone voice of his.

Off court "Nails" has a typically dry Australian sense of humor, but I don't see him around too much. He is usually off in pursuit of a "bird."

Mark Cox: There is a lot of quiet, thoughtful intelligence under mark's mass of blond curls. After graduating with honors from Cambridge University, he wrote himself into the tennis history books by becoming the first "amateur" to beat a professional when he posted wins over Pancho Gonzales and Roy Emerson in the very first Open tournament, the British Hard Court Championships at Bournemouth in 1968. But Mark didn't stay amateur long, and although he might like to spend more time at home in Surrey with his wife Allison and their son Julian, he seems much more at ease with the life of a straightforward contract professional.

Although I do not know him well, I have always found him to be a person of great integrity, in both his general attitude toward life and his conduct on and off the court. It is no surprise to me that he has emerged as a most effective member of the new Players Association committee. He has a solid game with a strong left-handed serve, but I think he has tended to underestimate himself in the past. Winning his first WCT tournament in Cleveland in August 1972 may provide just the encouragement he needs to go for his shots.

Dick Crealy: Nothing much went right for Dick during 1971. He suffered a bad knee injury which forced him to miss several tournaments and he evidently became disenchanted with World

Championship Tennis in the process, because he quit the group at the end of the year and has now returned to the Independent ranks.

A tall, pipe-smoking humorist with a comical loping walk, Dick was credited with one of the more original remarks of tennis folklore during a match in New Zealand when he hit a ball into the bottom of the net and told himself severely: "That was an abortion of a shot. You ought to go on the pill."

Dick is one of those characters who has too many theories for his own good. One month he would decide that running five miles a day and practicing for four hours is the best way to prepare for a tournament, and the next he would be staying up late, having come to the conclusion that relaxation and diversion put one in a keener, fresher frame of mind for match play. He's an engaging personality but I don't think he's really discovered what is best for him.

Owen Davidson: Although he re-emerged briefly to reach the men's doubles final with Newcombe at Forest Hills in 1972, "Davo" retired from full-time competitive tennis to take a teaching job at the Houston Racquet Club. Having coached the British Davis Cup to the Interzone Finals in 1969, he has already proved his worth in that sphere of the game. Obviously he can bring out the best in people, for Graham Stilwell has never played better than he did that year under Davo's influence.

Davo seemed to lose interest in his own game toward the end of his playing career, but at his best he was tough on court. He had a really dangerous top-spin forehand, and although his sliced left-hander's serve didn't hurt you, you couldn't do much with it either. As a typical fun-loving Aussie, Davo is missed on the tour. It is certainly more difficult to find out what's going on now, because he was our verbal gossip columnist. Nothing ever happened on the circuit that Davo didn't get to hear about sooner or later—and usually sooner.

Phil Dent: John Alexander's contemporary and doubles partner, Phil is another young Aussie with good potential. In fact I think he may even be a better player than J.A. except for one thing—his temperament. He is prone to get nervous at vital moments, while Alexander is much tougher on the big points. But Phil is quicker than J.A. and has a greater variety of shots. He has a good sense of humor and I have had a lot of fun with him, but as a player he is in danger of becoming intimidated by Alexander's stronger personality. Bob Lutz suffered from this problem while he was partnering Stan Smith early in his career, and only since they split up has Lutz realized his full potential. I am not suggesting Alexander and Dent split up, because they have the makings of a really top-class doubles team, but somehow Phil has to start believing in himself as a singles player, too.

Cliff Drysdale: I never knew Cliff very well until last year; now I find him stimulating company. He exudes charm and self-confidence, but he is far from being just the handsome playboy that he might appear at first glance. He has a wide range of interests and is a skillful ambassador for South Africa, even if the die-hard Afrikaner Nationalists think otherwise. Somehow he manages to remain loyal to his native country without ever condoning the policy of apartheid. In fact he has often spoken out fearlessly against his government's policy and did his best to try to persuade them to grant Arthur Ashe a visa to play in Johannesburg.

As a player Cliff has tightened his game considerably in recent years. Although he was usually placed above me in the world rankings, I used to handle him pretty easily at one time, but he is a much more formidable opponent now. His forehand has improved since he changed the grip on that stroke, and of course his double-fisted backhand is a weapon we all try to avoid. For someone who was reputed to have stamina problems, he has maintained a very high record of consistency on the WCT tour and has never dropped out of the top five places since the points system was instigated.

In an effort to see more of his family, he took a position as touring pro at the WCT-owned Lakeway Tennis Village in Texas in January 1972. His wife Jean, who is the sister of the former

South African Davis Cup player Gordon Forbes, is always a most welcome addition to the tour when she travels with her husband.

Ismail El Shafei: This is the man they call the Omar Sharif of tennis and not without reason. "Izzy" has dark good looks and a natural, easy-going charm. He makes friends easily and also seems to have relatives scattered all over the world with whom he often stays during tournaments. We share a passion for back-gammon, but I usually back out and let my regular opponent, Tom Okker, take him on. His cunning Middle Eastern tactics are too good for me. But we get along well and occasionally spend time together after the matches.

The only Egyptian to have reached world class as a tennis player, Izzy is similar to Carmichael in that he often plays better against the top players than his equals. He beat Laver twice in 1970 and Ashe twice the following year, and I always have a tough time wearing him down. He is strong and muscular, never seems to get tired, and is very acrobatic, especially at the net. He is always lunging for volleys very close in and jumps well for the overhead. He whips a dangerous double-fisted backhand and has a strong left-handed serve. I don't think we've seen the best of him yet.

Roy Emerson: For me, Emmo is the best example of a cham-pion that tennis has seen for the past decade. During the years of his Wimbledon triumphs in the middle sixties, the game could not have had a better ambassador. He always had time for people and for kids—just as he still has—and could keep any party going till dawn with his stories, his hilarious banter, and his famous hip-wiggling dancing. He is just as good at it now but he tends to take more care about the number of hours he reserves for sleep because at 35 there is no way his body can do what he asked of it at 27. At the Pacific Southwest in Los Angeles one year he consumed innumerable cans of beer during the course of an all-night party and a few hours later went out on court, apparently as fresh as a daisy, and breezed past Tony Roche in the semifinal, 6-4, 6-4. I never knew how he could do it, nor am I suggesting that anyone should try to follow Emmo's example as far as his nocturnal activities are concerned.

But then the kids never saw that. What they saw was this incredibly dedicated champion going through a one-and-a-half-hour full-scale practice session every morning, even when he had to play singles and doubles that afternoon. Speed and physical fitness were the key to his success, and even though he is a little slower now he is still a formidable competitor whom most of us find hard to beat. He was so dominant during that period of 1964–66 that it is only recently that many players have overcome a certain inferiority complex about playing him. I have often had trouble beating him in the past, mainly because of his speed and the way he tees off on my serve. And he can still beat me—as he proved after I led by a set and a break in the CBS-TV Classic at Hilton Head, South Carolina in 1972.

Brian Fairlie: This stocky little New Zealander is probably the hardest working guy on the tour. He's always out there practicing, often with his doubles partner, Izzy El Shafei, and if only he played like he practiced he would be very good indeed. He has good strokes but he could use a bit more on his serve. He used to be injury prone during his amateur days, but seems to have gotten a lot stronger since joining the tour.

Argumentative on the court and boisterous off it, nevertheless he has quieted down a bit since his marriage.

Frank Froehling: As I mention in a later chapter, Frank Froehling—the 6'3" Spider Man, as he is called—signed with WCT at the start of 1972.

Andres Gimeno: While Manolo Santana was grabbing all the titles and all the glory for Spain at Wimbledon and Forest Hills in the mid-sixties, Andres was slogging around the backwater stadiums and deserted arenas of the old pro circuit. Along with

Gonzales, Rosewall, Laver, Buchholz, MacKay, and a few others, he helped keep the ailing tour alive until the infusion of new blood and the advent of Open tennis put it back on its feet.

Having signed with Jack Kramer back in 1960, Andres had become so much a part of the pro game that it was a shock to hear that he decided to leave WCT and join the Independent ranks at the end of 1971. But Andres was anxious to consolidate his future in Barcelona as a teaching pro and coach—possibly to Spain's Davis Cup team—and to do this it was necessary to reestablish ties with his Association. It was a wise move for him but he is missed on the WCT tour. We miss the endless stream of funny stories he used to tell in his thick Catalan accent, and we miss him as a colleague to whom one could always turn for some small favor or kindness. In manner and bearing, Andres is very much the traditional Spanish gentleman. Years of demanding competition against the likes of Gonzales and Rosewall had made him one of the toughest percentage players in the business. He made very few mistakes, and even on his backhand, which, as we used to say, couldn't break an egg, he was always forcing you to play good shots to survive because of his cunning placements.

Pancho Gonzales: There is, of course, one player who has most of his greatest achievements behind him but who remains a world-renowned personality in the game, and even though he has reached his middle 40s he is still no pushover on court. I refer, naturally, to Pancho Gonzales.

Pancho was an idol of mine, as he was to many kids taking up the game in the fifties, and it came as a real shock to find he was mortal when I eventually got to play him in practice during Davis Cup training sessions. Even so, I was in awe of him in those days and although, as coach to the squad, he tried to improve my game in various ways, I think he only ended up confusing me. It was a hopeless relationship really because I don't think Pancho has much respect for people who are in awe of him. When Open tennis arrived in 1968 and I got the chance to play him in proper competition, I found I could beat him quite easily and did so on

the two or three occasions we met. Obviously he was past his
prime by then, but it sort of shattered the myth nonetheless, and
since then we have become good friends. A few years ago John
Newcombe, Tony Roche, and I stayed at his ranch at Malibu for
a few days and it was fun seeing Pancho in a domestic setting,
cooking for us and his children and generally giving us a great
time.

On court in his heyday Pancho was not quite so tame. He was
one of the few players I have ever known who played better when
he got mad. Instead of it hurting his form—as it does most players—a real raging temper would bring out the best in Pancho and
it would be his opponent who would suffer. People really used
to be afraid of that temper. On one occasion a group of us flew
to Japan for some pro tournaments in 1969 right after Pancho
had been involved in a wild flare-up at Anaheim, California. By
the time we got to Osaka, Pancho's mood was even blacker, and
when he went on court for his match we could feel that famous
temper simmering below the surface. I remember we were all so
scared he would burst into one of his racket-throwing fits that
none of us would sit in the front row to watch. He had started
using metal rackets by then and we were not about to get in the
firing line.

Of all the players I have seen, I would have to rank Pancho
Number One—not necessarily on stroke production or natural
skill with a racket, but simply because, at his best, he could beat
everybody else. Hoad, Rosewall, and Laver all had more talent
but none of them could get consistently on top of Gonzales until
age began to take the edge off his reflexes. His superb service and
his relentless will to win made him, quite simply, a winner. In
many ways he still is.

Ron Holmberg: Whenever injuries depleted our ranks, WCT
had a willing reserve in Ron Holmberg, who frequently stepped
in to fill a gap in the draw. Ron is now the tennis pro at West
Point. Despite his lack of mobility—an ample girth was, perhaps,
the only thing that stood between him and the very top of the
tennis ladder—he can still give most of us a good game. No

American player of my generation could equal Holmberg's touch play and much of that basic natural talent remains.

Rod Laver: To my mind, Rod's total dedication to the pursuit of winning makes him the most formidable champion of all time. Anyone who can go on winning week in and week out as he has done over the years has to be a fantastic player. Is he the best player in the world? Many people ask that question and by way of an answer I would say this: Rod's "high" is higher than anyone else's. He is the most spectacular shot-maker I have ever seen, and at his peak he is definitely better than any of us. But he has been hitting some lows in the past couple of years as well, and a little of the aura of invincibility has fallen away.

I beat him three times in 1971—the year that he won an incredible $290,000—and was a little disappointed to find that he was beginning to search for excuses to explain away his defeats. In Dallas, it was his back that was hurting him and in Tehran he said the balls were impossible to play with at that altitude. These were very untypical reactions for Laver or for any top Aussie, but I suppose that it was understandable to a degree. Ever since he won his second Grand Slam in 1969, each defeat has been accompanied by the inevitable question, "Is Laver slipping?" Nowhere is it tougher than at the top, and when you are as used to winning as the "Rocket," defeat becomes doubly difficult to accept. Nevertheless, Rod Laver doesn't need excuses. He has been, and still is, too good for that.

I have never had occasion to room with Rocket and only recently have I come to know him really well. His basic shyness, coupled with the icy champion's streak that is evident in his character, made him seem a little aloof at times. But he can let his hair down in the best Aussie tradition when the beer is flowing. He also takes great delight in being at home in Corona Del Mar, California, with his lovely wife Mary and their son Ricky.

Tom Leonard: An ambitious young Californian with a mane of carrot-colored hair, Tom joined WCT midway through 1971.

He had achieved little of note on the Independent circuit, but with WCT he quickly proved himself to be a fighter and a player who hates to lose. After one defeat in Cologne at the hands of Torben Ulrich, whom he felt he could have beaten, Tom bashed his steel racket into a rectangular shape in a fit of locker room rage. Normally he conserves most of his energy for his biggest weapon, his serve. He also returns well off the backhand, and if he maintains his fierce competitive spirit, he should improve.

Bob Lutz: It took Bob a few months to realize he was no longer just Stan Smith's doubles partner—they had split up when Lutz joined WCT and Smith remained an Independent at the end of 1970—but as soon as he did, his considerable talent began to blossom. Somewhere along the line Bob started to believe in himself and realize that it would take only a little more practice and serious training for him to become a leading member of the group. The transformation produced rapid results, for Lutz swept through the field to win the Cologne title in October 1971 and go on to reach the final in Barcelona the following week. Up to that point he had never beaten Laver, Emerson, or Okker. He beat all three in three days in Cologne and then took Laver and Emerson for a second time in Barcelona. It was quite an awakening, and from now on all Bob's dreams will be real. However I hope his nightmares aren't, for he seems to have plenty of those. I roomed with him a couple of times last year and discovered that with Bob in the next bed, the nights are never silent. He is always talking in his sleep and once, in Sydney, he suddenly sat bolt upright and said in a frantic voice, "Stolle!" Then he flopped back on the pillow. Fred must have aced him.

When he is not sleeptalking or taking a bath—frequent long baths, often two or three a day, are among his many passions— Bob is either reading, listening to music, chatting up a girl, or amusing us all with his droll wit. He is a hip Californian who shared his Sausalito pad with Jeff Borowiak for a while and is a lot of fun to have around. As a player he is immensely strong— quick for his bulky build and blessed with a good feel for the game. Few players have a better eye for the acutely angled volley. So far I have been able to handle him pretty easily, beating him four times out of four in 1971.

Robert Maud: In contrast to Lutz and Borowiak, who are very much products of their generation, Robert seems to hang on to the more old-fashioned values, probably as a result of his traditional South African upbringing. He's a quiet, pleasant person who often seems puzzled and upset when he has to handle all the apartheid questions that are continually being thrown at a South African abroad.

As a player, he's a real fighter who did better than many people expected during his first year with WCT in 1971. He has a good serve and one of the best overheads on the tour, but the rest of his shots can't hurt you. What can hurt is the way he will run down everything in sight and refuse to accept defeat. You have to work to beat him.

Frew McMillan: Frew played a lot of good tennis with very little to show for it in 1971. He was always running into a Laver or an Ashe in the first round, playing brilliantly and losing. I think that may have had something to do with his decision to leave WCT at the end of the year. Also I think he missed having a good regular doubles partner, for Bob Hewitt had remained Independent and in the sixties they had formed one of the greatest doubles teams in the world. Frew tried several partners when he joined WCT but with little success. This did not surprise me, for Frew plays doubles differently from anyone else and it is not easy to fit in with his style. He hits a double-fisted shot on both flanks and generally chips off the right-hand side and hits through it on the left. The chip can be very effective and consequently Tom and I normally serve to Frew's backhand, especially if he's playing with Hewitt. There is little you can do off the chip except push it back, often too high, and with Bob always looking for the chance to cross and put away the "poached" volley, that is inviting disaster.

Although he is South African by birth and upbringing, Frew

has married a charming English girl and maintains a home in Bristol, England. He is an interesting character with a quick, sarcastic wit. Sometimes I find it a bit too abrasive for my taste.

John Newcombe: When John won Wimbledon for the third time in 1971, I felt sure that when his game was on, he was the best player in the world. Not week in and week out, perhaps, but given the big occasion he would come through as the toughest and the best prepared competitor. He may well recover that zest and dedication, but it will require an even greater effort now, for he has slipped from the pinnacle and the road back up is always harder.

His problems began when he arrived at Forest Hills in 1971 lacking match practice after three weeks of coaching at his tennis ranch in Texas. He lost in the first round to Jan Kodes and then injured his knee while winning the doubles title with Roger Taylor. Although he played a few tournaments later in the year, he wasn't really fit again until 1972, and by then he had lost a little of that solid, steamroller quality that makes his game so formidable. But I am sure he will regain his confidence, and tennis will benefit when he does, for he really has the interests of the game as a whole at heart.

He is one of the few players to have made a deliberate effort to develop a more interesting personality on court. Realizing his style was methodical and even dull to watch, Newk began breaking it up with a few gestures and antics. Some people say it is upsetting his concentration and that it seems contrived. I don't agree. All John is doing is letting a little of his off-court personality, which is anything but dull, seep into his play. Off court, in fact, he is terrific fun. Since he and Tony Roche and Tom and I often end up in the later stages of the doubles, we are frequently together during the last couple of days of a tournament when most of the other players have already moved on to the next town. Consequently we have spent a lot of time together at discotheques, night clubs, and restaurants all over the world, and there are few people whose company I enjoy more. Newk can be a real ham at times, as anyone who saw his takeoff of Marlene Dietrich at the Monte Carlo Ball one year will agree. He is also a natural leader and was the instigator and president of the original International Tennis Players Association. There was a time around 1966–67 that Newk beat me seven straight times but I, too, have gotten tougher since then and I was very content at beating him three times out of five in 1971.

Tom Okker: Obviously I'm biased about Tom because he's not only my doubles partner but my best friend as well. We have a great relationship on and off the court and have developed an understanding—a philosophy of life, if you like—that enables us to ride the rough and the smooth. We never blame each other for a defeat in doubles. If we lose, we lose together and can even laugh about it right out there on the court. It may be a bitter laugh, but at least it is a harmonious one. When we play each other in singles it is very competitive and our record is amazingly even. We had four wins each against each other in 1968, Tom was two and one over me in 1969, and we were two and two in both 1970 and 1971. We both go out on court with the intention of beating the hell out of the other as quickly as possible, and even if we got into a row during the course of a match, it would not impair our friendship.

We have become very close over the years. Tom and his wife Annemarie, a typical down-to-earth Dutch girl with an understated but sparkling sense of humor, have stayed at my parents' home in Evanston during tournaments at McGaw Hall and I have often visited the Okkers in Holland, where I have always been made to feel completely at home. Tom is an incredibly lively person—a real bundle of nervous energy. Even when he's sitting down and supposedly relaxing, he'll be scratching his knee or jumping up to look at something that caught his eye. He has a sense of humor that often borders on the outrageous and generally packs an awful lot of living into that tiny, wiry frame. He is called, aptly enough, the Flying Dutchman, and he is certainly incredibly fast on court. I think he has a very exciting game to watch with that incredible top-spin forehand. But then, as I said, I'm biased.

Charlie Pasarell: Midway through WCT's European tour at the end of 1971 I was saying that Charlie ought to be winning more often, that he had resorted to aimlessly belting the daylights out of the ball, and that he had lost direction as a tennis player. A couple of weeks later Charlie blazed his way into the semifinals in Bologna, nearly beat Laver in a real thriller, got married back in Los Angeles, won our little African Grand Prix when he and his bride Shireen joined Arthur, Tom, and myself on their honeymoon, and continued to play great tennis when the tour started up again in 1972. In fact by the time he lost to Drysdale in Hollywood, Florida, in March, he had been a semifinalist in three out of the previous five WCT tournaments—not bad going. But then Charlie was ranked Number One in the United States after his performances in 1967 and there is no question that he can be a devastating player when he's in the mood.

He comes from a wealthy Puerto Rican family and there is much of the proud Spaniard in his makeup. He is a great thinker and talker about the problems confronting tennis and was one of the founding members of the Players Association. The year Philadelphia held the ITPA Championships Charlie and I went down there to discuss rules and guidelines with that progressive pair of promoters, Ed and Marilyn Fernberger, and I was surprised how tough and earnest Charlie proved to be as a negotiator. He has a strict set of principles and he stands by them. He's a good friend, too—the sort of guy who would give you the shirt off his back if need be. He's a marathon match player—his classic 112-game losing fight against Pancho Gonzales in 1969 set a Wimbledon record for longevity—and a marathon joke-teller. He kept going with one after the other for an hour and a half in Sydney recently and spent much of the time laughing so hard himself that he couldn't get to some of the punch lines.

Nikki Pilic: Pronounce that "c" as a "ch" and you have the senior partner of that well-known Yugoslavian tennis firm of Pilic, Jovanovic, and Franulovic. Nikki's the instant expert on any subject you care to bring up. We all know that he can't be a

lawyer, doctor, architect, and historian, but in his amusing frac-
tured English he has a good try at making out that he is. In fact
he did study law and is pretty well informed on a lot of subjects,
which makes for interesting conversation. On court he's a great
showman, and crowds that think they are going to hate him as
he starts arguing and gesticulating over doubtful line calls usually
end up loving him. Appropriately enough for a great ham actor,
he married a beautiful girl called Mia. She is not a ham but she is
a well-known Yugoslavian actress.

Nikki fancies himself as a shot-maker so we always ask him
about his top-spin backhand lob. He insists he can play that, too,
but with his type of grip there is no way he can do so. But he
does have a good whippy forehand and an excellent chip on the
backhand. For so tall a man, he gets very little height on his
serve because he throws the ball so low but, perhaps because of
that, it is difficult to read and he still hits it with great power.
He's a much better player than his 1971 record suggests because
he had consistent bad luck in the draws. For weeks on end he
would run into Ashe or Drysdale in the first round and consequently was never able to build momentum and confidence. All
that changed in the second half of 1972 when he reached the
final in St. Louis and from then on started doing greater justice
to his talents.

Dennis Ralston: Two badly injured knees put an end to any
hope Dennis had of continuing on the WCT tour in 1972 but
as soon as he rejoined the Independent ranks he gained quick
reward by being appointed U.S. Davis Cup captain. It was no
surprise to me when he made such a fine start in the job, either,
for he was an excellent Davis Cup coach during the previous
four years.

It is a strange contradiction in Dennis's character that he should
be so patient and painstaking as a coach—especially with kids—
and yet so hot-tempered and moody in other areas of his life. He
is a lot more mellow now, but when he first burst onto the tennis
scene he was notorious for his sulking and temperamental outbursts. I think part of the problem was that there is no place

Dennis would prefer to be than right back home in Bakersfield, California, with his wife and three kids. The globe-trotting life of a tennis player always grated on him more than the rest of us. And yet when he wasn't being homesick, Dennis managed to live in style. I always think of him as the big spender of the group, the one with the most extravagant tastes. This was another contrast in his character, for in many of his attitudes toward life he is essentially conservative; however, there is nothing very conservative about the way he plays craps, blackjack, and roulette. He risks a lot but he is either very good or very lucky, for I have often seen him walk out of the casino at the Caribe Hilton in San Juan, Caesar's Palace in Las Vegas, or the Playboy Club in London with more money than he brought in. Again in contrast to his moody disposition on court, I find Dennis enjoyable company. He has many good ideas for the development of the game and he has no doubt enjoyed putting them to the test in his role as Davis Cup captain.

As a player Dennis has always given me a lot of trouble. He beat me in the quarterfinals of Wimbledon in 1965 after I led by two sets to love, and the fact that I pulled the reverse trick on him a couple of months later in the final at Berkeley—winning the tournament after trailing by two sets—was only partial compensation. One of my problems with Dennis was that he always served well against me. The double faults for which he was notorious never seemed to materialize—much to my disappointment. Before his knee trouble he had a clean, crisp game and, at his best, I always thought of him as one of the top players in the world.

Cliff Richey: In March 1972, just before the peace agreements were worked out with the ILTF, Cliff made the smartest move of his career and accepted a four-year contract with Lamar Hunt. The peace formula precluded Hunt from signing up any more players or renewing existing contracts; this meant that Cliff would enjoy the benefits of a huge guarantee of over $100,000 a year as well as having his air fares paid to WCT tournaments for longer than most of us.

No one could say that Richey had not worked for that kind of security. Although he takes a more relaxed attitude toward life now, Cliff and his sister Nancy had been brought up by their father—a teaching pro in Texas—to eat, think, and sleep tennis. One of the gutsiest players in the game, Cliff never knows when to quit.

I shall never forget the horrific sight of Richey staggering and groaning around the court against Nikki Spear of Yugoslavia in the French Championships a few years ago as cramps seized hold of every muscle in his legs. He was obviously in agony and continually collapsed writhing onto the dusty red clay, only to pick himself up again and battle on. When I saw him in the locker room afterward, I asked him why he hadn't defaulted, as there was no way he could have won in that condition.

"Well, you never know," replied Cliff, "the guy might have fallen down and broken his leg."

We call him "Bull" and sometimes he acts like one on court. In the Washington Star tournament in 1971 during his match against Andres Gimeno he tripped over a section of the service line tape that had been pried loose from the clay court. As far as Cliff was concerned that was the last straw. He was 2-4 down in the tie break, it was hot, he wasn't playing well, and even the court itself seemed to be conspiring against him. So in a fit of rage he reached down and yanked the whole service line tape right out of its moorings and held it above his head. I was watching the match with a group of players, and seeing Cliff standing there, red in the face and dripping sweat with the remains of the service line hoisted above his head, was just the funniest spectacle in the world. We nearly died laughing.

Richey is a very intense but vastly amusing conversationalist off court and he has become much easier to get along with now that he no longer feels it necessary to "psych" people out before a match by pretending he hates them.

As a player Cliff's tenacity is his greatest asset for he has always had to make up for a weak service. He has added power and penetration to his first serve through sheer hard work on the practice court, but his second delivery still tends to be too short.

Considering how serious a handicap this can be on fast surfaces, it says much for Cliff's fighting qualities that he has battled his way into the semifinals of Forest Hills twice in recent years.

Tony Roche: Tony's severe arm injury, which forced him to quit the circuit for six months in 1971 and even threatened to put a permanent end to his career, was a sad blow to the game and to WCT in particular. Many experts thought Tony was destined to succeed Laver as the world's best player and he was showing signs of proving them right in 1970 when he beat Rod to win the U.S. Pro Championships and then reached the Forest Hills final for the second straight year before losing to Rosewall. Tony had also been a finalist in the first Open Wimbledon in 1968 and there is no doubt that this naturally gifted left-hander would have achieved even greater things had not injury intervened. I only hope that Tony's second elbow operation in September 1972 will enable him to make a complete recovery.

I used to think his backhand volley—a masterly punishing stroke—was the best single shot in tennis. I am not sure whether it was the arm problem or the switch from wood to metal racket that was the cause, but I felt he lost a little confidence in that shot and in his game as a whole in 1971.

Like Newcombe, his lifelong friend and doubles partner, Tony is great company. We have had some memorable parties over the years, and in particular I will never forget one all-night session of liar poker in Mexico City. After a few beers—a few by Aussie standards, a lot by anyone else's—Tony can get really funny. During the French Championships one year all the players went to a party at the Club Privé, or the Psychedelic, as it was then known. It was the fashionable thing at the time for girls to wear scarves around their heads, Red Indian style. So Tony, quickly followed by Fred Stolle, took his tie off and tied it around his head in imitation. Soon everyone was dancing about with their ties tied round their heads, which seems damned stupid in the cold light of day but not at 3:00 A.M. in a Paris discotheque. By some unspoken agreement, it has become a signal between us now to denote when a party stops being just a party and becomes a GREAT party. So whenever you happen to run into a bunch of tennis players with ties around their heads, beware. It means there's something special going on. And it will all be Tony Roche's fault.

Ken Rosewall: If I become a teaching pro, this is the man my pupils will get to see on film, to learn from, to study, to admire. Not Laver, Newcombe, Okker, or anyone else. Just Ken Rosewall. He's my type of player. Playing tennis day in and day out, I would rather have Kenny's game than anyone's. His stroke production is classic, his speed uncanny and apparently effortless, his eye for the opening faultless. He is exciting to watch, not because he hits the ball hard, which he doesn't, or because he uses top spin or under-slice, but simply because his strokes are beautiful.

Since my victory at the Albert Hall I have had a terrible time trying to beat him, and I lost to him nine straight times in 1971 and 1972 before finally beating him in Quebec City. Like all players with whom I have trouble, it is his quickness that bothers me most. His fleetness of foot is fantastic. He has this disturbing ability to follow a service return into the net without your realizing it. You never see him coming nor do you hear him coming. He seems to tiptoe about court and suddenly he's there in that one spot that you were quite sure it would be impossible for him to reach. The worrying thing is that he seems, if anything, to be getting better. I think that he is one of the few players who have benefited from switching to metal rackets. His aluminum Seamless frame, which he started using just before winning the U.S. Pro Championships in Boston in 1971, seems to have given him a new lease on life at 37. His little serve, which was always deceptively deep and accurate, now has more zing in it, and there is a greater punch to his volleys as well. At any rate he became the first World Champion of Tennis in November of that year and no one deserved the honor more. When he repeated the feat by winning the second WCT play-off finals in May 1972, it only confirmed his extraordinary and seemingly tireless talent.

I respect him greatly as a man. He turned professional in 1956, and in the ensuing fifteen years he has done more to foster and maintain interest in the pro game than anyone else. He takes his craft very seriously and keeps himself in great physical condition. Like most Aussies he enjoys a beer, but he rarely does anything to excess and reserves his vacations for the times he spends with his wife and their boys at home in Sydney. He has a deep burning pride of performance and it is sometimes comical to see him hang his head in shame after mis-hitting a forehand when he is in the middle of disecting some poor unfortunate opponent 6-1, 6-0. To alleviate our frustration at watching this amazing little man make everything look so easy, we sit in the stands on such occasions and chide him among ourselves. "Tut, tut, Kenny, you just missed a backhand by a quarter of an inch. That's the first one you've missed in three weeks and it really won't do." It's about as bad an attempt at gentle sarcasm as his nickname "Muscles." He was called that because he didn't have any as a kid. He doesn't have many now. But he does very nicely without them, thank you. Very nicely indeed.

Ray Ruffels: Ray can be a dangerous opponent when he's playing well—as he proved by reaching the final of the WCT event in Cleveland in August 1972. He has the advantage of being a left-hander, which many players find tough to deal with, and I think he could still improve. He has become stronger physically in the last couple of years and he is hitting his backhand better than he used to. A good victory over Stan Smith in the Embassy Championships at Wembley in November 1971 showed that he is capable of great things. Ray has formed a solid doubles partnership with Carmichael and they did well to win the Rothman's title in Toronto early in 1972. Having a good doubles record can boost your confidence and help in the fight for survival on a tour as tough as this. And as doubles gains in importance and prestige, as I am sure it will, he should do well.

Ray can be quiet and withdrawn or boisterously funny depending on his mood, and he always seems to be in the thick of any after-hours Aussie activity.

Terry Ryan: A likable, keen South African, Ryan never signed a contract with WCT but joined the tour as a replacement for injured players toward the end of 1971. He's a better player than many people give him credit for and proved it by beating Nikki Pietrangeli in Bologna and in the last of five tournaments he played for WCT. He's a hustler who is always in good physical shape and he makes you work for your points.

Stan Smith: During this period of 1971–72, there were other leading players whose paths I crossed less often because they were not members of the WCT tour. Many were making a considerable impact on the game as stars of the Independent circuit—none more so than Stan Smith. By winning Forest Hills in 1971 and Wimbledon the following summer, Stan established himself as one of the top players in the world. Some people started thinking of him as the world's best but I don't think many players on the circuit regard him as such.

We all have a great respect for his game because he's tremendously strong and he keeps coming at you. He's a formidable sight when viewed from the other side of the net and you have to be decisive and unwavering with your strokes against him because that's the way he is. He has a good temperament and believes implicitly in his ability to achieve his goals. His concentration is superb and it is almost impossible to get him ruffled. His enormous reach makes him very difficult to pass and he gets in very close to the net for the volley. One has to use the lob to force him back but it has to be a good lob because Stan's agility —formerly one of the weaknesses of his game—has improved considerably in recent years and he can really get himself up off the ground to reach the high ball now.

All this makes him a very tough man to beat, but most players feel that he must prove himself consistently, week in week out, against the likes of Laver, Rosewall, and Newcombe before he can be regarded as Number One in the world. I expect him to do very well on the WCT tour, but a lot of the boys want to get him out there and test his mettle in that tough environment. He also has to improve his clay-court play. He suffered a whole series of dismal defeats at the hands of lesser players on European clay during the early summer of 1972 but, of course, his superb Davis Cup victory over Nastase on clay in Bucharest will have given him much greater confidence now.

Off court, as well as on it, Smith presents the classic clean-cut American image. Raised in Pasadena, California, Stan now lives at the Sea Pines Plantation on Hilton Head Island, South Carolina, and represents the Sea Pines Racket Club as its tennis director. He gives the impression of having great purpose in his life: he seems to know where he is going and derives much comfort from his deep religious beliefs. Occasionally he appears almost embarrassed by the wealth tennis has brought him and often shrugs off his success by stating simply, "I'm basically a very lucky sort of person."

Graham Stilwell: Probably the most genuine humorist on the tour, Graham has a real deadpan Cockney wit. By throwing a couple of casual remarks into a conversation, Graham can break up a whole party, and once you get him going, it can get hysterical.

One night in Stockholm he came to the aid of a colleague who was having great success with a girl until a Swedish TV producer barged in and started getting overprotective. There would have been no way to shake him off had it not been for Graham, who started fixing the intruder with his Cockney banter. "Fancy your chances, then, do you?" He came straight out with it in front of everyone with that look of knowing innocence. And then he carried on from there, making terrible puns out of everything the poor man said until the Swede, whose normally excellent English had been straining to keep pace, finally retired in confusion. By that stage everyone was convulsed in laughter and the girl didn't even realize that she'd been left defenseless. It's tough running into teamwork like that.

Graham's talents don't end there. He has great natural ability as a tennis player but he got himself into a depressing losing streak soon after joining WCT, and 1971 must have been misery for him. He put on weight, lost all confidence in himself, and seemingly forgot how to win. But fifteen pounds of Stilwell disappeared over the Christmas holidays and he earned his reward with a fine victory over Ashe in Toronto. A few weeks later he followed that up by reaching the semifinals of a sixteen-man tournament in Macon, Georgia, and if he continues to train hard he will be a potential threat to everyone from now on.

Fred Stolle: Fred is a good companion and one of my favorite guys on the tour. Everything always seems to be a lot more fun if Fred gets mixed up in it, and he likes to get mixed up in most things. He also went into a decline as a player in 1971 but now appears to have regained his zest for the game and his pride as a professional. His performance in beating Newcombe and Drysdale to reach the quarter finals at Forest Hills in 1972 was vintage Stolle. Fred has always been a staunch pro who has little time for the hypocrisies of the amateur game and is not afraid to say so— a trait that hasn't endeared him to people in certain quarters. But Fred has always adhered strictly to the "Look after your mates" philosophy of life and is therefore a loyal friend.

He's a very straightforward sort of player who hits the ball hard and flat, better off the backhand than forehand, and with particular power on the serve. He has the frustrating distinction of having played in three consecutive Wimbledon finals from 1963 to 1965 without ever having won the title, although he did capture both the Forest Hills and French championships in his heyday. As with Emerson, the legacy of that dominance lives on and I still find him difficult to beat.

Allan Stone: A typical, happy-go-lucky Aussie from Melbourne, Allan proved he was serious about his tennis when he fought back from a bad beginning as a contract pro in 1971. Many players would become totally discouraged if they suffered ten consecutive first-round defeats as Allan did, but by the end of the year he was beginning to show he had what it takes. He's a little slow with his first shot and could improve his game by sprint training. But he has a good serve, which along with his cheerful determination, forms a sound basis for improvement.

His bride Jocelyn was a most welcome addition to the tour and

It is, of course, a fallacy that Torben does not care about his physical condition. He cares very much. It is just that he turns the rule books upside down—eliminates those sections that interfere with what he considers to be civilized living and adds a few items of his own. Like health foods and 1,500 mg of Vitamin C a day. (500 mg is usually considered sufficient.)

Torben is one of the most fascinating people I have ever had the pleasure of knowing. His interests and talents are apparently limitless. He plays the saxophone, writes a jazz column for a Danish newspaper, co-hosts a radio talk show in Copenhagen, has played more Davis Cup ties than any man still active in the game except Nikki Pietrangeli, and has made a film about the images tennis balls make when they are dipped in paint and hit into canvas. The man is an artist—in his fashion. The way his mind works is best illustrated by the reply he gave to a hard-nosed New York sportswriter a few years ago after he had just been beaten in a great Stadium court match at Forest Hills by that other ageless wonder, Pancho Gonzales. It was Pancho's devastating serve that had finally crushed Torben, so the reporter, looking for a good tough quote from a bitter loser, asked Ulrich what he thought of that serve. Torben stared at the man with those quizzical blue eyes and after his customary thoughtful pause said: "Well, it is a thing of beauty, really. I think it can only give pleasure."

At the end of 1971 Torben decided to leave WCT when his contract ran out so that he could have greater freedom to choose his tournaments and indulge in his numerous other activities. He was missed on the tour, but happily, he was not lost to the game as a whole.

In the last two or three years five European players have emerged as major forces in the world game, Zeljko Franulovic, Jan Kodes, Ilie Nastase, Manuel Orantes, and Adriano Panatta. In style, attitude, and ambition they are different from anyone in the previous generation of European clay-court masters except Manuel Santana, who set the standard they are all endeavoring to emulate.

In the past, clay-court experts like Nikki Pietrangeli, Fausto

seemed to fit in with the crazy life of a globe-trot
a lot better than many wives.

Roger Taylor: I find Roger an awkward an
gravating opponent, although my record has b
him over the years. We always have very tough
though I have won most of them recently, he us
make me feel that somehow I lucked out. We
problems off court, but sometimes I find him a
to get close to. He's a very dangerous player w
and his powerful left-handed game poses proble
He's a good competitor who came back strongl
year of nagging back injuries. For me his foreh
gerous than his serve; and his backhand, once
ness, has improved considerably. He can roll it
started chipping it cross-court like Laver—the
the delight of British fans at Wimbledon in 19
was going for his third straight Wimbledon title
won the Forest Hills Doubles title two straight y
combe in 1971 and Drysdale in 1972.

He had the reputation of being the great won
boy of the circuit in his younger days, but he h
ferent person since his marriage to the Scottisl
MacLennan and is very much the proud father
their beautiful daughters, Zoe and Katriona, a
him.

Torben Ulrich: Torben is a unique character l
If you ever want to drive a physical training
get him to tell you—as he surely will—that a
appearance and a regular early-to-bed, early-tc
two of the basic fundamentals for physical fitne
him with Torben Ulrich. Torben goes to bed a
four and six in the morning, sleeps until noon,
knows what, and spends many of his nights in
yet I have never seen a fitter 44-year-old in my
lean, wiry body of a man of 25, and if you ca
of it that is because his hair comes down to the m

Gardini, and Istvan Gulyas were content to play their tennis from the back-court in the traditional European style. They were masters of the art and looked upon grass as something fit only for cows and power-crazed Americans who relied on brute force instead of skill. The present generation quickly realized that, with the advent of fast indoor carpets and the sudden expansion of the dollar-laden world circuit, they would have to adapt if they were to get their share of the prize money and reach the top. As a result Nastase, Kodes, and the rest are far more complete tennis players. They have taught themselves how to volley as well as rally from the base line, and their game contains a far more aggressive element than that of their predecessors.

Zeljko Franulovic: When I first played Zeljko in 1968, I thought he was going to become the best of the European clay-court players. He has a natural attacking flair and seemed to be quicker than most in keeping the racket out in front of him on the volley. He enjoyed early success in America by winning the U.S. National clay-court title, which set him apart from most Europeans who do not enjoy playing on our clay. The balls are harder, the clay itself is firmer and gives a higher bounce. A more attacking game is required than on the red European dust and Zeljko adapted to it easily. Unfortunately he suffered a bad shoulder injury soon after winning the Argentine Championships in Buenos Aires at the end of 1971 and underwent surgery at home in Yugoslavia a few months later. It put him out of the game for almost a year.

Although he gives the impression of casual assurance on court, he is a shy, modest, and extremely likable person off it. Like Nikki Pilic, he comes from Split on the Adriatic Coast.

Jan Kodes: Jan's quiet, serious off-court personality matches his industrious style of play. This muscular Czech hits his ground strokes with tremendous power and it was his blazing backhand returns of service that helped him to eliminate John Newcombe in the first round of Forest Hills 1971 and reach the final—his first success on grass. By then, of course, he had already won the French Championships back to back in 1970 and 1971, and the following year he was a Wimbledon semifinalist. He is the kind of aggressive player who always puts a great deal of pressure on his opponent and he has now acquired a really sound first volley.

He took four months off at the start of 1972 to finish his studies in Prague and that seemed to take the edge off his game for the remainder of the year, but he will continue to be a threat to all of us in the future.

Ilie Nastase: By reaching the Wimbledon final and winning the U.S. Open at Forest Hills in 1972, Ilie Nastase established himself as the Number One player in Europe and quite possibly in the world. He has the greatest flair of any player in the game today, combining superb touch with surprising strength. The power in his arm and wrist enables him to take the ball out in front of him and do things with it that perhaps only Laver can match.

A crazy, amusing character off court, "Nasty" as he is called only half jokingly, is a very different proposition on it. He is quite the most maddening and distracting opponent I have ever faced. He will pull every trick in the book to annoy and upset the man on the other side of the net and, as a doubles team, he and Ion Tiriac are really a handful. I respect Tiriac as a person but I always suspected that he was encouraging Nastase to act the clown. Tiri is basically a very shrewd guy who rarely does anything without intent but Nasty doesn't seem to have a serious side. I hope it dawns on him soon that he can win without the antics. Then this incredibly gifted Rumanian will receive the respect and world acclaim his talent deserves.

Manolo Orantes: Winning the WCT tournament in Barcelona in October 1971 proved to be the turning point in Orantes' career. He beat Rosewall, Lutz, and myself to win the title, and he quickly proved it was no fluke. After winning a major tournament in Madrid in the early spring of 1972, he went on to take the Italian, Belgian, and German titles and then reached the semifinals at Wimbledon—a remarkably consistent record by any standards.

Unlike Manolo Santana, who guided him through his formative years on the circuit, "Little Manolo," as he is called, does
not have a great deal of flair but he has a quick eye for the passing shot and now that he is no longer bothered by the cramps
which affected him as a teen-ager, he is a tough and durable
fighter. He is a happy, friendly sort of guy to have around on
the circuit, although we will be seeing less of him than most because as of this writing, along with Gimeno and Nastase, he was
one of the few top players not to sign up for the new, two-group
format WCT tour.

Adriano Panatta: When I watched Panatta play Ken Rosewall
in Bologna in November 1971, I realized that I was seeing a
potentially great player in the making. He was still only 21 then,
but despite his baby-faced good looks, he is tall and strong with
an obvious talent for the big game. He has excellent footwork and
this gives him time to spare in making his strokes—even on a
surface as fast as Wimbledon's Center Court, where he played
so well against Neale Fraser and Jimmy Connors in 1972. He
still has a lot to learn but he has the stamp of class that promises
great things in the future.

These, then, were the players who dominated the world game
during those troubled but fascinating years of 1971 and 1972—
years that saw power struggles between the ILTF and WCT divide
the game for a few disastrous months and then stitch it together
again to begin, hopefully, a new era of peace and unity.

The International circuit will continue to grow and change
with the times, but to give the reader some idea of what it is like
to be a part of that strange, nomadic world we call "the circuit,"
I kept a diary of the last leg of the 1971 WCT tour which began
in Berkeley and swung on through Vancouver to five hectic weeks
in Europe before the climax of the $100,000 play-off finals in
Houston and Dallas. The following chapters are taken from that
diary—a strict personalized view of the pro tour and the people
who live on it as seen through the eyes of one of the players
involved.

13

MY WORST MATCH

The last leg of the WCT tour which was to take us from San Francisco to Bologna, Italy, before returning for the $100,000 finals in Houston did not get off to a particularly auspicious start for me. In the Redwood Bank International at Berkeley, I struggled through to the quarterfinals and then fell on my face against Ken Rosewall, losing 6-1, 6-3. There was a reason, if not a particularly valid excuse, for that. I was unfit after a week's vacation at home—a problem that I knew I could put right with a little hard work.

But the next week in Vancouver it was a very different story. There was a reason for what happened there as well, but there was absolutely no excuse for it. None at all. It makes me ashamed to think about it now, let alone admit it, but the fact is that Tom Okker and I threw a match. The cynics who became convinced way back in the days of the Kramer circus that all professional tennis was rigged may shrug their shoulders and say: "What's so extraordinary about that? Aren't you always throwing matches?" The answer is no, never. Never before in my life, either in singles or doubles, have I ever gone on court with the intention of losing. And I can assure you that after the experience in Vancouver, I will never do so again. It was without question quite the worst thing I have ever done in tennis. I have never been so embarrassed, never felt such loss of pride. Winning tennis matches has never been easy for me. I have always had to work hard for any success I have achieved, so it is entirely illogical for me to deliberately lose a match I know I can win. No one in any walk of life can prostitute whatever talent he is lucky enough to possess and still retain his self-respect. To my mind, there is no worse form of self-abuse than that.

So why did we do it? Well, there was a little crazy logic behind our decision—or at least there seemed to be at the time. Amazing as it may seem, Tom and I had decided to throw the doubles in Vancouver some two months before—as soon as we heard that the following tournament in Cologne was due to start on the same Sunday as Vancouver ended. After Wimbledon we had been in five out of six WCT doubles finals and we were getting fed up with struggling into town for the next week's tournament a day late. Even when one is traveling between places no further apart than Louisville, Boston, and Toronto, the two- or three-hour journey takes its toll and leaves you at a considerable disadvantage in the singles against players who have arrived a couple of days earlier.

I am convinced my success in Tehran, where I beat John Alexander in the final, was largely due to the fact that I had left Rome midway through the previous week and was therefore thoroughly acclimatized to the court conditions and high altitude by the time the tournament started. Conditions were not going to be the problem in Cologne—just the flight, a fifteen-hour haul through eight time zones which promised to be a real killer for anyone having to go straight on court after arrival.

Rather than face that, I saw the opportunity of breaking the journey in Chicago, and satisfying a personal wish at the same time. A cousin of mine, Kay Riessen, was getting married on the Saturday of Vancouver and I had special reasons for wanting to be there. It was to be an outdoor, modern-generation type of wedding; Andy, the groom, works in pottery, wears his hair long, and is not exactly the type my essentially conservative family is used to. I felt it important to get there if I could so that there would be at least one other Riessen present in jeans with his hair over his ears. It would be the only chance I would have of breaking another seven-week spell away from Sally.

All these factors somehow seemed to add up to a sound rationalization for our throwing the doubles. As it turned out, nothing added up because nothing went right. I didn't even make the wedding, as I had to play Rosewall in Vancouver on the Friday night. (Wedding or no wedding, there was no question of my wanting to "tank" that one. I played my guts out and lost 6-3, 7-5.) I eventually arrived in Chicago the next day at 4:00 P.M. —an hour too late to attend the celebrations. So Kay and Andy had to go without my moral support. It was ironic, really, because it had been a guy with hair even longer than Andy's— Torben Ulrich—who had ensured that our whole rotten little plan would be publicly exposed.

I don't know what kind of amusement Lady Luck got out of throwing Ulrich and Roy Barth across our paths in the first round, but from our point of view it was a pretty cruel twist of fate. Here was the one week of the year when we were praying for a tough first round—someone like Rosewall and Stolle, to whom we could quietly lose without any fuss or loss of dignity. But no, for the first time on the tour we had to draw Ulrich and Barth, the least successful doubles pair of all.

The fact that under normal circumstances they would not have had a hope in hell of beating us was only part of the problem. The other part had to do with the sensitivity, personality, and moral outlook of that uniquely extraordinary Dane, Torben Ulrich. Most players are only too delighted when they realize that their opponents are not trying. Certainly Tom and I are. We gobble them up because we're hungry. On every occasion but this, we have a real desire to win.

But to Torben there are more important things in life than merely winning. I suppose it is his Viking blood that makes him take fainthearted opposition as a personal insult. Certainly he took our decision not to tell him of our intention as an affront to our friendship. I probably don't think as deeply about these things as he does, so I overlooked the fact that he might feel hurt that we had not taken him into our confidence. It was a mistake—just as the whole thing was a mistake.

Right from the start, throwing a match didn't prove to be as easy as we had imagined. Normally there should be nothing very difficult about it at this level of the game. Any tennis match between top-class players is decided on the outcome of a few vital points, and all you have to do is make sure you lose them. You don't have to be a great actor, either. Any good player can volley a fraction long when he's 30-40 down on serve and no one will be able to tell he didn't intend the ball to go in. Nevertheless a convincing "throw" does require a certain level of expertise from one's opponents, and in the first set, to our considerable concern, it was not forthcoming from Barth and Ulrich. Barth, in particular, was in terrible form and no matter how easy we tried to make it for him, he still managed to drop easy volleys into the bottom of the net.

But with the kind of practice we were giving them, they had to get better, and so eventually this charade of a match began to follow the required script and all seemed well when Torben reached 40-15 on his serve at 5-4 in the second set. Two match points. But the proud Dane wasn't going to let us slink away into the night that easily. To my enormous embarrassment, he ballooned two serves way out of court for an unmistakably deliberate double fault. If the public hadn't caught on to what was happening before, Torben's gesture of disdain suddenly let them in on the secret. Even a tennis novice doesn't need to be told that you don't chuck away match points like that for nothing.

But worse was to follow. On the second match point, Torben served to Okker—a condescending, gentle little serve which Tom made the mistake of returning. But still Ulrich refused to deliver the coup de grace. Allowing the volley to fall off his racket, he let the ball plop into the net. Deuce. I nearly died of shame. It was 1:00 A.M. by this time, but to my horror I realized that there were still a lot of people in the stands. They were booing now, and whistling too, just as they had every right to do. "Why don't you all go away?" I thought miserably. "Why don't you all go home and let us finish off this mess in peace?"

But of course that would have been more than we deserved. As a paid performer, be it boxer, singer, juggler, or tennis player, there is no way you should be allowed to cheat the public and get away with it. That in effect was what Torben was saying and of course he was right. I started to panic a bit at this stage and said to Tom: "This is too embarrassing. Don't you think we ought to try and win it now?" But he felt it would be worse to turn back, and I suppose it would have been an even greater discourtesy to our opponents to suddenly get up off our backsides and snatch away the victory we had been trying so hard to give them a few seconds earlier.

Mercifully Barth settled the issue for us by crossing for winning volleys after Torben had obliged by putting his next two serves in court. But Ulrich was not mollified. He refused to shake hands with me as we walked up to the net and it was only a couple of days later that I heard just how much reason he had to be offended. The afternoon before the match he had asked if he could borrow my car for an hour or two. Naturally I agreed, not even bothering to ask him what he wanted it for, which was none of my business anyway. But I heard later that he had driven to the airport to change his plane bookings to Copenhagen on the perfectly natural assumption that he and Barth were going to lose to us in the doubles. He was already out of the singles. So I suppose he felt I could have saved him a trip by letting him in on our secret.

Happily the incident did not have any lasting effect on our friendship. Although I don't necessarily dig his scene, Torben and I have always had a good understanding and I was delighted a couple of nights later when he made it known that all was forgiven with a typical little gesture.

I was sitting in the players' enclosure at courtside, having gone along out of curiosity to see Ulrich and Barth play Ashe and Lutz in the next round. Incredibly, Ulrich and Barth won that one, too, and as Torben changed ends, preparing to serve for the match, he came up to me, clasped my arm, and said in that deep, intense way of his, "What should I do now?"

Laughing at the expression of mock panic that was visible beneath his heavily bearded features, I said, "Just get your first serve in, Torben." He strode off to the base line with that superbly athletic gait, nodding gravely at the pearls of wisdom

I had offered him, and proceeeded to serve out obediently for victory.

Their success in beating as good a pair as Ashe and Lutz was the only small crumb of comfort Tom and I could cling to, for the memory of our performance two nights before was still hard to live with. I felt particularly bad about the fact that it had happened in a tournament of one of our best sponsors, Rothmans. They have always been very good to us. They are well-organized, they run four excellently promoted and presented tournaments for us in Canada, and at a time when we were struggling to attract good sponsors, we ought to have shown them greater respect.

As I said, players throw matches far less than some members of the public like to believe. And when they do, financial gain, in my experience, has never been the motivating factor. Rather the opposite. When a player throws a match he usually decided that the prize money at stake is worth less than the chance to make an early start for home after a long tour or maybe to spend a couple of days with a girl friend somewhere en route to the next tournament.

Only once have I been approached about the possibility of getting someone to throw a match for financial reward, and even that was not in a proper tournament. It happened during a Pro-Am Celebrity contest at the Le Club Internationale at Fort Lauderdale when I was partnering a guy who turned out to be a professional gambler. He had some sucker who was prepared to bet huge sums of money with him on the outcome of various matches, and he kept drawing me into corners in the dressing room to ask me how much it would cost to get so-and-so to lose his match.

Because of the nature of the event, I didn't think much about it at first, but later I began to realize how dangerous the whole concept is to our game. I remembered the basketball bribes and the pro football scandals and I thought, "Heavens, we mustn't let this sort of thing creep into tennis—at any level." I don't think anyone accepted money to take a dive that day, and I guarantee that no one I know would even entertain the idea in a Championship match. But it is something we will all have to watch out for if betting on tennis matches becomes legalized in the States as had been suggested. It works all right in England, where official odds are laid on players for Wimbledon, but even there you can only bet on the outright winner of the tournament —not on individual matches. The danger would arise if betting were allowed in head to head situations in the early rounds. There is no knowing what kind of temptation some players might have dangled in front of them by the type of character a betting situation attracts. Frankly, I think the whole idea is something tennis can do without.

14

THE JET-AGE TENNIS TOUR

TWA Flight 770 out of O'Hare Airport in Chicago got me safely to London. It usually does. That's the flight I normally take going to Europe because it leaves at the convenient hour of 7:30 P.M., enabling me to sleep after dinner—especially now that 747s are used on the run. If I can get three seats to stretch out across, I have no difficulty in sleeping like a baby on a plane, which is a useful habit, as I seem to spend half my life 30,000 feet up. I like the people who work for TWA at O'Hare, too. They have always been kind to Sally and me and it is nice to get a little personal attention—especially when you are straggling home from some long, exhausting tour.

So I left the memories of Vancouver behind me and looked forward to better things in Cologne. That would be the seventeenth leg of the WCT tour. Three more to go after that, and then the eight-man play-off finals for $100,000 in Houston and Dallas in November. It was Monday, October 11, as the west coast of Ireland emerged with the dawn, and soon after that I started thinking about these things as I came out of a good sleep.

I was placed a solid seventh in the WCT point standings—16 points ahead of eighth man Roy Emerson, so I was in no danger of losing my place in the play-offs. That was satisfying, but it was still no time to relax. Starting with the Quebec tournament back at the end of July all the remaining tournaments of 1971 were counting double because WCT was switching their playing year

141

from May to May instead of following the regular calendar year. The need to attract television was the principal reason behind this. February, March, and April are the only months when sports coverage on TV is not dominated by either baseball or football, so these would obviously be the best months to televise the final run-in for the WCT play-offs in May. To effect the change, Mike Davies, WCT's Executive Director, decided to merge the latter half of the 1971 tour with what would then become the first half of the 1971–72 season. As a result there was another $100,000 waiting for the top eight to fight for in just seven months' time. So this was indeed no time to relax in the battle for points.

Points, as I kept telling everyone, was the name of the game. I had been considered something of a fanatic about points at the start of the tour when I began keeping charts of who had won what where, but soon most of the guys became as obsessed with them as I was, as the play-offs and their massive cash bonus loomed on the horizon. Even those players who had no chance of making the top eight started talking in terms of points rather than prize money or individual matches won. To them, it was a matter of pride. In addition to the graduated prize money, points were also awarded for excellence. In other words you had to reach the final to make any real advance up the table. First-round winners received one point, second-round winners two points, semifinalists four, the losing finalist seven, and the winner ten. Before Cologne only eight players had made it through to a final: Laver, Okker, Drysdale, Newcombe, Rosewall, Ashe, and myself—who were the top seven front-runners and as a group way ahead of the rest of the field—and Alexander, who had lost to me in the final in Tehran.

It was a tight, select little club and the other players were beginning to despair of ever breaking into it. All that was to change in Cologne, but of course I had no way of knowing that as I sat in the European terminal building at London Airport waiting for the Lufthansa flight to take me to West Germany. Suddenly there was a call over the loudspeaker for Messrs. Ulrich, Stolle, and Barth. It turned out that they had come in on a Pan

High-rise apartment blocks dwarf my throw-up in downtown San Francisco as I serve to Joaquin Loyo-Mayo during the Redwood Bank International at Berkeley. For the first few days a couple of matches were scheduled at the Golden Gateway Tennis Club there so that businessmen and office workers could get to see some tennis during their lunch hour—one more good idea from one of the best tournament directors in the country, the former touring pro Barry MacKay. *Credit: Richard Evans*

Sally and I pose for Tom Okker in Dutch national costume during one of our many visits to Holland. "Old Dutch" is a fine restaurant at Volendam, just north of Amsterdam. *Credit: Tom Okker*

Gregarious Roy Emerson is never happier than when he's surrounded by people. The day before this photo was taken Emmo survived a severe electric shock from the towel railing in his Fort Worth hotel. Apparently none the worse for wear, the indefatigable Aussie tells some admirers about it at the Colonial Country Club. *Credit: Richard Evans*

Am flight a couple of hours earlier and so I went over to join
them as they straggled into the terminal from the Pan Am Clipper
lounge. It was a typical sight which airline officials the world
over must be getting used to by now—a motley group of haggard-
looking tennis players, weighted down with rackets and an assortment of carry-bags marked Dunlop, Head, Adidas or Slazenger.
On the plane we were joined by Bowrey, Davidson, and Ruffels,
who had stopped over in London; so along with Arthur Cole,
the director of the British magazine *Tennis World,* there were
eight of us who eventually arrived in Cologne to find a guard of
honor waiting for Japanese Emperor Hirohito but no reception
committee waiting for us. It was not pomp and circumstance we
were looking for—just a ride to the Esso Motor Hotel. Finally
two BMWs did turn up, and all eight of us stuffed ourselves and
our baggage into them and wearily completed the last leg of a
9,000-mile journey.

To my relief, I discovered that I did not have to play my first-
round match against Roger Taylor until the following day, so I
went down to the Sportshalle, a large indoor arena that holds
about 6,500 people, and practiced for a bit. I tried to stay up as
late as possible that night to get onto the new time schedule, but
by ten o'clock I was beat. And by 4:00 A.M., of course, I was
wide awake again. A couple of hours later I gave up trying to
sleep and was down for breakfast at 7:20 A.M. Unlike most of
the players on the circuit, I am habitually an early riser and frequently find myself breakfasting alone.

But on this particular morning I had company and plenty of
it. A whole group of players were already in the dining room,
including several I had never set eyes on at that hour of the
morning. Bob Lutz looked as if he was witnessing the break of
dawn for the first time and Charlie Pasarell admitted that he had
never had breakfast at that hour before in his life.

A few hours later a group of players started meandering on
court in a daze for a practice session at the Sportshalle. It was
easy to spot the ones who had just stepped off a plane. Rod
Laver's eyes had sunk back into their sockets, becoming almost
indistinguishable from the large blotchy freckles on his forehead.

Roy Emerson, his suntan bleached through lack of sleep, clambered up laboriously into the umpire's chair, and until it was his turn to use the court he kept himself awake by offering a running commentary, through the microphone, of the antics going on below him. His deep Australian baritone dropped octave by octave until it was little more than a grunt.

It was Tuesday, the third day of the tournament which, as I mentioned before, had been optimistically scheduled to start on the same day that Vancouver ended; but still fewer than half the players were in any condition to play proper tennis. Allan Stone, Brian Fairlie, and a couple of others were going through the motions of hitting balls through the vast emptiness of the hall, but you could have taken away the balls and they would hardly have known the difference. It was like a dream sequence. More specifically it reminded me of Antonioni's "Blow Up." Faces masked in white miming their way through a parody of a pantomime of a tennis match. It was unreal.

Torben Ulrich, to those who don't know him, appears to be in a perpetual surrealist dream, but as usual he got his wits together faster than most, as was demonstrated by an incident that I heard about later. A few of the boys decided to have a look around the largest sporting goods fair in the world, which was on display in the huge complex of exhibition halls just across the parking lot from the Sportshalle. To get to the front entrance, it was necessary to take a shuttle bus which left every fifteen minutes or so, free of charge. Torben was sitting near the front of the bus, waiting for the driver to return from his coffee break. As usual he was attired in jeans and a well-worn pullover. And his hair, of course, was flowing way past his shoulders. He did not, to put it mildly, look remotely like anyone in a postion of authority.

But when a Teutonic-looking gentleman with sleek, blond hair climbed aboard and started to move down the bus, Torben stopped him gently and said in *English,* "Your pass, please." Without a second's hesitation, the man whipped out some sort of document—presumably a regular ID card, for no passes or tickets were required for the bus—and showed it to his bearded

inquisitor. Torben stared at it gravely for a second and then said,
"Okay, thank you very much." Again he spoke in English. Meanwhile Mark Cox and Terry Ryan were trying desperately to sup-
press a fit of giggles across the aisle, Torben simply stared out into space with the satisfied expression of a man who has proved a
point. To him it was merely an amusing sociological exercise.

"The Germans, you know," he explained afterwards, "are so
uptight about authority that they will accept it from absolutely
anyone. You notice how the man didn't even think of querying
why I should be talking to him in English on a German bus in
the middle of Cologne."

That night I played Taylor and discovered just how fast the
court was. The only service break came right at the end of the
third set when Roger faltered to give me a 6-7, 7-6, 6-3 victory.
That's how fast it was. No chance of returning well, no chance of
interesting rallies. As winning is the name of the game, all you
can do is wait for the other guy to slip in a few poor serves and,
in the meantime, make damn sure you don't do so yourself. It's
tedious to play and tedious to watch—two very good reasons
why bad grass and very fast indoor carpets should be scrapped.
Whether they realize it or not, the public is getting cheated and
that, of course, defeats the whole purpose of the exercise. Sportface, which is the carpet WCT now uses almost exclusively in
the United States; Uniturf indoors; and the excellent French
carpet made by Sommer called Matesoft are the only ones which,
in my opinion, match up to the required standards of speed and
bounce.

But no matter how it is achieved, a victory is a victory and it
was pleasing to have one under my belt at the start of what was
obviously going to be a hard slog through Europe. As it turned
out, it was harder and a little more painful than I had expected.

15

EUROPE ON THE TENNIS CIRCUIT

Forty-eight hours later I was hanging upside down, suspended by the backs of my knees from a towel railing in my hotel bathroom wishing I was a monkey. A tail, I thought, would have come in very handy just then. As I was wearing nothing much in particular, I was also wondering whether or not this might be an appropriate moment to take a suppository. Such are the strange thoughts and unlikely positions that befall a globe-trotting athlete.

I was not adopting that position for my amusement, but rather as a result of doctor's orders. The previous day—only coincidentally, I am sure, October 13—I had felt something go in the lower left-hand side of my back while practicing with Tom. By the time we came to play doubles against Ulrich and Barth that evening I could hardly move. But, as you might imagine, this was one match I had no intention of losing even if it cost me more than it was worth in physical discomfort. It was one week to the day since our dismal performance against Torben and Roy in Vancouver, and we wanted to make it very clear to them that there was going to be absolutely no chance of a repeat. With Tom doing all the running and chasing for me, we beat them fair and square and felt a little better for it.

But my back didn't feel any better and the next morning I set off in search of a doctor whose address I had been given. I eventually found his office, which was situated above an electrical appliances shop on one of Cologne's main shopping streets.

On the second floor a nurse, looking prim and efficient in a bleached white tunic, sat at the end of a long corridor. The walls were bare and bleached white, too.

"Ah, and you are ze tennis player, yes?" she said with a tight smile. "Mr. Riessen, yes?"

At least the Germans never have any trouble with my name.

"Herr Doktor is expecting you," she added, and swept me into an adjoining room. There Herr Doktor was keen to give me all sorts of injections, but luckily he understood the basic rudiments of the English language like "No!" and "Not on your life!" so I managed to avoid the needle, as I have done throughout my playing career. Maybe the time will come when I am in such agony that I will succumb, but until that happens I am going to stay away from cortisone or any other pain-killing injections. Pain is a warning signal that you are damaging your body by moving in a certain way. If you switch off that signal artificially, you have no idea what you may be doing to yourself. Tendons, cartilages, and discs may get ripped to shreds and damaged for life before the cortisone wears off. I can understand players using it before a Wimbledon final or some similar occasion, but under normal circumstances I prefer more natural methods of treatment.

Once I had gotten this point across to the doctor, he promptly put away his needles and started jerking and twisting me about like a chiropractor. I didn't know my limbs could be bent in so many ways but by the time he had finished, the pressure and tightness in my lower back seemed to have eased slightly. After that I was handed back to the nurse, who told me to pull down my pants "just so" and then stuck me under a heat ray lamp. It was all very efficient. Before I could escape, the doctor reappeared to tell me that the best way to relieve the pressure on my back was to hang upside down with my legs hooked over a bar or railing. I knew that to be true, for several of the guys on the circuit have bad backs—probably the most common complaint among tennis players—and many had been told to indulge in similar exercises.

In fact one American firm had developed a portable machine consisting of bars which you can fix in a doorway of your hotel

The film star grin belongs to John Newcombe during lunch on the terrace of the beautiful Real Club at Barcelona in October, 1971. Credit: Richard Evans

The ever-cheerful Egyptian Ismail El Shafei, pictured at the Colonial Country Club in Fort Worth during the WCT tournament there in August, 1971. Credit: Richard Evans

After months of painful rehabilitation following surgery on his elbow, Tony Roche proved that he could do more with his left arm than lift a paper cup in the Washington Star tournament in July, 1972. In sweltering humidity, the popular Aussie completed his brief comeback bid by beating me in the final. Credit: Richard Evans

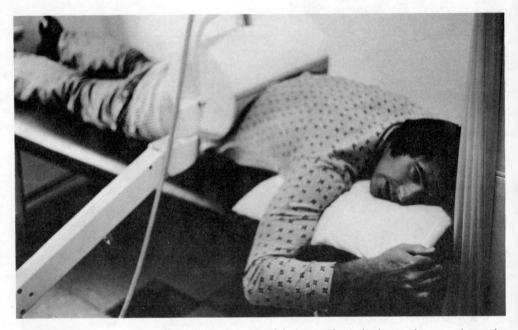

It really wasn't that painful, but I don't look too happy about the state of my back as I get some heat treatment at a doctor's office in Cologne during WCT's 1971 swing through Europe. *Credit: Richard Evans*

bathroom or wherever. Apparently a salesman for the company had turned up a few weeks before at the Pacific Southwest in Los Angeles and persuaded Cliff Richey and a few of the boys to help him demonstrate it in the locker room. The sight of Cliff hanging upside down, getting pinker in the face by the second, was obviously too much for the crowd of players that had gathered round. Wisecracks flowed thick and fast, most of them highly uncomplimentary to the machine in relation to Richey's position on it. The salesman made the fatal mistake of not seeing the joke. A sense of humor is the number one priority in a job like that, and of course his refusal to see the funny side of it only fed the audience more ammunition. I don't think he ended up selling many of his firm's contraptions, although the basic idea was absolutely valid.

So I took the good doctor's advice about finding something to hang upside down from and also, with somewhat greater reluctance, accepted his prescription for suppositories. I learned later that European doctors nearly always favor anal as opposed to oral dosage, which is better, I suppose, than puncturing the skin with needles, but not much.

So that was how I came to be suspended arse-upwards in my bathroom. For all the good it did me that particular evening, I might just as well have stayed there, for I blew a perfectly good 6-3, 4-3, 40-15 lead against Andres Gimeno in our second-round match and sank without trace in the third set. It wasn't my back that was the problem. After all the attention it had been getting it felt reasonably good. It was simply that I pulled my gutless wonder act after Andres played really well to get back into the second set. I got so cautious and nervous that I seemed incapable of hitting the ball. It was pathetic.

I was furious with myself when I got back to the locker room, and without even bothering to shower I pulled on a sweater and a pair of jeans and got the hell out of there for a walk. I often feel the need to be by myself after a bad loss. This time especially, I felt as if I would only be rude and say things I would regret later if I sat around the locker room moping. So I went off for a half hour's stroll around the half-deserted streets of Cologne.

It was cool and damp after some light rain, and the headlights of the Volkswagens and BMWs dazzled the eye as their beams glistened on the glassy asphalt. But I didn't notice much. I was too busy lecturing myself about my defeat. There was no way one could afford to lose matches from a set and a break up on a tour as tough as this. I was supposed to have put performances like that behind me. It was no good merely setting them up for the knockout blow—you had to deliver it as well. And you had to counterpunch, too. Fifteen-forty down on your serve at 5-1 —*that* was the moment to get tough, really tough. I had watched John Newcombe do it so often. Just when you thought you had him with two break points against his serve, he would crack down on you, springing to the net for the volley just that fraction of a second faster and punching the shot away just that inch deeper so that suddenly it was you who was back on the defensive. An inch, half an inch, a tenth of a second—these were the terrifying margins that divided the quick from the dead in our league. And always the ultimate test comes at those two or three moments of crisis that suddenly erupt along the rocky path to victory or defeat. The big points. Anyone can hit great winners at 15-love. Only champions hit them consistently at 30-40. Tougher on the big points, Marty, tougher, tougher, tougher . . .

Out of the corner of my eye I caught a passerby giving me a quizzical look as I strode back toward the Sportshalle, head down, hands thrust deep into the pockets of my jeans. I don't think I was actually talking out loud, but I must have cut a strange figure on the streets of Cologne that evening all the same. Not all my thoughts had been pertinent to the loss I had just suffered against Gimeno but they had provided the sort of personal pep talk I needed. In tennis confidence plays such an enormous part in winning and losing that it is necessary to keep reminding yourself of the strengths of your game as well as the weaknesses. I, too, had become tougher on the big points— there was no question of that. I hadn't established myself in seventh place through sixteen tournaments by caving in when the going got hot. I could stand the heat all right—most times,

The gentle Dane Torben Ulrich—one of the unique characters of the game—prepares to give Roger Taylor's wife Frances and daughter Zoe a helping hand on the terrace of No. 3 Court at the Foro Italico during the Italian Championships of 1971. *Credit: Richard Evans*

The Paris-based *New York Herald Tribune* becomes an essential source of news when we are on tour in Europe. Here in a shopping mall near the magnificent Cologne Cathedral, I pause to catch up on some football scores back home. *Credit: Richard Evans*

anyway. It was just the occasional lapse, the sudden slip backwards to old bad habits that was so annoying.

But no matter. There was always next week and the week after
that. Finding myself back at the Sportshalle, I returned to locker
room, showered, and felt prepared to meet the world once again.
The walk, as always, had done me good. I checked the other
scores and found that the rookie on the tour, Jeff Borowiak,
had beaten Fred Stolle, which was hardly surprising the way
Fred had been playing, and that Cliff Drysdale had pulled his
usual psycho act over his doubles partner Nikki Pilic. It was all
mental between those two, as it is between so many players.
Tennis is such a mental game. You can get great psychological
blocks about certain players that take months or even years to
break down. Cliff "owned" Nikki and no matter how well Pilic
played there seemed to be nothing he could do about it. As we
say, it was all in the mind.

I found one of the drivers who was ferrying players to and
from the Esso Motor Hotel—a hip young German with shoulder-
length hair and a somewhat fatalistic sense of humor—and
prepared myself for another nerve-racking ride through the center
of Cologne. The tournament had been loaned a couple of new
BMWs—spectacular cars that our two drivers could not resist
driving at spectacular speeds. Each trip was like a practice run
for the Nürburgring but we always seemed to survive.

Whether the Esso Motor Hotel would survive a week of WCT
was another matter. It wasn't that we were particularly rowdy but
simply that our hours didn't seem to fit into any known Teutonic
timetable. The first night they said that the restaurant closed at
11:00 P.M. and one couldn't even get coffee any later. As matches
were finishing at midnight or after ,that was obviously no good at
all. So the next night the boys who got in around ten just sat
tight at their tables, which were then continually expanded by
late arrivals. By the end of the week the management had sur-
rendered. The restaurant stayed open until the last hungry tennis
player had been fed. At $24 a night, we didn't think it was too
much to ask.

Local boy Jeff Borowiak sought out Arthur Ashe's opinion when he was offered a WCT contract during the Berkeley tournament in September, 1971. They talked about it on the roof of the clubhouse and the next day Borowiak signed. *Credit: Richard Evans*

There were various players dotted around the dining room when I went in, including, at one table, the unlikely pair of Borowiak and Rosewall. Kenny was winning world titles when Jeff was two, and their life styles are just about as dissimilar as that age gap would suggest. The scene between the two of them was fascinating. Borowiak, with his mass of long black hair cascading down onto his threadbare blue pullover, was busily picking the impurities from his salad. Lifting some watercress out of the bowl with his fork for closer inspection, he eventually put it in his mouth.

"Hmm, now let's see," he said dubiously, "if this is really fresh it should sort of melt in the mouth and go down in one swallow."

The watercress passed the test and Borowiak asked the waiter for a jug of hot water. He then produced a crumpled paper bag from under the table, extracted a bottle of molasses, and started stirring when the water arrived. Rosewall's face was a portrait.

Jeff, of course, is a health food nut who carries around his own supply of nutritious cereals, honey, and molasses. He is also a musician of considerable ability, having majored in music at UCLA and toyed with the idea of becoming a concert pianist. Jeff has theories on most things, and before the week was out he was to engage Stolle in what was probably Fred's first conversation about Bach. Jeff reckons Rosewall and Bach have much in common. In fact he thinks Rosewall plays tennis like Bach composed music, seeing similarities in tempo, style, and productivity. Fred, who had never viewed his doubles partner in quite that light before, was prepared to give Borowiak a hearing because Jeff had just beaten him on a tennis court twice in three weeks. That, in Fred's book, entitled Borowiak to a modicum of respect.

Having brought another jug of hot water, the waiter eyed Jeff's bundle of health food, which was now spread around the table, and said, "It is goot that not everyone brings own dinner. Ve vould be out of work, no?"

"Bloody right," muttered Rosewall who was secretly enjoying the experience.

After dinner a crowd of us decided to go to a discotheque. It was a fairly typical group—Emerson and Stolle, Allan Stone and his wife, Ashe and a Jamaican girlfriend named Nancy Burke, who had flown down from her job in Heidelberg for the week, and John and Micky Konrads, two friends from Paris who happened to be in town. John is a former Australian Olympic swimmer who now represents a sporting goods company in Europe. Tom Okker was also with us, and he had the only bad experience of an otherwise enjoyable evening. When we got ready to leave at about 2:30 A.M., he found that his $200 pigskin coat had been stolen. That did nothing to improve Tom's mood.

He wasn't any happier a couple of days later when Bob Lutz beat him in the semifinals. Lutz, who was in hot pursuit of Roy Emerson for eighth place in the points table, had taken both Emerson and Laver in previous rounds for the first time in his career and was going through the tournament like a Panzer division. I was not surprised he had beaten Tom; in fact I had predicted it, for Bob had a momentum going and was obviously gaining in confidence daily.

I was also right with another forecast—Borowiak beat Drysdale. After watching Jeff a few times during the week, I had come to the conclusion that we were underestimating him a little. He has a very solid game, moves well, and obviously, in his first tournament as a contract pro, he had nothing to lose. None of us—save possibly for Lutz, who had played him often in California—were familiar with his game and on top of that he had the advantage of filling Newcombe's Number One seeding spot in the draw, as Newk was still injured. But even with all that going for him, he still had to put it together out there on court. That isn't easy against a player as consistent as Drysdale, but Borowiak managed it—playing a cool tie-break to win 7-6 in the third. Gimeno, who tends to be more nervous than the rest of us against players he does not know, also found Jeff too tough to handle in the semis, and so in his very first WCT tournament our new hippy from Berkeley had reached the final. That was quite an achievement, but we would be after him in

While I went off to practice for a match in the French Championships in 1971, Donald Dell, agent, lawyer, and friend, took some of his clients for a stroll down the Champs Elysee. From left to right, Tom Gorman, Dell, Charlie Pasarell, Stan Smith, Arthur Ashe, Bob Lutz. *Credit: Richard Evans*

On an outside court at Rome's Foro Italico, a familiar Roman scene. Nikki Pilic (center) and Cliff Drysdale, who seems to have learned a few gestures from his partner, argue with the umpire while Arthur Ashe tries to blot it all out of his mind by attempting to balance the ball on the top of the net. Dennis Ralston, partially hidden, looks on. *Credit: Richard Evans*

earnest from that moment on and he wouldn't find it quite as easy again. Lutz came through as expected in the final to win his first WCT title and so gain entry to the exclusive winners' circle. Emmo was looking glum. His hold on that precious eighth position—which meant a ticket to Houston for the $100,000 play-off finals—was beginning to slip.

The nerve in my back had been improving slowly all week and Tom and I had managed to fight our way into the doubles final, where we staged one of our greatest comebacks against Laver and Emerson. At two sets to love down, and 5-6, love-40 in the third, you can safely be said to have one foot in the grave and the other on a banana skin. But just in case anyone had any doubts as to our fighting qualities after Vancouver, Tom and I saved those three match points plus one more before winning 6-4 in the fifth. It was a pretty astounding victory, considering Rocket and Emmo hadn't lost a doubles since before Wimbledon. Afterwards Tom had to drive back to Amsterdam with Annemarie and his father, but I thought a little celebration was called for, so I joined in one hell of a party back at the hotel where beer and schnapps flowed until the early hours. The Berkeley boys, Lutz and Borowiak, were already hard at it when I got back, and as I was rooming with Bob that week I didn't see much point in going to bed and having him stagger in on me in the middle of the night.

There was nothing wrong with the party at all execpt for the Monday morning that followed it. We were all booked on early flights to Barcelona via Frankfurt, and one look at Lutz told me Lufthansa was going to have a "no show." He made a brave effort, actually getting up and making it down to the dining room, where he stared two eggs in the face for a couple of minutes, changed to a color that was more in keeping with the green decor of the restaurant, and staggered back upstairs. I found him semiconscious and fully clothed on his bed when I returned to get my bags, so I left him there to sleep it off.

Bob said afterwards that he was pleasantly surprised that I hadn't made any attempt to force him up even though it was obvious he was going to miss the plane. Well, for a start I knew there were later planes he could catch, and anway I don't believe in forcing unwanted assistance on people. Bob had been hung over before and he had caught later planes before and he didn't need me to wet-nurse him.

As it was, I had quite enough on my hands with Borowiak. Punctuality is not one of Jeff's strong points and as we had agreed to travel together, I felt obliged to wait around for him. In the end we both nearly missed the plane. From his point of view it would probably have been better if we had, for it was a really bumpy flight and Jeff suffered from airsickness most of the way. I cheered him up with a little black humor—telling him about the time lightening struck a plane I was in, and of another occasion when the pilot made a botch of the landing in Boston and had to roar back up at the last minute and swing around for another try. Jeff loved that.

We eventually made it to Barcelona to be greeted by a warm October sun and the very different atmosphere of Spain. After dropping our bags at the hotel, Jeff and I went straight to the beautiful Real Club for some very necessary practice. WCT had really done it to us this time, scheduling a tournament on slow European clay immediately after the fast carpet of Cologne. As pros it is our business to be able to play on any surface at any time, but no one finds it easy to make such a dramatic switch in so short a time. Our problems were increased by the fact that this was one of eight WCT events in 1971 that were opened up to a few of the top Independents, and since many of them had been practicing in Barcelona for several days before our arrival, they had a considerable advantage. They made the most of it, too.

We discovered that Marty Mulligan, a clay-court specialist since he left his native Australia for Italy several years before, had already scored a first-round upset over Arthur Ashe, and that was only the start of our troubles. One appreciates the difficulties facing WCT's European director John MacDonald in arranging a workable tournament schedule, but greater care must be taken in the future to avoid sudden changes of playing surface. It is not a question of making things easier for ourselves,

although it would help if we all played under the same circumstances. Rather, it is the paying customer who suffers most, because he just doesn't get to see the standard of tennis of which we
are capable. It was no coincidence that the worst tennis of the
European tour was played in Barcelona. That was a shame, because once you get in the groove it is possible to play the most
crowd-pleasing tennis of all on clay. And we should never forget
that as pros, it is our business to entertain.

The difference in playing conditions was apparent to Jeff
and myself as soon as we stepped on court. The slowness of the
surface requires one type of adaptation in strategy and shot-
making, while the balls themselves necessitate quite another, for
they fluff up very quickly and soon feel like lead weights compared with those used on a fast, smooth court. I was due to play
Taylor again in the first round the next day and I knew it was
going to be tough because we have this rivalry going between us.
I was on a winning streak against him, but that didn't make life
any easier because I knew he would be particularly keen to beat
me. I was so right. Roger got off to a great start and won the
first eight games to lead 6-0, 2-0.

At that stage I decided I had better begin doing something different, so I changed rackets. I had had one of my Dunlops
loosely strung in the hope of finding it easier to get the heavy
balls back over the net. But I had been all over the place with it,
slugging everything out of sight. So I switched to one that was
tighter strung and struggled back to lead 4-2 in the second set,
and after one more moment of crisis when Taylor had me 15-40
down on my serve at 4-all, I got on top and eventually won 0-6,
6-4, 6-1. That was better. I had fought well even if I hadn't
played particularly well. Maybe the pep talk I had given myself
during that walk in Cologne had done some good.

Later Jeff Borowiak, Bob Lutz—who had arrived apparently
none the worse for wear from Cologne the previous evening—
and I went off to a good little restaurant called the Alamente,
which we had found just around the corner from the hotel.
We were pleased with both since the Arenas Hotel, which
was modern and comfortable, cost only $12 a night and the

Alamente offered a succulent array of dishes in a great Spanish atmosphere at very reasonable prices. We enjoyed one of the most pleasurable aspects of touring in Europe—a good meal, a little wine, and fun-filled conversation. Jeff was on about the pros and cons of pot smoking and the use of other drugs, and as he has considerably more liberal views on the subject than I do, it turned out to be a pretty stimulating evening.

The week continued to go well for me. The following day I beat Andres Gimeno 4-6, 7-5, 6-0, which was very satisfying not only because I did it on his home court but also because Emmo had told me that Andres thought he "owned" me after his victory in Cologne. The hell he did. (I will describe this match in detail in the instructional section of the book.)

But although Andres was obviously disappointed at losing so early in the tournament in front of his own crowd, there were, as usual, no hard feelings between us, and the next day he invited me to join his wife Cristina, Tom and Annamarie Okker, and Arthur Ashe on a trip up the coast to La Scala. There was some land there that he was proposing to buy and he wondered if we might be interested in coming in on the deal. Apart from the land, which seemed to offer a good investment as it was situated right on the coast next to a yacht club, the drive through the beautiful Spanish countryside in Andy's Mercedes was most enjoyable in itself. We had an excellent lunch in the village before heading back to the club. It was a nice diversion, for it provided a rare opportunity to get away from the tight routine of hotel-club-restaurant-hotel that one is almost obliged to follow during a tournament.

On Friday I made it to the semifinals with a 3-6, 6-4, 6-4 victory over John Newcombe. I still didn't play as well as I would have liked but Newk, who was playing his first tournament since his knee injury at Forest Hills, was not at his best either so I scraped through. Even so, I was elated at having beaten him again, as it gave me a 3-2 record against the Wimbledon Champion.

By this time, of course, the rest of the field was thinning out and things did not look good for WCT. Of the four semifinalists,

two were Independent pros, Mulligan and the left-handed Spaniard Manuel Orantes, who was the heir apparent to Manolo
Santana on the Spanish Davis Cup team. Orantes had played
well to beat Ken Rosewall in the quarters, but he was helped by
one of the worst line calls I have ever seen at 5-6, 15-40. That's
one of the few drawbacks of playing in Latin countries, as far
as I am concerned. They'll rob you blind given the slightest
opportunity.

Apart from myself, the other WCT survivor was the incredible
Herr Lutz, late of Cologne. Apparently taking the change of
surface in his great loping stride, Bob had overcome both Emerson and Laver for the second straight week—writing himself a
ticket to the play-offs in Houston at Emmo's expense in the
process.

Lutz versus Mulligan and myself against Orantes was the
semifinal lineup, so it was a straight fight—WCT versus the
Independents. When we arrived at the Real Club on Saturday
John MacDonald relayed messages of good luck from WCT's
Executive Director Mike Davies, who was sweating it out back in
Dallas. This was the eighteenth leg of the tour and so far only
one Independent had made it through to a WCT final. In May,
Jan Kodes, the hard-hitting Czech had done so in Rome but
Laver had nailed him there before he could get his hands on
one of our titles. Neither Davies, nor indeed any of us, wanted
an outsider to win one of our tournaments so the pressure was on.
While Bob went out to do battle with Mulligan inside the packed
Center Court, I finished off an early lunch under the trees on
the patio of the lovely old clubhouse. For no logical reason, I
was starting to get bad premonitions about my match and I was
glad when a nice-looking Spanish girl asked me if she could have
an interview for a local magazine. It provided the diversion I
was looking for until it was time to go on.

Lutz finally struggled past Mulligan in a ragged match full of
unforced errors, and then we had to hang around for fifteen
minutes because some VIPs had not arrived. Orantes, who
comes from Barcelona, was already a big name in Spain, having
been dubbed "little Manolo" as he grew up in Santana's shadow,

and the whole town seemed to be catching a touch of autumnal tennis fever. I knew it was going to be rough out there, and after the kind of calls Rosewall had gotten I wanted to make it plain right from the start that I was not going to get bullied into accepting bad decisions.

I got an early chance of doing so and nearly caused a riot in the process. At 2-all in the first set and 30-love on my serve, I hit what was undoubtedly an ace. From where I stood I could see the mark an inch inside the center line. But the linesman called it fault. "Right," I thought, "this is where we make our stand." So I walked up to the net and beckoned with my finger for the center-line judge to get up off his chair and come and look at the mark. The crowd was incredulous at first because no one could understand why I was making such a fuss. There could hardly be a less critical, less dramatic moment of any match than 2-all, 30-love, first set. But that was precisely the point. I didn't want to start arguing when the whole match hung in the balance later on. I wanted to let them know right there and then that they were going to have a fight on their hands if they tried to pull any fast ones on crucial points. I still think it was sound tactics and I would do it again—except for one thing. I wouldn't beckon with my finger. It was that small gesture that made everything backfire for it brought the crowd down on my back like the wrath of God. Apparently it is considered very rude and uncivilized to beckon someone in that manner in Spain, where strict codes of behavior are still rigidly enforced. To the spectators I was simply carrying on like a brash, arrogant Yank who didn't know how to behave himself in someone else's country. I didn't realize this at the time, of course, and anyway I expected a little hostile reaction when I started arguing. I certainly wasn't trying to win any popularity contests out there. But when the line judge finally hauled himself out of his chair and pointed to a different mark in an attempt to support his decision, I got really mad and marched around to Orantes's side of the net to circle the correct one with my racket.

By this time the tournament referee had come on to court to tell me, over the explosion of noise that was erupting from the crowd, to stop "angering the public," as he put it, and get on with the match. Either that, he said, or I was to leave the court. For a split second I thought I might do just that, but I dismissed the idea immediately and stopped at the water cooler to take a drink instead. I wasn't going to give Orantes that easy a passage to the final. The crowd was still going mad, whistling and booing and yelling well-worn phrases like "American Go Home." The sheer intensity of that amount of noise can get pretty unnerving and I realized that I had probably unleashed a flood of animosity that would engulf me later on.

There was nothing for it but to get back on court and hang in. For a time I managed to do that with great effect. I grabbed the first set 6-3; broke immediately in the second, and had two points for a second break at 2-0, 15-40 on Orantes' serve. That's where I lost the match. I had him reeling and I didn't deliver the knock-out blow. I played safe when I should have ridden my luck and blazed away with everything I had. Manolo saved that service game and slowly started to work his way back into the match with good lobs and nicely judged passing shots that had me lunging hopelessly at the net. I could feel the tide turning and Orantes could, too, for his play became more confident and more aggressive with every point. As an experienced clay-court competitor, he knew that a set and a break was not much of a hill to have to climb when your opponent was losing his footing on the other side. Orantes had climbed it many times before, and when I double faulted twice to lose that second set, I knew all my premonitions had been correct. I lost confidence and direction and the harder I tried to reassemble what had been a winning game only minutes before, the deeper I became en-tangled in that mesmerizing red clay. The crowd, which had quieted down a bit during the first set, started up again with their chants and their yells, and afterwards Cristina Gimeno said she would blush if she told me some of the things they were shouting. "They were very rude," she said apologetically. It wasn't their rudeness that bothered, although that sort of thing does get to you in the end. It was my growing inability to mount any sort of a counterattack. I was becoming more helpless by the minute, and

I lost the third set 6-0. In the locker room during the break Bob
Lutz tried to bring me out of my depression, but I was in one of
my fatalistic moods by then and I knew I was beaten. The fourth
set went to Orantes 6-1, and after match point the crowd went
berserk, lifting Manolo up on their shoulders and carrying him
around the court as if he were a matador. I must admit I did feel
a bit like a dead bull.

Strangely, the crowd seemed more excited about Orantes
reaching the final than they did the next day when he beat Bob
to win the title. By that time I was in London, but I understand
that Lutz got two or three really bad calls—so bad, in fact, that
the crowd suddenly seemed to feel guilty about it and started
whistling their own line judges. Orantes played well to win and
deserved his success, but in the end Bob got almost as big a hand
from Manolo's own crowd as Manolo did.

The girl who had interviewed me before the match salvaged
something from the ruins of the day by inviting me out to dinner
that evening. Her name was Nuria Beltran, and apart from being
a writer and a tennis player, she was also one of the few women
lawyers in old feudal Spain, where Women's Lib isn't exactly
the cause célèbre. She took me back to her parents' magnificent
apartment, which was full of paintings hanging from oak-paneled
walls, and then on to Boccacio, Barcelona's most exclusive discotheque. There the walls were lined with red velvet and the
service was almost embarrassingly attentive—a flick of an eyelid being sufficient to draw a discreet waiter out of the shadows.
I found Richard Evans, my co-author, lurking in some other
shadows on the dance floor and some time in the early hours
Nuria drove us back to our hotel and bid us good night on the
doorstep in very correct Spanish fashion. It had been a delightful
evening—just the sort of distraction a sore tennis player needs to
cure the ills of the day.

16

ON TO LONDON AND BELGIUM AND STOCKHOLM AND BOLOGNA . . .

There was a little familiar London fog hanging over Heathrow Airport when my flight touched down around noon on Sunday. I went straight to Lancaster Mews, where my friend Herman Schreuder, a Dutch Shell Oil executive, has a nice little apartment with a spare bedroom that he is kind enough to let me have whenever I am in London. It's like a home away from home now, and I never have to worry if Herman is there or not because George Nutt, a mechanic who works downstairs, always lets me in. I find London a comfortable place to be. You can take it hard or take it easy, relax or hit the town. If you want to join the boys for a night out you don't have to look any further than the Playboy Club for a bit of gambling or the Saddle Room or Tramps for dancing. Arthur Ashe, Bob Lutz, Dennis Ralston, or Charlie Pasarell will be in one or the other.

But that particular evening Herman took me to a good restaurant on Fulham Road called The Hungry Horse and I knew I was back in London when people started recognizing me. They weren't mistaking me for Roger Taylor or Charlie Pasarell, either, as frequently happens in other parts of the world where people have only a hazy idea of who's who in the tennis fraternity. In England they know their tennis as a result of the saturation TV coverage given to Wimbledon and a few other tournaments during the year. A couple of days later when I went to get a cholera shot at a West London hospital, the nurse, who had not even been

171

given my name, said simply, "Well, we'll have to put it in your left arm, won't we?"

It's sort of startling when you are not used to it. But I must admit it makes you feel good.

I felt less good about tennis in general that week. Along with about half my WCT colleagues I was in London to play the Embassy Championships at Wembley, which was a regular Open tournament, not a WCT event. In the first round I was drawn against Bob Hewitt, the talented Independent pro from South Africa, and when I got to the stadium for practice at ten o'clock on Monday morning I found that Bob was the only other guy around. So we hit for a while and of course I found myself having the inevitable problems of trying to readapt to another ultra-fast carpet. The balls were much lighter than in Barcelona and flew all over the place.

When we started the match a few hours later, I hung in there for a bit, losing the first set on a tie break, but Bob wrapped it up by taking the second 6-4. Somehow I couldn't get worked up about it either way. It was already my thirty-fourth playing week of the year—originally I had planned on playing only thirty— and there were still three tough ones to go. In a way, I rather welcomed the thought of a few days off in London. There were many little personal matters that I had to attend to like the cholera shots, changing air tickets, and another series of visits to the faithful Dr. Sohickish near the Queen's Club.

My back had still been giving me some trouble and the doctor was very cheery about it, telling me that if I didn't take care I might end up spending a month in bed. That scared the hell out of me. Dr. Sohickish thought that I had knocked the hip joint fractionally out of line and that some fluid had gotten in which was aggravating a nerve. He gave me massages and heat treatment and all sorts of exercises to do, like arching my back and hanging from my hands. He also told me that I should not sit up straight because that only put more pressure on my back. "Sit as round-shouldered as possible and stick your stomach out," he said. I thought I was round-shouldered enough, but I followed instructions for a few weeks and the problem cleared up. But all that slouching around was terrible training for backgammon.

On Thursday Charlie Pasarell and I flew over to Brussels to join Tom and Arthur on a series of one-night exhibition matches through the Low Countries; they had been arranged by the Belgian Davis Cup player Eric Drossart in conjunction with Stella Artois Beer, the sponsor. Eric is getting into the sports promotional business in Europe and he had set up a good tour with matches in Liège, Antwerp, and Brussels. The crowds were not very large, but the fact that all the matches were televised locally probably accounted for that. I lost to Arthur in Liège and then beat Tom in Brussels and Charlie in Antwerp. There was $1,000 to the winner and $500 to the loser, so it was worth our while to get out there and play a bit.

On the plane coming over Charlie told me that Donald Dell had been hit by a car outside the Westbury Hotel in Mayfair the day before. A lot of the boys had been to see him in the hospital, but as I had been staying in a private home, I had not heard about it. Apparently Donald had been sitting in a friend's car that was parked across the street from the Westbury when he realized that he had left some documents back in his hotel room. He had only arrived in London that day and stepped straight out into the street looking left instead of right. As usual his head was full of 95 different things and none of them happened to be telling him that in England they drive on the other side of the road. A car accelerating away from the light caught him broadside, took his legs out from under him, dumped him head first onto the road, knocked him unconscious for about 45 seconds, and broke his leg. In a strange way, it probably did him good. It brought him up short with a bang and gave him 24 hours flat on his back in Charing Cross Hospital to ponder life at his leisure. As usual he had been working seventeen hours a day on a global basis at breakneck speed, and now that he nearly had broken his neck, he had time to ask himself whether it was worth it. To Donald the answer probably was "yes," simply because he is incapable of operating at any other pace. But he did admit to

Charlie, Tom Gorman, Zeljko Franulovic, and a few of the boys who went to see him in the hospital that it had made him realize how easily expendable we all are.

That was my reaction, too, when Charlie told me the whole story. It just reminded me how quickly we can die. Anybody who flies as much as we do hardly needs reminding of that fact, but I am lucky in that I'm generally not uptight about flying. I have bad spells in which I get scared to death, but they last only a month or so and then I seem to come out of it—basically, I suppose, because I enjoy the excitement of getting on a plane to go to a different place and also because I am able to rationalize this fear in my mind. I just pick up a flight timetable and have a look at all the hundreds of flights that go to London or Chicago each day and I think, "Good heavens, look how many times they make it!" Considering the congested air space over big metropolitan areas, the airlines' safety record is something of a miracle.

But although I have a basic faith in most airlines' ability to get me where I'm going in one piece, troublesome thoughts still cross my mind during the bad spells—especially on the last leg home after a long tour. "If this plane lands safely, I'll see my wife again." I try not to let myself think like that but it is at such moments that you suddenly realize all the things you meant to do and never managed to fit in, all the things you meant to tell people you care about and never got around to saying. It is all very melodramatic, but when you fly an average of twice a week, year in and year out, even the most sanguine among us have to have moments when we agree with comedian Shelley Berman, whose observation about the takeoff must pass through everyone's mind: "And it rolls and it rolls and it rolls, doesn't it? And you think, 'To hell with science, tonight it's not going to make it'."

Anyway most of our traveling around Belgium was done by car and, statistically speaking, that can be twice as hazardous. Before driving down to Antwerp on Sunday, I had lunch with Dick and Betsy McKinney, who have a lovely house in Brussels just a few minutes' walk from the Leopold Tennis Club. Dick, whose 6'3" frame is topped by a shining bald head, works for

Procter and Gamble in Belgium. As usual, he was kind enough to ask me to stay there. But we had gotten in late the night before and all I really wanted was a quick bite to eat and some time to myself to relax and sleep. It seems strange, perhaps, to opt for another hotel room when you have a chance to be with friends that you don't often get to see. It is difficult, too, not to give offense, but unless you happen to be a total extrovert who craves company morning, noon, and night, it is essential to guard your privacy on tour—for no other reason really except to gather your thoughts, to unwind at your own pace, to write some letters, or to phone home. Betsy understood this when I declined their invitation, but I'm not so sure about Dick. Maybe it was just his naturally quick, probing attitude. He's a very sharp guy who is always questioning me about how I play tennis, why I play tennis, and what my motives are for doing this or that. At any rate, I spent a very enjoyable time at their house the following day and even got in a little basketball practice with Dick and his son Christopher.

Early next morning we were off again and this time Stockholm was our destination. We changed planes at Copenhagen, where I remembered to buy some duty-free cigarettes and whiskey for Ingrid Bentzer and Madelene Pegel, two good friends from the days on the old amateur circuit, who would appreciate the gift because of the exhorbitant cost of living in Sweden. Lars Myhrman, one of the dedicated group of tennis enthusiasts who always make the players so welcome in Stockholm, was there to meet Arthur, Charlie, and myself at the airport, and after the long drive into the city, we checked into the opulent Grand Hotel, which lives up to its name in being one of the grandest in Europe. Thankfully, the tournament had arranged a discount for the players; we pay our own hotel and living expenses on tour—WCT pays for the air fares—and Stockholm really is incredibly expensive, certainly more costly than any other city I have visited, including Paris and New York.

The social activity in Stockholm is always hectic, and even if there is no actual party going on, there is always action to be found at Alexandre's, the number one discotheque in town. But it just wasn't my week for nocturnal activity and, unlike some of the boys, I had a very uneventful few days, which was exactly the way I wanted it.

I had a tough time beating Nails Carmichael on Monday evening. I lost the first set 6-1 on the fast tiled court of the Kunglehallen, a well-appointed indoor tennis stadium that looks much more modern than it really is. That goes for many buildings in Sweden, which says a lot for Scandinavian design. But the scenery wasn't my prime concern out there against Carmichael, and I had to concentrate hard to get back into the match. Finally overcoming Nails' rugged game, I closed it out 7-5 in the third.

The next few days were taken up with routine tennis activities. Tom, Arthur, and I had some pictures taken for VS—the gut we use in our rackets—and one afternoon I deputized for the absent Dennis Ralston, whose knee problems were keeping him home in Bakersfield, California, at a Coca Cola-sponsored clinic for eight Swedish juniors. I practiced with them for about an hour and found that they all hit the ball quite well, especially on the serve, which seems to be most Swedish players' strong point. Certainly it had seemed that way on the opening night of the tournament when the country's most promising young player, Leif Johannson, pulled off an amazing upset by beating the titleholder Stan Smith. Apparently, the slightly built teenager hit so many unreturnable serves that Stan never got into the match.

Roger Taylor struck a blow for WCT in our continuing battle against the Independents by ousting Ilie Nastase, also in the first round. The day before, Nastase had played superb tennis to win the Embassy Championships at Wembley over Rod Laver in a thrilling final. By then, there was no doubt that "Nasty" had established himself as one of the most exciting and talented players in the world, capable of breathtaking performances on his day. But consistency and concentration over the long haul were still his biggest problems.

On Thursday my problem was Arthur Ashe. It was one of those occasions when I felt really great as I walked on court—confident after my victory over him at Wimbledon that summer and quite sure that I would play well again. Arthur wiped me out 6-3, 6-1. After months of mediocre performances, Art had suddenly found his touch again. Apparently Brian Fairlie had been instrumental in bringing about this dramatic change. While they were practicing together soon after arriving in Stockholm, Brian asked why Arthur seemed so afraid to hit out at the ball and really go for his strokes. In his typical manner, Arthur thought to himself: "Hmm, good question. Why am I so afraid to hit out at the ball?" Failing to come up with a reasonable answer, he promptly decided to have a swing, and when it comes to hitting tennis balls few can give them a mightier whack than Arthur Ashe. To his surprise, he found that most of his shots were going in, and he simply went on swinging, right through me and right through the tournament.

There is nothing much you can do with Art when he gets hot like that except pray for rain. It was the rain splattering onto Ashe's glasses that enabled Jan Kodes to turn the match around in their semifinal at Forest Hills two months before, but as the roof of the Kunglehallen didn't leak I had no such luck. Nor did Kodes when he and Ashe met in the final. It was a mighty ball-pounding duel with the muscular Czech fighting his way back from two sets to one down to lead 4-1 in the fifth. As usual, he was blasting his backhand service return down the line at a hundred miles an hour, and at that stage Arthur seemed to be in dire trouble. But, having built up his form and confidence through the week—he had demolished Okker and Gimeno with as much ease as he had beaten me—he did precisely the right thing and went for broke. Blazing away at everything, he stopped Kodes dead in his tracks with some incredible high-velocity power hitting and roared through to his first WCT title of the year.

Nevertheless Kodes had had his moment of glory in the quarterfinals when Laver was leading by 6 points to 2 in the third-set tie break (with a few exceptions only the final on the WCT tour was played over the best of five sets). It takes something very special to stop the Rocket when he is that close to victory but Jan had something very special to offer. With a magnificent do or die assault, he unleashed more of those explosive service returns and crunching volleys to win the 6 straight points needed for victory. Laver was stunned.

Stockholm was turning white under its first snowfall of the year as Tom Leonard and I made a 5:30 A.M. getaway on Saturday —bound for Bologna, Italy, and the last leg of the twenty-tournament WCT tour. It turned out to be a very long day. After another change of planes at Copenhagen, we went into a holding pattern over Milan in the hope that the weather would improve. But after being bumped around the sky for a while, the pilot decided to cut his losses and divert to Genoa. It was a rough trip —even worse than the one from Cologne to Frankfurt three weeks before. But our troubles did not end on the ground. We still had to make it to Bologna, and after investigating the various possibilities with a Milwaukee businessman who happened to recognize me, we opted for a two-hour bus ride through the rain-swept mountains to Milan and from there a train down to Bologna. Although Tom and I bought ourselves first-class tickets, every compartment seemed to be packed. Climbing over children and suitcases, we went through the familiar Italian ritual of fighting tooth and nail for a place to sit and then watched the smiles light up as everyone got settled and realized that they were not really mad at each other after all. It was all a bit of a wasted effort on my part, for I noticed a middle-aged woman standing in the corridor and gave her my seat. She spoke a few words of English and kept on asking me if I was all right and did I want my seat back? Even though I ended up standing for an hour and a half, the trip was kind of fun and, as usual, I enjoyed being back amid the vital, volatile atmosphere of Italy.

Fourteen hours after our departure from the Grand Hotel in Stockholm, Tom Leonard and I eventually stepped onto the station platform at Bologna, having used just about every method of transportation available to get ourselves across Europe, short of boat and bicycle. We were just about to make the final stage on four wheels when the porter shook his head and pointed across the street. Our hotel was right there, 100 yards away. Tired as we were, we thought we could just about make it on foot.

Armed with a coat that looks like a relic from the Russian front, Bob Lutz is well equipped to face Stockholm's first snowfall of the winter in November, 1971. But Fred Stolle considers it no time for picture taking and heads for the warmth of the Kunglehallen. *Credit: Richard Evans*

Still pointing dramatically to the mark my ace made on the red clay of the Real Club in Barcelona, I start walking back to my side of the net during a semifinal clash with Manuel Orantes in October 1971. I didn't appreciate the call. The crowd didn't appreciate my reaction. *Credit: Richard Evans*

Rothmans, breaking into Europe for the first time as tennis sponsors, were in charge of the promotional side of the tournament in conjunction with the veteran pro promoter Carlo della Vida, and between them they had done as good a job as might be expected. There were posters and streamers all over this interesting old city, and with Nikki Pietrangeli, Adriano Panatta, and a few of the lesser Italian players who had given us so much trouble in Rome the previous May also included in the draw, interest was running high.

Some of the early-round matches were being played at the nearby town of Modena and I had to drive over there on Monday for my first-round match. Ironically I was drawn against Tom Leonard, my traveling companion and roommate for the week. I beat him without any difficulty in straight sets. The next day I handled Graham Stilwell 6-2, 6-1 at the Pallazzo della Sport in Bologna and was very pleased with the way I was hitting my ground strokes. The Uniturf court was not too dissimilar from the rubber tiles at the Kunglehallen and it was great to be playing on a court that offered the same type of speed and bounce two weeks running. The heavy Pirelli balls were a help, too. You could really hit them without fear of losing control and as a result everyone felt free to go for their shots.

With the play-off finals due to start in Houston the following week, all the top players seemed keen and in top form. The lack of any readjustment problems with the court meant that the tennis opened up at a high standard right at the start of the week and from then on simply got better and better. I don't think I have ever seen more great tennis packed into a week's play than I saw in Bologna. Two of my own matches were not only the most exciting I had played all year, but they also produced longer rallies and better points. This was because both players were at the peak of their form, moving well and hitting well. When you get players of our standard doing that, on a good surface with balls that we can hit hard yet still control, the results can be fantastic. This was what we had all been aiming for—this was pro tennis.

By the middle of the week the Bolognese crowd was beginning to realize that they were seeing something exceptional. They had been a little subdued early on because Terry Ryan had beaten Nikki Pietrangeli and, apart from Panatta, none of the other Italians had been able to live with us the way we were playing. Finally Panatta, a strong young player with a good serve who I feel sure will become very good in a few years, got them going by putting up a fine performance against Rosewall. Even though Adriano lost 6-3, 6-3, he made Kenny work for his points and the little Maestro responded by producing his whole repertoire of beautifully tuned strokes that were a joy to watch. Even in their disappointment, the crowd was full of admiration for such a virtuoso performance.

For the fifth time that year I played Roger Taylor and we had our best match by far. He seemed to be moving well again after his back problems and we were both all over the court, chasing down impossible "gets" and prolonging rallies by sheer speed and anticipation. Roger won the second set on a tie break, but a crucial double fault by him late in the third enabled me to finish it off 6-3, 6-7, 6-4 with a running forehand that clipped the net, jumped over his racket, and landed on the line. He gave me one of his "You lucky devil" looks, and for once I had to admit he had a point—although I had played well.

That evening Arthur Ashe, Nikki Pilic, and I had dinner back at the hotel. A soup called tortellini in brodo—a specialty in Bologna, according to the maître d'hôtel—was becoming a regular part of my diet, just as my favorite raw fish had been in Stockholm the week before. In between keeping an eye on Brian Fairlie who was busy at a nearby table chatting with a striptease artist who happened to be staying in the hotel, Art and I argued with Nikki about what one should demand of a wife.

"I expect her to give up ev-er-y-ting for me—but ev-er-y-ting," said Nikki, who had been married all of four months to a beautiful Yugoslavian actress.

"Come on, Nikki, why should a woman give up anything for you?" kidded Arthur, suspecting, as I was, that Pilic was only half joking. Woman's Lib hasn't hit Yugoslavia, either. But I must say that Mia, the new Mrs. Pilic, had looked quite liberated at her wedding reception, which was held at the Connaught

Rooms in London during Wimbledon. Trust Nikki to get married during Wimbledon. He's not a shy man. There was tons of publicity and the party was one of those that qualified as GREAT. You could tell that just by taking a quick look at Ken Rosewall as midnight struck. He had a beer in each hand and his tie tied around his head. If that was the state Ken was in, you can imagine what the rest of us were like.

There was no problem about eating late in Bologna. The city has the best reputation for food in the whole of Italy, and Carlo della Vida and Rino Tommasi of *Tennis Club* magazine knew many of the fourteen excellent restaurants that stayed open until four in the morning. I doubt if the restaurant at the railroad terminal just across the street from our hotel would qualify as "excellent" in culinery terms, but it was good enough for a bunch of hungry tennis players who had just come off court at midnight or later. By the end of the week it had been turned into a sort of gathering point for the latecomers and other insomniacs. Passengers waiting for the night express to Venice, Rapallo, or Florence were treated to the all-night ritual of waiters bringing yet another bowl of minestrone, yet another plate of spaghetti or ham and eggs, not to mention the bottles of beer and white wine that were always cluttering the long table. One night two old men sat riveted and stared, unblinking, at Torben Ulrich for at least half an hour. Only when he tossed his pigtails over his shoulders, flexed his muscles by raising Nails Carmichael off the ground with a backlift, and then swept out with a cheery wave, did the two old fellows look at each other and give a shrug of speechless bewilderment.

But none of these festivities had any effect on the tennis, which continued at its dizzy pitch of excellence. I was to play Rosewall in the quarters and, having lost to him five times out of five for the year, I decided on a new strategy. I would chip and come in on his serve and sacrifice power for accuracy on my own delivery. At 6-0, 1-0 to Kenny, those tactics went out the window and I decided to go down hitting. I nearly didn't go down at all. I began penetrating his defenses with some good returns and took the second set 6-3. A bad line call cost me my serve at 3-all in the third, but I broke back immediately and reached match point on his serve at 5-6. But my attempted backhand cross-court winner was out by a foot. The rallies were long and spectacular and the crowd was loving it. A good backhand winner down the line —a shot I had been going for on most of the big points—and a double fault by Rosewall helped me to snatch a 3-0 lead in the tie break; even though he recovered for 4-5, I still felt I was in a great position because I had to win only one of his two serves to have match point with my own to follow. But those little deliveries of his are so deceptive and so tough to handle, and he held on to both of them to lead 6-5—match point. I put in a good serve, checked fatefully on a first volley that I might have put away, hit a sound smash going backwards, and then got that sinking feeling as I stretched for a backhand volley and watched the ball plop off my racket and into the net. It had been great spectator tennis and we got a big hand as we walked off the court, but I was depressed at having lost after getting so close.

One of the revelations of the week was the form of Charlie Pasarell. Like Arthur the week before, he had suddenly rediscovered his confidence. Cliff Drysdale, who had been beating Charlie without much difficulty up to then, found himself wiped off court in straight sets. Charlie swept on into the semifinals— the first time he got that far in a WCT event—and there proceeded to engage Rod Laver in what many veteran watchers of International tennis described as one of the greatest matches they had ever seen. Although he had been playing well throughout, Pasarell trailed by two sets to one simply because Laver had been playing better. But Charlie stuck with it and soon had the crowd, which was partially enveloped in a haze of cigarette smoke, cheering him on as he leapt about court, pulling off a series of spectacular winners with backward tilting overheads, lunging volleys, and blockbuster passing shots that only a man who is bursting with confidence would dare go for against Laver. The fourth set went into the tie break and Charlie won it. With both players having had innumerable nerve-racking chances of making a decisive breakthrough, the fifth set also went into the tie break and by this time the packed, smoke-filled arena was steaming with tension. Three times Pasarell held match point in that tie break with his serve to follow. Three times Laver countered with the streak of genius that makes him a champion. Then Laver had three match points himself, but he too lost them all. Eleven-all. Tie break. Fifth set. Semifinal. A minimum of $2,500 on the line—$7,500 if the winner went on to take the whole tournament. It no longer mattered that there was not an Italian down there on court. The galleries were as excited as if Pietrangeli had been playing Laver in a Davis Cup Challenge Round. They screamed their way through the last two points as volleys, smashes, and drives were rifled around court and then erupted in a gigantic roar as poor Charlie lost control of a volley to give Laver a victory by 13 points to 11 on the Australian's fourth match point.

After that the final was something of an anticlimax, although it, too, was good match. Ashe, blasting Rosewall off court in the semis, reached the final for the second time in as many weeks, but with Laver on the other side of the net some of his confidence drained away, as it always does when he is faced by the only leading player in the world who he had never beaten. Arthur hung in there for a while with some good serving and the occasional sweeping backhand service return, but he never really threatened to break Rod's hold over him.

So despite his slump in midsummer when he went from May to August without a tournament victory, Rod Laver ended up firmly on top of the WCT points table with 87 points—thirteen more than his nearest rivals, Rosewall and Okker. He had won four WCT titles—a feat equaled by Rosewall and Newcombe. It was interesting to note that no one outside the eight players who had now qualified for the play-offs had won a tournament, and each of those eight—Laver, Rosewall, Okker, Drysdale, Ashe, Newcombe, Lutz, and myself—had earned himself at least one WCT crown.

By the time Rino Tommasi, the game's statistical genius, was poring over all these fascinating facts and figures back in Bologna, I had made it home to Chicago. But again it had not been easy. I don't know what I had done to annoy St. Christopher but it became obvious that I was one traveler he wasn't taking very good care of. My journey began when I got up at 6:00 A.M. and went to Bologna airport to catch a plane that didn't exist. Having been informed of this fact in the cold light of dawn, I tried to make it back to the railroad station in time, but the taxi stalled. When I did get there, everyone yelled *"Retardo, retardo"* at me when I inquired about the express to Milan. So I checked back into the hotel for a couple of hours' sleep and set out for Milan later in the morning with Tom Okker in his rented car. My new plan was to fly to London and catch a 3:30 P.M. flight out of there for Chicago. To my utter disbelief I was told that that flight didn't exist either, so I screamed goodbye to Tom, who was heading back to Amsterdam, leapt into a cab, and headed for the second airport, which is on the other side of the city. I got taken for $25 by the driver and was then told that there were only first-class seats left on the Alitalia flight I was trying to catch nonstop to Chicago. That meant $190 extra. Sally didn't believe it when I told her, but I was actually prepared to cough up the extra cash, so desperate was I by that time to get home. However, there is always a shaft of sunlight in the bleakest days and Alitalia eventually put me in first class without demanding any extra payment. I was just beginning to feel content with life when we were informed that we were making an unscheduled stop in Montreal. They wouldn't let us off the plane at Montreal Airport so we stewed on board in unbearable heat for 40 minutes, and it was a very weary tennis player who finally staggered into our new house on North Dayton Street that evening.

Apart from helping Sally to get the house in shape, there were a hundred and one personal details to attend to after seven weeks on the road, and for the next three days I never stopped. In retrospect I realize that I didn't spend enough time preparing myself mentally and physically for the play-off finals that were coming up in Houston at the end of that week, and I paid the price. At the time, I felt that a few days' break from the game after so long a tour would do me good, but it didn't work out that way. As soon as I started practicing in Houston, I realized I wasn't hitting the ball well and on Friday, to my utter disgust, I went out and played my worst match of the year against Tom Okker, losing

6-3, 6-3, 6-0. I was never happier to get off a court in my life. Ron Bookman, WCT's publicity officer who later became associate publisher of *World Tennis* magazine, came into the locker room afterwards to ask Tom and me to come upstairs for the press conference. But I declined. I just felt that there was nothing I could say at that moment which would reflect kindly on the playing conditions, WCT, or tennis in general. Obviously my attitude was clouded by the fact that I had played so badly—and that, of course, was my fault—but even so I didn't think much of the conditions at the Hofheinz Pavilion. The lighting was terrible —the film crew who made such an excellent movie of the finals will testify to that—there was a continual distraction of noise coming from the walkways up at the back and people kept moving in and out of one's line of vision as they emerged from the tunnel at the back of the court. Even if I had won I wouldn't have felt that the conditions matched the standards expected of so important an occasion, and of course having lost I was doubly critical. But Tom had played well and that was that.

In the other quarterfinal matches, Ashe beat Drysdale in a good battle, Laver whipped Lutz, and Rosewall was much too sharp for Newcombe, who had still not recovered properly from his knee injury. In the semifinals Okker couldn't handle the clinical accuracy of Rosewall's game, and Laver maintained his total dominance of Ashe. So the two little Aussies had made it through to the first World Championship of Tennis final that would earn $50,000—the biggest prize in the history of tennis— for the winner and $20,000 for the loser.

The match was to be played five days later in Dallas, WCT's operational base, so while I returned home, Rod and Ken were feted around the Big D at luncheons, dinners, and press conferences as part of the expertly handled promotional buildup. Everybody expected Laver to win, but Rosewall had other ideas and pulled off a brilliant 6-4, 1-6, 7-6, 7-6 victory in a match that was every bit as good as the occasion demanded.

Nobody deserved the title of World Champion of Tennis more than the 37-year-old wizard from Sydney. No one had worked harder to keep pro tennis alive during its darkest days; no one

Tennis shorts double as bathing trunks as Arthur Ashe takes a dip in Dakar. Credit: *Richard Evans*

Is this the way you play *boule*? Well, probably not, but here at Dr. Fourteau's house in Dakar, Arthur and I try to learn the French form of bowls, which is played on gravel in village squares all over France. *Credit: Richard Evans*

I don't really have James Bond fantasies but you would never know it from this shot, taken as I descend from the Lagon Restaurant in Dakar, Senegal, for a little underwater exploration. Charlie Pasarell looks on. *Credit: Richard Evans*

Dr. Raymond Fourteau, a friend of tournament promoter Marc Brissac, laid on a sumptuous lunch for us at his house outside Dakar soon after we arrived from New York for the start of our Marlboro Grand Prix tour of six African nations in December 1971. Here Arthur (foreground) and Sally enjoy a joke after a pre-lunch swim. *Credit: Richard Evans*

Tom Okker, who made a brief attempt to grow a goatee in Africa, was the terror of the merchants wherever we went. He entered into the spirit of bargaining with a vengeance and haggled over the last cent. Here Tom and his wife Annemarie look at some lovely wood carvings at a market in Yaounde, the capital of the Cameroons.
Credit: Richard Evans

This was the beach at Libreville in the Gabon where I got bitten by a dog and had to have rabies shots as a precaution. But before that happened we all enjoyed the bathing. Here Annemarie Okker, Sally and I wait to be submerged by another wave. *Credit: Richard Evans*

had given greater esthetic pleasure to the true lovers of the game over a greater number of years. Ken Rosewall is the player's player, and if never winning Wimbledon was the major disappointment of his life, then this triumph offered admirable compensation. I was delighted for him and I think my sentiments were shared by most of my colleagues on the tour.

It had been a long year for everyone—both stimulating and exhausting—but for four of us it was not over yet. If you want to know how we keep the pace—don't ask. I have no idea. All I do know is that the day after the WCT final—two weeks to the day since I had returned from Bologna—Arthur, Charlie and Shireen, his bride of 24 hours, Sally and I met at Kennedy Airport in New York and boarded an Air Afrique DC 8 for Africa! Just seven hours later, after an excellent flight, we arrived in Dakar, Senegal. Tom, who had flown back to Amsterdam from Houston to pick up Annemarie, had arrived shortly before us and so we were all set for a three-week swing through six countries on a working vacation that was officially billed as a Marlboro-sponsored African Grand Prix. Privately, we called it Charlie Pasarell's honeymoon. I don't know how Charlie managed it, but he certainly played better tennis than I had succeeded in doing on mine. Although I beat him in the first tournament in Dakar, he ended up winning the Grand Prix, which was a good wedding present, as there was a total of $25,000 prize money at stake.

Marc Brissac, who had been organizing tours to French-speaking African countries for many years—including one I had been on in 1969—was in charge of operations, and although too many official U.S. Embassy functions kept creeping into the itinerary, which was not Marc's fault, we all had a great time. Arthur, of course, was the big star and it was because of him that an additional stop in Lagos, Nigeria, was added to the tour. Arthur had been there on a State Department tour with Stan Smith the year before and was asked to return by popular demand. After Lagos we flew back along the coast, making leisurely stops in our Air Afrique Caravelle at places like Cotonou, Lomé, and Accra before arriving at Abidjan, capital of the thriving Ivory Coast. There we resided in splendor for a few days at the magnificent Hotel Ivoire, which calls its swimming pool Le Lac because it is just that—a lake. The hotel also boasts a casino and an indoor ice rink—the only one in Africa—and it was on the cement floor of the rink that we played our matches. The local skating enthusiasts weren't very happy about having their ice removed for a few days, but we got good crowds and the make-shift surface turned out to be about the best we encountered on the whole trip.

It was in Abidjan, on December 4, that I celebrated my thir-tieth birthday with a most enjoyable dinner at the hotel and I started to think of myself, without much success, as an old pro. I didn't really feel that old.

Libreville in the Gabon was the next stop and the least enjoy-able one for me. Apart from the hotel, which Sally and I moved out of because our room was so filthy, I got bitten by a dog while playing with a soccer ball on the beach. After frantic at-tempts to find the owner and much heart-searching during the next stop at Yaoundé in the Cameroon, I decided to play it safe and start taking the required series of rabies shots. As they have to be injected into your stomach they are extremely unpleasant. But the end result of catching rabies is a very certain and a very rapid death so I considered it the more practical alternative. As it turned out, the dog was healthy but the cable containing that happy piece of news did not reach us until we were out on safari at the foot of Mount Kenya eight days later. By that time a suc-cession of doctors had penetrated my stomach with a series of alarming looking needles, one of which was gaily produced out of a rusty sardine tin.

But although I could have done without the dog, the sheer scope and diversity of Africa made the whole trip unforgettable. From a tennis point of view there is much that can be done to foster the already rapidly growing interest in the game that exists in many countries, especially in the area of breaking down the old colonial atmosphere that lingers on at many tennis clubs. Although the clinics we gave attracted hundreds of apparently eager African kids, spectators at the matches themselves were predominantly white. The high price of tickets in places like Abidjan and Libreville obviously had a lot to do with this, but it is also true that tennis clubs are considered the last bastions of a colonial age and are not the sort of place the average African would want to visit. All this is slowly changing, of course, but it will take time, and on future tours of this kind I would like to see greater efforts made to include Africans in every facet of the visiting players' program. Arthur, I know, will work toward this goal.

By Christmas we were home again and home for good. Or at least for what remained of 1971. Three weeks into January the WCT tour was due to start up again. By then World Championship Tennis was officially banned by the autocratic rulers of the old amateur game, which was now desperately trying to be as professional as we were. It was tragic for tennis as a whole, but not for us individually. We were part of a strong group that had a strong schedule laid out for 1972. It was a new challenge.

17

A NEW YEAR—THE TOUR ENDS
IN A CLASSIC DUEL

The Christmas vacation lasted all of two weeks. Almost before I had digested Sally's turkey I was back on the practice court, preparing for the first WCT tournament of 1972 at Richmond, Virginia. As I have explained earlier, the WCT year had been switched for television purposes so it ended in May, and to make the transition from a November final as easy as possible, the last ten tournaments of 1971 were being counted as the first half of the 1971–72 schedule. So Richmond was, in fact, the eleventh leg of the new tour and another $100,000 play-off final was looming only four months away.

Once again I was solidly in seventh place in the points standings—well clear of the eighth man. I knew that I only had to play with reasonable consistency to maintain my position. But of course I was aiming to do more than maintain it. I wanted to improve on it—to climb higher up that tough ladder. It was an ambition I eventually fulfilled, but not before many frustrating weeks had passed. The brief two-week break should, I felt, have worked in my favor. I was still in the groove and I arrived in Richmond in good shape. I played that way, too, in my first-round match against Frank Froehling, an old foe but a newcomer to the ranks of World Championship Tennis. Along with the athletic Australian Terry Addison, Frank had been signed by WCT to replace Dennis Ralston, whose knee problems had forced him to quit the competitive game for a year, and Andres Gimeno, who had decided to consolidate his future in Barcelona by re-

197

joining his national Association after more than a decade as a contract pro. Andres wanted to teach in Spain and obviously his chances of being appointed coach to the Spanish Davis Cup team would be greatly enhanced if he became part of the national setup. As it turned out, Andres, who had never managed to reach the final of a WCT tournament, got a new lease on life as a player amid the independent ranks and won the French Championships —the first major title of his career—in May 1972. Later in the year he also beat Stan Smith in the Davis Cup in Barcelona, although the United States won the tie 3-2.

Gimeno's decision to leave WCT when his contract ran out at the end of the year was influenced, in part, by the fact that the ILTF ban on Lamar Hunt's players went into effect on January 1, 1972. From that moment on we were a bunch of outlaws as far as the tennis establishment was concerned and, at the time, no one had any idea how long the war would last. In fact a settlement was not long in coming, but even so it was an absurd position for the game to be in at such a crucial stage of its development.

So when we regrouped in Richmond we had this feeling of being very much on our own—a small band of top professionals determined to prove that we could survive, ban or no ban, simply by playing a higher standard of crowd-pleasing tennis than anyone else. The crowds we attracted in the ensuing weeks and the eventual success of the NBC live television coverage of the finals on Sunday afternoons helped us achieve that goal. But it wasn't that simple at the start, for despite the arrival of Froehling and Addison we were somewhat depleted in number at Richmond as Dick Crealy, Torben Ulrich, and Frew McMillan had also left the group, and the World Champion himself, Ken Rosewall, was missing because of family illness back home in Australia. The sponsor, Fidelity Bank, wasn't too happy about Rosewall's absence but we tried to make up for what we lacked in quantity with quality. I think we succeeded, too, for, like myself, most of the boys had returned to the circuit in good physical condition after the short layoff, and the standard of tennis reached heights not far short of those we had touched in Bologna.

I played well to beat Froehling in straight sets, thus avenging to a small degree the defeat he had inflicted on me in the fourth round of the French Championships the previous May. I had played some of the best tennis of my career during the first two sets of that match in Paris, but Frank has always been less worried by the mysteries of European clay than most Americans and he hung in there to beat me in five. Frank handled Arthur Ashe in the next round and so reached the semifinal of the French in his first year back on the International circuit after an absence of more than five years. It was a fine performance and one that ultimately led to his selection for the Davis Cup Challenge Round against Rumania at Charlotte, North Carolina, in October 1971 and then his WCT contract. In retrospect that whole run of success had probably started with his fight back from two sets to love down against me in Paris, and while I was pleased for Frank that he had been able to re-establish himself so quickly, I was equally pleased to show him that life on the WCT circuit was not going to be quite that simple.

I got a taste of just how tough it could be myself in the very next round at Richmond when I ran into Charlie Pasarell, who was still playing as if life were one long honeymoon. Although he had deposited his bride Shireen in their new apartment in Los Angeles after our African safari, Charlie had brought his African form with him. Even though I won the first set and had chances to break in the second and third, I could never really get hold of Pasarell's booming service and he brought my anticipated good start in the year to an abrupt end. Tom and I won the doubles, which was encouraging, but my arm began to develop some soreness in the elbow and that, coupled with the loss to Charlie, seemed to set me back. I found myself in a rut and for the next two months I couldn't break out of it. The quarterfinal round of each tournament presented a psychological barrier that I found increasingly difficult to crack.

Meanwhile the tour developed into the "Rod and Kenny Show." Laver won Richmond over Cliff Drysdale—who had also started the year in super form—and then in Philadelphia the following week Laver and Rosewall staged the first of their 1972 finals.

Unlike a couple that were to follow, this match was a fine contest, with Rod, the eventual winner, showing off his masterly stroke-play after Ken had won the first set. There were 11,800 tickets sold for Sunday's play, and throughout the week a total of 58,000 spectators poured into the spacious Spectrum. The turn-out was a big boost to our morale. WCT was proving it could still fill the large indoor stadiums. But if we provided the talent to attract the customers, there was no doubt who had provided the platform to display that talent in Philadelphia. That tire-lessly enthusiastic husband-and-wife team of Ed and Marilyn Fernberger had built big-time tennis from the bottom up in the city, and the success of the 1972 U.S. Indoor Championships was largely due to their dogged persistence over the years. Marilyn had coaxed, cajoled, browbeaten, and finally shamed a regiment of volunteer workers into service by talking faster, working harder, and sleeping less than anyone not running for President. (I don't think Marilyn is running for President, but with her one can never be sure.) At any rate she seemed to have half the housewives of Philadelphia mobilized in one way or another, and over the years the tournament not only grew in size but increased in efficiency. By 1972 it was one of the most smoothly run tournaments I have every played in and from the competitors' point of view everything was made much easier by the presence of former Wimbledon Champion Vic Seixas as referee.

Obviously Vic has an intimate understanding of a player's problems, and furthermore we knew that we couldn't pull any fast ones on him. As a result, the usual complaints about untidy scheduling of matches were cut to a minimum and for once an aura of mutual respect existed between the players and the referee. I wish this were more often the case, but really qualified referees are difficult to find.

From a personal standpoint Philadelphia was frustrating and once again the name of my frustration was "Rosewall." I had overcome the problems of a sore arm to beat Ray Ruffels in the first round and survived match point against John Alexander before beating him 7-6 in the third to reach the quarters. That was where Rosewall was waiting for me. I was playing well—well enough, I thought, to beat just about anybody else in the tournament, but Ken still had my number, and although we staged a fine match, full of long rallies and exciting points, he beat me in the end.

The Eastern seaboard was caught in the grip of winter and most of us had a tough time getting up to Toronto for the following week's tournament. A strike at Toronto Airport didn't help matters and eventually I took the opportunity of spending a night at home in Chicago before finding a flight that could beat both the strike and the weather and make it into Canada. The warmth and luxury of the Sutton Place Hotel, which is owned by a big tennis enthusiast, David Dennis, provided a welcome sanctuary from the biting Canadian winter, but it was a few hours before I could start enjoying it when I finally got into town. Not for the first time on our tightly scheduled tour, I had to make a mad dash straight to the stadium from the airport and go right on court. Ruffels was my first-round opponent again and after beating him I had what amounted to a virtual walk-over against Tony Roche. The Australian left-hander had rejoined the tour after an operation on a damaged nerve in his elbow and although he had suffered through weeks of rehabilitation exercises back home in Sydney, the injury was still giving him a lot of trouble. All the sting and power had gone from his game and he was serving at less than half pace. It seemed as if it was going to be some time before we saw the real Roche in action again. Although my own arm problem was nothing compared to Tony's I had been following his lead and packing it in ice after every match in Philadelphia. The treatment seemed to work because I was completely free of pain by the time I started playing in Toronto; so I wasn't even able to offer it as an excuse for my poor showing in the quarterfinal.

Once again it was Rosewall. Once again he beat me. It was getting to be a habit—and a sickening one at that. I seemed incapable of figuring out a way to beat the guy. It had, of course, built up into a problem of confidence by this time. You don't get defeated by someone nine straight times without getting a little psyched out about it. And when a player of Rosewall's caliber walks on court absolutely certain he can win, it takes something very special to burst the bubble of super-confidence that surrounds every move he makes. I produced nothing sharp enough nor special enough to do it in Toronto, and, as Tom and I lost early in the doubles, I was back home in Chicago sooner than anticipated for a week's rest before the start of the next tournament at the David Park Courts in Hollywood, Florida.

I didn't fare any better there, either. After winning twelve straight games to beat Brian Fairlie 6-1, 6-0 in the first round, I lost to Mark Cox. It was the first tournament of the year outdoors and on clay, and although I had done well on that surface the previous year, I felt listless in the heat and I was starting to worry about my singles game. I wasn't playing particularly badly, but in this select company I wasn't playing well enough to win, either, and winning is the only thing that counts. My form cost me the chance of selection for the U.S. team that played Australia in the World Cup event in Hartford, Connecticut the following week and although some of the Aussies were surprised that I wasn't chosen, I couldn't complain. Charlie Pasarell and Bob Lutz had been playing well and they got the second and third singles spots behind Arthur Ashe. As it was, we were trounced after a series of very close matches but that gave me no satisfaction either.

In fact the only satisfaction I was getting at the time came from the doubles. Tom and I had hit a good streak in Florida and, as luck would have it, we got ourselves on nationwide television as a result. That was the second tournament NBC was televising on a weekly basis for the remainder of the 1971–72 tour and fate was not being particularly kind to them. In Toronto the first televised final turned out to be a dismal affair as Laver crushed Rosewall in one of their most one-sided encounters. Then, with everything teed-up to go live for the Rosewall-Drysdale final at 3:30 P.M. from the David Park Courts in Hollywood, dark thunderclouds appeared on the horizon and at 3:29 P.M. *precisely,* it started to rain. In one of his more memorable remarks, WCT's popular road manager Bill Holmes—nicknamed "Sher-

John Newcombe, depressed at missing another easy shot against Roger Taylor waits to be handed his racket like some immobolized relay-runner, during the Rothmans International at the Toronto Coliseum in February 1972. Newk was in the middle of a bad spell at the time but like all champions he pulled out of it eventually. *Credit: Richard Evans*

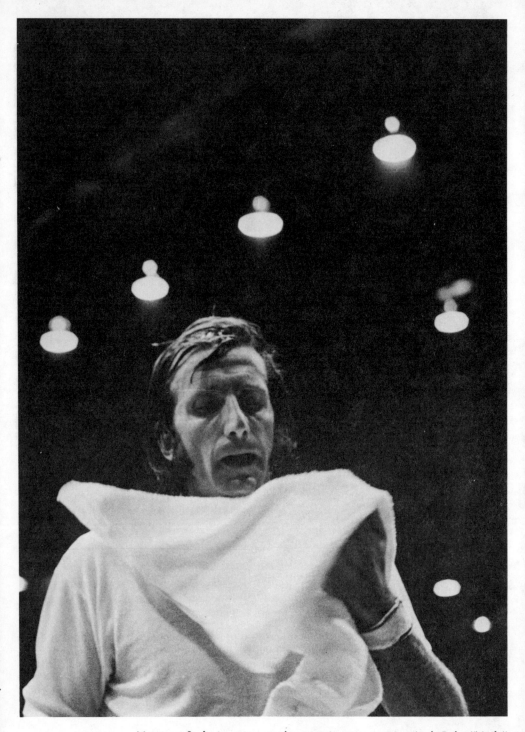

No one finds it easy at the top in pro tennis. And Bob "Nails" Carmichael, a self-made player, finds it harder than most. Bob's face tells a story of sweat and struggle at the Toronto Coliseum as he towels himself down between games while playing Ken Rosewall in February 1972. As always, Bob played well against Ken. But he lost. *Credit: Richard Evans*

lock" by the players—was heard to mutter, "God just has to be an Independent pro."

Certainly neither WCT nor NBC was getting the best breaks in their pioneering attempts to bring tennis into the homes of America's sporting public but at least somebody up there had a soft spot for Tom and myself, for on this occasion we were the beneficiaries. Our doubles final, in which we had outplayed Rod Laver and Roy Emerson in surprisingly decisive fashion, had been taped as a precautionary measure and now, while the frustrated fans sat under dripping umbrellas in the steamy Hollywood heat, the nation got to see Okker and Riessen play doubles. If nothing else, it was good for the ego.

Our doubles form carried on into Chicago the week after the World Cup when the fifteenth leg of the WCT tour landed in my backyard, so to speak. After the early rounds had been divided up between the Le Grange high school and De Paul's Alumni Hall so as to bring pro tennis to as many parts of the metropolitan area as possible, the tournament moved up to my old hunting ground at McGaw Hall on the Northwestern campus at Evanston. Tom Okker, of all people, put an end to my hopes of excelling in front of my own crowd by beating me in a good three-set match in the quarters, but as soon as he joined me on the same side of the net for the doubles it was a different story. We were hot at the start of the week and by the time we reached the final, where "Rocket" Laver and Emmo were waiting for us once again, we were pretty much ablaze. This feeling of total, intuitive harmony with one's partner is, to my mind, the most exhilarating sensation in the whole game of tennis and that Sunday afternoon at McGaw Hall I felt as if Tom and I were unbeatable. Without wishing to be immodest about it, we probably were. Everything we tried came off and Laver and Emerson, who had the most consistent winning record of any team on the tour, couldn't touch us as we streaked about court in euphoric unison, feeling as if we were treading on air.

A couple of days later I came down to earth with a bump on the slow green clay of the Sea Pines Plantation Courts at Hilton Head Island, South Carolina. CBS was filming its Television

When you are playing well in doubles, partners move as if connected by an invisible string. Tom Okker and I had one of our best spells during the Kemper International in March 1972, and here, in the final at McGaw Hall, Northwestern University, Evanston, we won the tournament by beating Roy Emerson and Rod Laver. *Credit: Richard Evans*

Classic which was to be shown in thirteen weekly segments throughout the summer months and which promised more great exposure for tennis. On a surface that was ideal for long, crowd-pleasing rallies, there were some tremendously exciting matches played during the tournament, which was won ultimately by the indefatigable Rosewall. I only got to participate in one of them, however, as I lost in the first round to Emerson after leading by a set and a break in the second.

I was really depressed by the state of my singles game by this stage, and when I returned home for a week's break before picking up the WCT tour again in Houston, I resolved to do something about it. What does a player do to break out of a losing streak? He just works. There is no magic formula, no secret substitute. He simply gets out on court for as many hours as body and mind can stand and hits tennis balls—thousands of them. He hits them hard and soft—working through the full range of his storkes with meticulous care, smoothing out any kinks or rough edges that may have crept itno his backswing or his service action or his footwork. In other words, he takes himself back to school. It is a long, tedious grind and provides just one example of how a professional tennis player's life is not all fun and games and girls and parties. People who come into contact with us on the circuit tend to see three main facets of our life—playing matches for huge sums of money in front of large crowds, lying around at a party in somebody's luxurious home, or rushing through an aiport to catch a plane to some distant and exotic place. All that makes up for a large part of our strange existence and I'm not complaining. I think it's a great life. But there is this other side of it, too, which few people get to see unless they happen to belong to one of the many families who are good enough to put us up at tournaments all over the world. Then they might catch a glimpse of a bleary-eyed tennis player dragging himself out of bed early in the morning to go off for a couple of hours' practice and maybe a little roadwork before playing his match that afternoon.

It is the mental discipline required that makes it especially tough. Unless you are on Davis Cup duty, there is no coach there to force you to practice. Unlike a member of a football or basketball team, you won't get fined or even cursed out if you say "to hell with it" and stay in bed. It is all a question of self-motivation. If you want to get to the top and, even more important, if you want to stay there, you have to drive yourself. It doesn't really have much to do with how naturally gifted you are, either although obviously some players do need more time on the practice court than others. No one better illustrates my point than Rod Laver. No player in the world has more natural, God-given talent than "Rocket," and yet if you get to a tournament long before play is due to start or wander round the back-courts late in the evening, the man you will see out there most often, working harder and more conscientously than almost anyone else, is the first millionnaire of tennis himself—Rodney George Laver.

So I knew what I had to do and I wasn't particularly upset when my hard work routine failed to pay immediate dividends. It takes time—as I discovered at the River Oaks Country Club in Houston. After beating Ruffels again in the first round there, I lost to Bill Bowrey, who was way below me in the WCT points table. It was a bad defeat for me but, as I have mentioned before, Tex has always given me trouble and, with my game in a state of half-completed rehabilitation, I suppose I was a ripe target for him. At any rate, I persevered with the extra practice sessions for an hour each morning and afternoon, irrespective of whether I had to play singles and doubles on any given day, and soon I started to feel the benefits.

It was in Houston that I received a little extra incentive from a source I usually pay heed to—my wife. Sally gave me a friendly ultimatum when I phoned her after my loss to Bowrey.

"I'm not going to join you on weekends any more unless you're still in the singles," she told me. "I don't enjoy watching doubles much anyway so it's up to you."

Sally had a job which was keeping her in Chicago during the week, but she had been in the habit of flying to wherever that week's tournament was being held every Friday night. Now she was telling me that I would not get to see her unless I was still in the singles. As the tournament format was structured, that meant I would have to reach the semifinals every week. It was a tough assignment, but that incentive, coupled with my extra practice sessions, seemed to do the trick. One week later I was on the phone from Quebec City telling her: "Come on up. I'm in the semis. I've just beaten Kenny."

I had, indeed, just beaten Rosewall and of course this long-awaited victory gave me a tremendous psychological lift. I beat him 4-6, 6-3, 7-5 in a fine match in which my strong serving proved to be the decisive factor on the Sportface carpet. I was doubly elated by the victory because I had not only beaten my old nemesis but I had cleared that troublesome quarterfinal barrier for the first time that year. Keeping her side of the bargain, Sally was among the crowd at the magnificent new Laval University Sports Complex by the time I walked on court to face Arthur Ashe in the semis, and although I lost the first set in that match, too—decisively enough by 6-1—I was not deterred. For the first time in weeks I was superbly fit and bursting with confidence and although I had always had trouble beating Arthur in the past, I suddenly felt certain I could turn the match around. And sure enough, as soon as my first serve started finding its mark, I did—taking the last two sets with comparative ease 6-4, 6-3.

Quebec City was one of four tournaments sponsored in Canada by Rothmans, and to fit the occasion Sally had brought my Albert Hall Champions Blazer with her from Chicago. It was a jacket designed by that famous tennis couturier Teddy Tinling and awarded to players who had won the Rothmans event at London's Royal Albert Hall. At that time there had been only three winners—Rod Laver, Cliff Richey, and myself—and although I had been the first to receive the honor in 1970 I had somehow never found an opportunity to wear the blazer. Sally, who is more fashion-conscious than I am, decided that the Rothmans' wine and cheese party on the Saturday night was the ideal occasion and so I turned up in the jacket, feeling a bit like a peacock in my green and blue striped plumage, and, inevitably taking a good deal of ribbing from the witty Rothmans executive George Phillips and the boys. I didn't give them much chance to get into their stride, however, as Sally and I and a friend of ours were determined to sample one of the many good French restaurants to be found in Quebec City. Following directions to one called Le Traite du Roy situated in the fascinating old section of the city, we enjoyed an excellent meal and even indulged in a crêpe flambé as a final luxury. I was in great spirits and felt quite capable of handling a crêpe flambé, as well as my opponent the following day—even if my opponent's name was Rod Laver.

Obviously I have great respect for Rocket's talent but, unlike some players, I always relish the challenge of meeting him on court. This was partly because, win or lose, we always seemed to stage fast, entertaining matches and partly because I didn't always lose. Far from it. I had beaten him three times the previous year and there was evidently something about my game that he didn't like. I was determined to make sure he didn't begin to get a taste for it in the final.

As it turned out, Rod didn't have much of a taste for anything the following day. He was badly out of form and although he took a set off me, I never felt as if I would lose my grip on the match. Maintaining the pressure with my serve and volley game, I found myself winning my second WCT title—the previous one had been in Tehran almost exactly a year before—and the $10,000 that went with it, far more decisively than I had imagined possible.

But I was overjoyed once the realization sunk in and I felt it was ample reward for all those hours on the practice court. For the first few days in Quebec I had risen every morning at 7:00 A.M., so that Brian Fairlie, my willing practice partner, and I could be on court at 7:30—a good hour and a half before any other players arrived to stake their claim on the only two practice courts available. Brian and I would then stay on for a bit, sharing half a court with two other guys, as is the custom on our tour when courts are in short supply. One does not practice doubles under these conditions but simply uses half the court. This method is fine for improving one's accuracy but it doesn't really give the chance of getting a proper physical workout.

At any rate, the results of these early morning sessions were now plain enough. After beating Mark Cox, who was in good form at the time, having just won a sixteen-man WCT event in Macon, Georgia, I had swept past Rosewall, Ashe, and Laver— three of the best players in the world—in three straight days. I felt this was another milestone in my career and I was determined there would be no turning back.

Despite a bad loss to Rosewall in the quarterfinals at Charlotte, North Carolina, the next week, I did, in fact, maintain my improved form for the remainder of the 1971–72 tour. I was so confident after my success in Quebec that I had little difficulty shrugging off the Charlotte defeat, especially as conditions there were so bad that I was never able to play my natural game. It rained throughout the match and the weather was generally so miserable that I kept my track suit on the whole time. I am not in any way trying to belittle Kenny's win. He beat me 6-2, 6-0 and obviously mastered the conditions much better. It is simply that a player has to make private rationalizations—or excuses, if you like—to himself from time to time in an effort to maintain his confidence. For the moment you allow yourself to become depressed by an isolated defeat, all the weeks of hard physical conditioning can suddenly count for nothing—another example of how "it's all in the mind."

From Charlotte we flew to Denver, the beautiful mile-high city, where tournament director Ray Benton and his associates from the sponsor, United Bank, had done an excellent organizational job at the Denver University Arena. Large and enthusiastic crowds were entertained by some thrilling tennis during the week, and I was lucky enough to participate in one of the most nerve-tingling matches. When John Newcombe led me by a set and six points to two in the second-set tie break, I was in the rare and unenviable position of having to save four match points to stay alive. Before the advent of the twelve-point tie break—the first player to win seven points with a two-point margin takes the set —it was impossible for a player to be down more than three match points in any single sequence, i.e., 40-love or love-40, depending on who was serving. But in this new age of tie-break tennis one could be as many as six match points down if the other guy ran away to a 6-0 lead in the tie break.

On this occasion it was four and that was quite enough as far as I was concerned. After I had taken one point off Newk's serve to make it 3-6, I remember telling myself that I only had to hold my own two serves for 5-6 to be back in it with a chance. This I managed to do, whacking down a morale-boosting ace on the second one. There is no point in playing defensively in a situation like this, so I went for an aggressive service return on the next point and won it. Four straight match points saved! I couldn't remember having done that before and, as so often happens when a player lets slip a great chance of victory, the momentum switched dramatically. I went on to win two more points to take the second set by eight points to six in that tie break and hammered home my advantage by winning the third set 6-3.

That put me in the semifinals and, as a result of another jubilant phone call home, it put Sally on another late night flight out of O'Hare Airport. She was there to see me beat Roy Emerson in straight sets the following day and so, for the second time in three weeks, I was facing Rod Laver in the final. Rod was generous enough to tell reporters afterwards that he had no idea how he was going to beat me when the match reached 4-all in the third set. Well, like an idiot, I showed him how.

For some strange reason, I suddenly become unsure whether to serve to his backhand or forehand in the ninth game. Indecision at that stage was fatal. I lost my rhythm and promptly served three double faults. Inevitably I lost my serve as a result and that was all the help Rocket needed. He ran out a 4-6, 6-3, 6-4 winner. I was mad at myself for blowing another chance of beating Laver but it had been a good match—one of the most exciting and spectacular finals NBC had televised up to that time, according to people who watched on the box. That, I suppose, was some small consolation.

Las Vegas was the scene of the twentieth and final leg of the tour—and it was some scene. Alan King had warned us it was going to be quite a week when Sally and I caught his show one night in Chicago. For once Alan wasn't kidding. He had enlisted the full cooperation of Caesar's Palace for the week's festivities, and although a lot of the money no doubt found its way back into the hotel coffers through the insatiable optimism of Alan's New York gambling friends in the casino, the original outlay for the week was reportedly $650,000. It wasn't difficult to see where the money went. The players, tennis writers, and a large number of Alan's personal friends were given free rooms. This same group plus additional guests were invited to a midnight Tom Jones show also for free; there was a poolside party with dancing to two bands one night, and on another evening in the Bacchanal Room Alan gave a sumptuous four-course dinner for about thirty people which began with two huge lobsters per person. Peter Duchin and his orchestra had been flown in from New York and they were the star attraction at the Saturday night ball, by which time the place was crawling with famous faces, as King was also running a pro-celebrity tournament over the weekend just in case anyone had any breath left.

But perhaps the most amazing aspect of the whole week was the amount of work that got done both on the court—where some excellent tennis was played in the Alan King Classic—and off it, where some high-powered behind-the-scenes activity was in progress regarding the formation of a new Tennis Players Association.

Cliff Drysdale, Arthur Ashe, Mark Cox, Ray Ruffels, and Ismail El Shafei had been elected to the committee, and there was a new mood of determination among many of the players to see that this time the Association achieved something worthwhile. Arthur, Charlie Pasarell, John Newcombe, and I had been involved in a previous attempt to organize the players some four years before, but there had been too few incentives at that time to pull all the various factions of the tennis-playing world together.

Now it was different. The peace agreement that had been formulated between ILTF President Allan Heyman and Lamar Hunt a few weeks earlier had created a whole new situation and the incentives for presenting a united front were both obvious and urgent. Briefly, the agreement called for Hunt to allow his players' contracts to run their natural course and then expire without renewal. He would also cease signing any new players to contracts. In return, the ILTF would sanction 26 WCT tournaments during the first four months of each year. Hunt would be allowed a virtual exclusivity in that period of the year, as the ILTF promised to schedule no tournaments with more than $20,000 in prize money against the $50,000 WCT events. For the remainder of the year everyone would be free to play the traditional International circuit which would be run by the ILTF. In this way the distinction between a contract pro and an Independent pro would eventually disappear as our WCT contracts expired and everybody, at long last, would become simply players.

This peace format, which was accepted almost word for word from a plan presented by Jack Kramer and Donald Dell and enthusiastically supported by the U.S. LTA Vice-President Walter Elcock, was as good a compromise as one could reasonably hope for considering the upheaval in the game at the time. But from the WCT players' point of view, there was one obvious drawback. As our contracts with Hunt ran out, we would automatically find ourselves back under the jurisdiction of our national Associations and, through them, the ILTF: That was not an arrangement that had worked every well in the past and now, with the game blossoming into a multimillion-dollar sport, there was no way that professional players could tolerate having their lives run by amateur officials. The formation of a strong Players Association seemed to be the only answer. By laying down our own bylaws and enforcing a strict code of behavior and discipline, we could be answerable only to ourselves.

It would take a great deal of hard work and compromise on our part, but most players quickly saw the advantages of working toward that goal. The Independents—headed, ironically, by that old contract pro Andres Gimeno—were working on a similar idea at about the same time, and we wanted to get together with them eventually so that the top 60 or 70 players in the world would then all come under one Association. Several meetings had already been held among the WCT pros and, with the committee elected, several important steps were taken in Las Vegas.

Donald Dell, one of the few people who had an intimate knowledge of the peace formula details at that stage, flew into town for a late-night meeting with the players. He explained to us precisely the terms of the agreement between Hunt and Heyman; now the obvious question of who we should go after for the job of our Executive Secretary came up. The names mentioned were Jack Kramer; former British Davis Cup captain John Barrett, a sound and progressive student of the professional game's development; Mark McCormack, better known for his involvement with golf but also an agent for Rod Laver, Roger Taylor, and a few other tennis players; Bob Briner, and of course Dell himself.

Some of the Aussies were wary of Donald's commitments to his own players and felt that he would be more interested in furthering the careers of Ashe, Smith, Lutz, Riessen, etc. than tending to the needs of the Association as a whole. The players who knew Donald had no such fear but, surprisingly, the most eloquent endorsement speeches came from Cliff Richey—who had signed with WCT the week before Charlotte as Hunt's last big-name pro—and Ray Ruffels, two players who had never been connected with Dell's organization. However it was decided that it would be better to seek some less controversial figure and Donald agreed to act as our legal counsel along with his law partner Frank Craighill. Then by general consent the committee turned to Bob Briner, the original Executive Director of WCT who was well liked by the original members of the group. Briner had become General Secretary of the Dallas Chaparells basketball team in the meantime, but he answered our call and the following night he, too, was meeting with us at Caesar's Palace. With our organization still in its infancy, Bob could not risk giving up a well-paid job then and there, but he did agree to help us out with administrative work on a part-time basis for the remainder of the year.

So something worthwhile was achieved in between the festiv-

ities, and there was even time for tennis. Pancho Gonzales, the
tennis director at Caesar's Palace, and his son Richard, ran the
tournament with the kind of skillful scheduling and eye for detail that come only from a wealth of experience. With the courts
just a few steps away, most of us managed to grab the opportunity
to collapse by the pool at some stage of the day and bask in the
95-degree desert heat.

I reached the semifinals with a remarkably straightforward
6-2, 6-4 victory over Laver and then got dumped by Drysdale.
Cliff and I hadn't met on court for about eight months and I
had forgotten how best to play him. I served to his backhand
too much and never really pierced his armor. Newcombe came
steaming through the other half of the draw to beat Drysdale in
the final and so win his first tournament since taking the
Canadian Open title in Toronto the previous August. It had
been a long, frustrating spell for Newk but, like myself, he had
pulled himself out of it with some grueling work on the practice
court.

Arthur Ashe took the opportunity to get a little class-work in
Las Vegas. Several players have favorite coaches they rush back
to whenever their game falls out of shape and in Art's case, he
always turns to Gonzales. With Arthur, it is usually his service
that needs attention when he runs into a bad patch and there is
no one better qualified to get the rhythm of that fine delivery
flowing again than Pancho, who is the owner of one of the
simplest and most beautiful service actions in the game.

By the weekend Alan King had his pro-celebrity tournament
in full swing. Although Charlton Heston, one of the game's
most fervent and active supporters, cabled his regrets from Rome,
most of the tennis aficionados from the entertainment world hit
town and the court area at the back of the hotel was an autograph hunter's paradise. George Peppard, Rod Steiger, Bill
Cosby, Steve Lawrence, Jim Franciscus, Ed Ames, George Mont-
gomery, Lloyd Bridges, George Plimpton, and designer Oleg
Cassini were among a host of celebrities. Many of them were
more than just pretty faces when it came to wielding a tennis
racket. Ed Ames, for one, is a fine player and he and Bill

were being played in Dallas. The site had been switched, too,
from the Memorial Auditorium to the Moody Coliseum, home
of the SMU basketball team—an arena that proved to be even
better for tennis, with its high-banked seating that gave spectators a closer and better view of the court.

Once again, the WCT staff under Lamar Hunt's personal
supervision had done a great job of organizing and promoting
the event and decorating the area. Even though some of the
leading British critics such as David Gray, Rex Bellamy, and
Lance Tingay had to stay at home to cover their own Hardcourt
Championships at Bournemouth, the international tennis press
was present in force as before. Rino Tommasi of *Tennis Club*
magazine in Rome, the chic and vivacious Judy Elian of
L'Equipe, Arthur Cole of *Tennis World* in London, and a still
sizable British newspaper crowd that included Jimmy Jones,
John Parsons, Frank Keating, and John Ballantine were there.
So, too, was the great Swedish champion of the fifties, Sven
Davidson, who coupled his role as a journalist with that of lobby-
ist for his seemingly endless list of radical ideas for the modernization of the professional game.

Lily Wollerner, who must have photographed every tennis
player who has set foot in the south of France since World War
Two, arrived, wide-eyed and wondering, for her first trip to
America. As someone said, for a European to fly straight into
the Big D was really taking the bull by the horns.

Some players attracted writers just by virtue of their national-
ity. Justin Dowling, the London-based correspondent for the
South African Argus Group, flew in to keep an eye on Cliff
Drysdale's fortunes, and Tom Okker's deeds were being chron-
icled by the jovial, pink-faced Nico Van Der Zwet Slotenmaker
of the Amsterdam *Telegraf.* Nico was quite a character and he
became the inevitable butt of Bud Collins' wicked humor when
the multi-talented Boston *Globe* columnist wore his master-of-
ceremonies hat at the lavish WCT dinner. "Nico's already filed his
story on the finals," Bud told his black-tie audience. "Tom Okker
won."

It was all good fun and, for my part, I was pleased as always

Bowrey brought the crowded week's activities to a close by be
ing Franciscus and Richey in a final that ended up on N
television, as the brevity of the Newcombe-Drysdale match
left the network with time to fill.

It was a happy note on which to end another tour. For m
of the boys, six weeks of vacation lay ahead before we regrou
in St. Louis for the first event of the new tour during the
week of Wimbledon. One of the most frustrating aspects of
peace agreement was that it could not be ratified by all the nati
that comprise the ILTF until one week after Wimbledon. T
meant that the ban would still be on and we would be ba
from competing in the world's most prestigious champions
in 1972. It seemed ridiculous, but once again the slow-mo
machinery of the ILTF stood in the way of immediate prog

But for the top eight players neither Wimbledon nor St. L
nor even the vacation, was uppermost in our minds as we ca
a late-night flight to Dallas. We were three days away from
second $100,000 WCT play-off final with another $50,000 or
line for the winner. I had fulfilled the task I had set myse
January—that of climbing above my seventh place finish in
1971 points table. By the time Las Vegas closed out the 1
72 tour I was in fifth position—five points ahead of Ashe
therefore the top American on the tour. It was a good fee

However the battle for the vital eighth position had devel
into a fierce neck-and-neck race in the closing weeks. Ch
Pasarell, who had had the Number Eight spot since the sta
the year, was being strongly challenged by John Newcombe
Roy Emerson, and when we arrived in Las Vegas all
players were within a point of each other. Even John Alex
and Roger Taylor had an outside chance if either of them re
the final. But the anticipated sprint down the final stretch
materialized. Two of the hottest contenders blew it at the
fence. Emmo lost to Ismail El Shafei and Charlie went do
Jeff Borowiak, also in the first round, so Newcombe was s
his place in Dallas long before he actually won the tourna

Unlike the previous November when the quarters and
had been played in Houston, all the rounds of the play-off

Another precision return off that incredible backhand, Ken Rosewall is on his way to his unforgettable five-set victory over Rod Laver at the Moody Coliseum Dallas in May 1972—a victory that gave him his second World Champion of Tennis title, and his second $50,000 check in seven months. *Credit: Richard Evans*

Ken Rosewall, the little man we call "Muscles," has done it again and
by the look on his face he doesn't seem to believe it. But the check for
$50,000 which WCT Executive Director Mike Davies is about to hand
over at the Moody Coliseum in Dallas was earned the hard way, through
three and a half hours of fierce competition against the man many
people still call the best in the world, Rod Laver. This was a feat that
assured him of a special place in the history of the game. *Credit:
Richard Evans*

Cliff Drysdale pounds a first serve at me during our quarterfinal match in the 1972 WCT play-off finals in Dallas. Cliff's racket is framed by the photo of reigning champion Ken Rosewall. *Credit: Richard Evans*

to see Asher Birnbaum, publisher of *Tennis Magazine*—the only serious rival to Gladys Heldman's *World Tennis* —and a fellow Chicagoan who has always taken a keen interest in my career.

So along with Temple Pouncey of the Dallas *Morning News,* Bridget Byrne of the Los Angeles *Herald Examiner,* and several other American sportswriters, the overseas correspondents really helped put the world spotlight on Dallas. In all but one respect, the event withstood the examination magnificently. From the players' point of view, the one quarrel we had with the way things had been organized centered around the scheduling of matches. Mike Davies had decided that, as the top two seeds, Rod Laver and Ken Rosewall should be given the benefit of a day's rest—assuming they won—between the quarter and semifinal rounds. So instead of playing the top half of the draw on Wednesday night and the bottom half on Thursday, which would have meant that players meeting in the semis would have had an equal amount of rest, one match from each half was played on Wednesday and the remaining two from each half on Thursday. Several players, including Tom and myself, who were probably most vociferous about it, saw the inherent danger of this decision as soon as we heard about it in Charlotte several weeks before. We tried then to get Mike to change his mind and spoke to him again about it in Las Vegas. But he was adamant. What we feared was the possibility of a player becoming involved in a long, tiring five-setter and then having to go back on court 24 hours later against a man who had spent the previous 48 hours with his feet up. There was a minimum of $10,000 on the line for a player who could clear the semifinal hurdle, not to mention the pride and prestige involved. With all that at stake, this was no time for handicap tennis.

Our worst fears were realized, because that was precisely what happened. And the player it happened to was me. On that Wednesday Laver laid into Newcombe and annihilated his fellow Aussie with a barrage of shots that had Rocket's copyright written all over them and won 6-4, 6-4, 6-4.

The following night I met Drysdale and fell behind by two sets to love. I knew I had to start doing something different if I was going to prevent a repeat of our match in Las Vegas the week before. So I started serving to his forehand. I figured that I would just have to let him hit the occasional winner off that flank and hope that four of them didn't materialize in one game. They never did because, although Cliff's forehand has improved considerably in recent months, he is still not as consistant with it as he is with that deadly double-fisted backhand.

By switching the point of attack with my serve, I disrupted his rhythm and immediately I felt the pressure ease. My own first serve started to find its mark more consistently, and of the fifteen aces I served in the match, twelve of them came in the last three sets. Although it was a tough struggle right up to the last point, I never got tired and I was especially satisfied with the 5-7, 6-4, 6-2, 7-5, 6-3 victory, as it helped erase the painful memory of my deplorable performance against Tom Okker in the quarterfinals of the previous WCT play-off finals in Houston.

Although I knew that the long battle with Cliff must have taken something out of me, I was full of confidence and optimism when I walked on court to face Laver the following night. I just tried to put the fact that Rod had been given an extra day's rest out of my mind. The psychological edge was mine. I had beaten him five times out of eight in the previous eighteen months and I knew he didn't enjoy playing me as much as I enjoyed playing him. I was determined to make him aware of that fact from the first point on.

Like professional golfers who go through their round in meticulous and accurate detail for reporters in the clubhouse, tennis players tend to be very objective and honest critics of their own game. No one knows better than ourselves how we are playing and generally we are not reticent about commenting on our form—good or bad. If you hear a player come off court and say, "I really played well today," don't brand him as a big head. Because a day later that same player is just as likely to be telling colleagues, reporters, and anyone else who will listen that he couldn't serve, couldn't time his backhand, and generally played like a jackass.

So I have no intention of bragging when I say that for two

sets in the semifinals of the play-off finals in Dallas, I killed Rod
Laver. True, the corpse rose to live again but for those two sets
I was simply all over him. My service was working as well as it
has ever done. Time and again I aimed for the outside service line
when serving from the right-hand court and, more often than not,
I struck the mark. By standing three feet wide of the center line
to serve, I accentuated the angle of the delivery, swinging the
ball away in a ferocious, curving arc wide of Laver's outstretched
backhand. Even when he did manage to get a racket to the ball,
he either put it into the net or flicked up the easiest of returns that
I simply volleyed away into an empty court.

Rod was still not able to read my passing shots correctly and I
broke him twice to move into a 6-4, 6-4 lead. When I reached
break point three times on his service in the opening game of the
third set, I smelled victory. But I smelled it too soon. He wriggled
free and held on to that service for 1-0. That in itself would not
have been a disaster from my point of view but the next game
was. I led 40-love on my serve and then, as a result of some great
returns by Laver and a couple of lazy shots from me, he struck
back to take my serve for the first time in the match. That was
where it all changed. That was were the whole thing was won
and lost. It had nothing to do with fatigue. Having all but had
Laver under lock and key, I had allowed him to get his foot
back in the door. Against any player that is dangerous. Against
Laver it is fatal.

As the third set slipped away, I felt the sting go out of my
shots and venom desert my serve. Suddenly I was straining for
that extra stride as I rushed the net and hesitating for that crucial
tenth of a second as I reached for the volley. I knew what was
happening. I was getting tired. Laver knew it, too, and immediately he drew strength and confidence from my predicament. I
lost the third 6-1, and at 5-2 down in the fourth, I let him serve
out for the set with the minimum of resistance on my part. I
wanted to serve first in the fifth and conserve as much energy
as possible in the process.

But those lethal top-spin passers were coming at me like bullets
by this time and my legs were no longer responding to my des-

Rosewall from moving sweetly into the final with a neat 6-4, 6-3, 7-6 victory.

So after a day's rest on Saturday, the stage was set on Sunday afternoon for another Rosewall-Laver showdown. As in the previous final seven months, most people were predicting a Laver victory. What no one dared to predict was the kind of match one waits a lifetime to see—a nerve-racking, blood-tingling epic between two of the greatest players the game has ever known. By the time the match reached 6-all in the fifth set, we had seen both men's hopes ride the roller coaster of fate. Rocket had roared away to a deceptive 5-1 lead in the first set only to lose his service rhythm and see Kenny take the second 7-0 and win the third 6-3 to lead by two sets to one. At 1-3 down in the fourth, Laver fought his way back into the match and leveled it by winning the tie break seven points to three.

So as another tie break loomed in the fifth, it had come all the way down to the wire—the last stride, the last gasp, and for Rosewall, possibly the Last Hurrah. The television lights glaring down onto the court made the heat almost unbearable in the seemingly airless arena, and at 37 years of age Ken was beginning to show inevitable signs of exhaustion after nearly three and a half hours of grueling tennis.

NBC, nearing its fourth hour of live nationwide coverage, preempted three regularly scheduled programs to stay with it, and by the end a record tennis audience of 23 million people had tuned in as fans of other sports flicked dials and became caught in the spell, riveted by the sight of these two extraordinary Australians exhibiting their rare skills in a finish too fantastic for fiction. It was the greatest possible advertisement for the game.

Laver led 3-1 in that fifth-set tie break and then 5-3. The title-holder was within two points of losing his crown. Rosewall conjured up a backhand to grab another precious point for 4-5 but then it was Rod's turn to serve and he only needed two good points for the fifty grand, the diamond ring, the gold cup, the Lincoln Continental, which was being lent to the winner for a year and—probably most important of all to Laver—the pride

perate call for speed. They were like lead. I k
the problem was a genuine physical fatigue bu
was mental—that psychological weight of
settles over any player who knows that he h
grasp and has let it slip. I coaxed, urged, and ir
myself to get up and go. I called myself every
sun in an effort to recapture the spirit of con
driven me forward in the early stages. But it w
time Rocket was playing too well and he hamme
faltering serve all over the court, breaking it in
and the third . . . and the fifth. A game later, i
I had lost 4-6, 4-6, 6-1, 6-2, 6-0.

At the press conference afterwards I did no
to be offering the strange scheduling of matc
for my defeat because it was not a valid excus
having complained about it to Davies before
justified in having my say after it was all over
out that, although I might never have been abl
momentum after he had won the third and fo
have been unlikely to lose the fifth to love ha
off with an equal amount of rest behind us
were the losers, too, for instead of watching
they would have gotten to see a much close
who the eventual winner might have been. A
did not begrudge Rocket his victory. Anyon
from two sets to love down deserves his succe

In the other half of the draw the situatio
slightly different. Arthur Ashe, who was havir
secutive nights, had blasted his way past Ton
quick time on the Thursday, whereas Ken
before got himself embroiled in a long five
Lutz. So the scales were a little more evenly b
met Rosewall in the semifinal, but that didn
has to be serving at his best to beat Kenny an
occasion he wasn't—despite Gonzales's effort
Arthur missed 44 first serves compared to Ke
forehand also showing signs of collapse, he

and the glory. It was, after all, the only title worth talking about that had eluded him so far. Well, two good serves might have been sufficient against most players but not against Ken Rosewall. Moving into a solid first delivery, Kenny swept the return cross-court off that incredible backhand, way down low to Laver's forehand side.

Rod saw it coming as he has seen thousands of them coming off Rosewall's racket in the past, and from the moment it was hit he must have known it was hopeless. He streaked after it nonetheless, a blue-clad blur topped with streaming copper hair, and thrust his racket under the ball as it flashed toward the carpet. But he couldn't control the volley and it sailed out of court. Five-all. Again Laver cracked down a first serve at that lethal backhand and again the legendary stroke did everything its master asked of it. Taking the ball on the rise, Rosewall hit it straight and true for an outright winner. Laver, stranded in mid-court, just watched it go. At 6-5 Rosewall stood at match point, and after 3 hours and 34 minutes the end came quickly. Ken served, Rod blooped the return into the net, and the World Champion of Tennis was still a man called K. R. Rosewall, master of his craft. As a man and a player, my cup of admiration for him had long been full. Now it simply spilled over. However, one could not help but feel sorry for Rod Laver, for he had played his full part in making this a match that gave new meaning to the name of World Championship Tennis.

18

A NEW SEASON

The new World Championship Tennis season began on the day
Wimbledon opened—in St. Louis. It was strange to be so far
away from the traditional center of tennis activity during the
last week of June and one could not help feeling it was somewhat unnecessary, too.

The formula to end the division that had existed in the game
since the beginning of the year had still not been ratified by the
International body and, in any case, the Holton Classic in St.
Louis had been arranged way back in March, so no matter what
the player or the public felt about it, the battle lines were still
drawn long after the peace had been made. The slow-moving machinery of the tennis establishment, chugging along on its own
sweet way, ensured only that the WCT players—including John
Newcombe, the reigning Wimbledon Champion—would not get
to play in the world's premier championships.

Most of us, especially Newk, were upset at missing Wimbledon
but it was quickly evident that a week in St. Louis would leave
us with little to complain about. Jim Holton and his assistants
from the Holton Bank and Life Insurance Company went out of
their way to give us a good time, and there have been few tournament I have played in where greater attention was paid to the
players' needs. They put us up without charge at the Colony
Motel, and every little detail was thought of; and for that, Butch
Buchholz, the former Kramer touring pro, must take much of the
credit. Butch knows that things like the availability of practice

228

courts are what make a player happy, and whether we were missing Wimbledon or not, there were a lot of happy players in St. Louis.

On court, the new season got off to a strange start and never really recovered. Tony Roche, returning from the six-week layoff in better physical shape than he had been all year, started the ball rolling by beating Rod Laver in a very tight match in the first round. Certainly Rocket didn't recover from that shock opening for some time. He never got further than the quarterfinals for the next six tournaments and was languishing in sixteenth place by the time Forest Hills arrived.

Newcombe, who was flying to London to commentate on the second week of Wimbledon the next day, eventually won the St. Louis title—beating me in a close quarterfinal struggle on the way.

Nikki Pilic turned out to be Newk's opponent in the final, which was the first of many surprises that were to come, for Nikki had never gone that far in a WCT tournament before. After that, "surprises" became routine and by the time that sixth tournament was completed in Fort Worth before the break for the U.S. Open, no less than ten different players had appeared in the final. Newcombe and Mark Cox—the finalist in Louisville and the shock winner in Cleveland—were the only players to reach the final twice.

I made it that far once, battling my way past Carmichael, Ashe, and Newcombe, among others in the suffocating humidity that hung over the D.C. area during the Washington Star tournament in the second week of July. The peace agreement had been ratified by then, so co-tournament chairmen Donald Dell and Johnny Harris hurriedly turned it into the first "Open" of the new era by expanding the draw to 48 so as to include qualifiers from the local satellite tournament.

Most of them were total unknowns but none the worse for that, and they added considerable interest to the early rounds. Despite the incredible heat, which was as bad as anything I have ever experienced, crowds flocked to the public park courts at Kennedy and Sixteenth Streets from the first day on, and some of the qualifiers were not dazzled by the limelight—not immediately, anyway. One of them, a pale, slightly built teaching pro from Pennsylvania called Steve Siegel, showed how much can be achieved on clay by sheer determination and a willingness to run down every ball. Gutsing his way through every point, he took the first set off Arthur Ashe and held him to 4-all in the second. At that point either the heat or the sudden realization of what he was doing became too much for Siegel and, after losing the set, he rushed off court to be sick behind the stands. Poor guy. I know just how he felt. But even so I suspect he feels the whole experience was worthwhile, and although it was harder work for us, we certainly enjoyed having a little fresh blood in our tournaments again.

In a different way from Siegel, I felt pretty sick with myself when I reached match point against Tony Roche in the final and blew an easy put-away volley. For a fraction of a second my racket slipped through my sweaty fingers as I rushed up to take the ball. It was one of those things that neither the crowd nor even perhaps one's opponent ever sees. It is something all players try to guard against, which is why you see us toweling down so often or even playing with bits of towel hanging out of our shorts. When it does happen it's nobody's fault but your own, but you still tend to curse your luck—especially when it happens on match point! It was the turning point as far as Tony was concerned and he came roaring back into the match to win in three sets.

Despite my disappointment, I was pleased to see Tony playing so well again. But unfortunately his return to full fitness was short-lived. His elbow started hurting again in Boston two weeks later and by the end of August he was back in the hospital in New York, undergoing his second operation in ten months—this time having part of the bone chipped away. We are all keeping our fingers crossed that he will make a complete recovery.

Ashe won in Louisville the following week; Bob Lutz hit a terrific patch of form to win the prestigious U.S. Pro Championships at the Longwood Cricket Club in Boston, and in Cleveland

Cox won his first WCT title by beating Ruffels, who was making his first appearance in a final. Then Ken Rosewall, who had taken an extended vacation after his triumph in Dallas and had only rejoined the tour in Boston, reached the final in Fort Worth but lost a five-set marathon to Newcombe. So the Rod and Kenny Show which had dominated the tour only a few months before seemed to be over. Week by week the titles seemed to be up for grabs and everyone was grabbing them.

I had beaten Rosewall in the first round in Boston, making sure that I seized a good opportunity to reverse the usual trend of our matches by serving really well. I also notched up another victory over Laver in Cleveland, but despite these satisfying wins I was getting stuck at that quarterfinal barrier again—losing twice to Drysdale and once each to Newcombe and Ashe.

From a personal point of view Forest Hills was disappointing. I was seeded ninth and had the sort of draw that should have allowed me to play myself gradually into the tournament. But although I reached the third round, beating a rejuvenated Mal Anderson on the way, I never got my form or my confidence together. I suppose there are horses for courses in tennis, too, and Forest Hills has just never been my course.

Neither my mood nor my confidence was helped by the fact that my third-round match with Frew McMillan was switched from Court 10—which is hardly star billing in any case—to Court 18, which is no more than a practice court, backed up against the Long Island Railway tracks. It sounds and plays like a marshalling yard, and as the few spectators that can reach it are all of forty yards away, the atmosphere is nil. This may make me sound like a prima donna, but the fact remains that it is not the sort of location in which a seeded player hopes to find himself playing the third round of the U.S. Open. That, of course, is not an excuse for my loss and I do not offer it as one. It merely explains why I was not in the best frame of mind to take on a player as dangerous as Frew, and I paid the penalty. McMillan's double-fisted strokes seemed to serve him well on the uneven grass where his smothering style of shot, played off a short backswing, is well suited to deal with a bad bounce. After I dropped service in the first game, I was always struggling to get into the match and Frew played much too well to let me do so.

Tom and I were seeded Number One in the doubles, which was a nice compliment but neither of us had much confidence that we could live up to that ranking. It was simply a matter of our style not being suited to a fast, uneven surface. Our whole game is based on speed and the ability to pick up the half volley off the return of serve. On bad grass there is only a fifty-fifty chance of being able to get the ball back if it is returned to our feet. Unlike the big servers who try to put their opponents on the defensive with that first delivery, we launch a second-phase offensive, and at Forest Hills this is just not possible. So it was no particular surprise to us when we lost to the scratch pair of Mal Anderson and Clark Graebner.

But the mixed doubles was a different story. Margaret Court and I won the mixed title for the third time, beating Ilie Nastase and Rosie Casals late on Sunday evening just after Ilie had become the new U.S. Open Champion by beating Ashe in the men's final. It was good to be playing with Margaret again. Although she lost to Billie Jean in the singles, motherhood does not seem to have affected her game and in fact she seems to have gotten the business of playing and traveling with a baby down to a fine art. Having a willing husband around helps, of course, and Barry was more than happy to be left holding baby Daniel whenever Margaret had to go on court.

It was in many ways an important and significant Forest Hills. As the only major tournament of 1972 that would see all the world's best players gathered together, it stood on its own as a test of current form and world standing. But the state of the courts, which seems to get worse every year, and the use of the nine-point "sudden death" tie-break styles, gave luck too much of a head start over skill for it to be considered the definitive test.

As Tom Okker said, "This nine-point tie break is pure lottery. And when you use it on courts that give one bad bounce in every three, the whole thing becomes Russian roulette."

The majority of players felt that way and next year the players might have some say in the matter. At what may well prove to be a historic meeting, held in the Open Club underneath the Stadium Court during Forest Hills, 56 Independent and contract professionals signed up as members of the newly formed Association of Tennis Professionals. This was a merger of the two players' associations that had been in existence for some months, and as each man had to pay a $400 membership fee, there was little doubt that the players were serious about making it work and represent their interests.

Although he had become something of an establishment figure in recent years, it was felt that Jack Kramer was the best-qualified person to fill the role of chief executive and he readily accepted the post. Personally I feel that Jack has always been happier as a players' man than as a U.S. LTA official, and I think he has the players' interests at heart. He should do a good job for us.

Bob Briner, who was in the running for the top job, was elected as one of three nonplaying members on the Board of Directors—Benny Berthet of France and Britain's John Barrett were the others—and Cliff Drysdale was elected president, Andres Gimeno vice-president, Arthur Ashe treasurer, and Jim McManus and Ismail El Shafei joint secretaries. Four other players, Mark Cox, Ray Ruffels, Nikki Pilic, and Jaime Fillol, were nominated to the Board of Directors and the firm of Dell, Craighill and Fentress assumed the role of legal counselors.

It was a strong team—one that I envisage taking over complete control of the professional game in the coming years. Tennis has been through many changes since 1968—the year of the first Open—and the revolution is not yet complete. Traditional tournaments and long-standing centers of power and influence are bound to feel the draft as fresh winds of change blow through the pro game, adapting it still further to fit the modern requirements of this big-money, television-orientated age. Even World Championship Tennis, an organization that played such a vital part in putting professional tennis on the map, may find its power diminishing now that Lamar Hunt will hold no more players to year-round contracts. We shall see.

Despite all the frustrations and passing disappointments, it has been great to be associated with a sport that has achieved such a rapid growth in popularity and recognition. There is still much that all of us in the game can do to consolidate that growth, but it has reached a point now from which there will be no turning back. Tennis is the sport of the seventies, and if the people of all ages, backgrounds, and levels of ability who are taking it up now derive half as much pleasure and satisfaction from it as I have, they will find it more than worthwhile.

It may sound strange coming from a 31-year-old professional who has been competing on the International circuit without a break for fifteen years, but I think my best is yet to come. I feel I am still on the upward slope and have not yet reached my own particular peak. When I turned pro in 1968 I never thought I would become as good a player as I am today, and while I am all too aware of my limitations, I also have a fair idea of which particular aspects of my game can be improved. It will require more work, more hours on the practice court. There are moments when I wonder if the physical and mental strain, the constant travel, the long months away from home, and the never-ending battle to maintain peak physical condition are worth it. But then I get out there in a crowded arena, and suddenly I become caught up once again by the challenge of winning each point and then each game and then each set until the ultimate challenge of match point arrives, bringing with it the tingling realization of having to face the final crisis. Winning it justifies everything. There is simply no substitute for a match point won—no greater despair than a match point lost.

I don't know how many more match points I will win, but if my years in the game have taught me one thing it is never to underestimate what tomorrow can bring.

Up, up and away—but not quite. Arthur Ashe eventually crash landed against Ilie Nastase in the 1972 final of the U.S. Open, losing to the Rumanian in five sets. *Credit: Richard Evans*

Bob Lutz twists to flick back a lob against John Newcombe in the first round of the U.S. Pro Championships at the Longwood Cricket Club in Boston in August 1972. Bob's defeat of Newk set him on the road to the title, which he won by beating Tom Okker in the final five days later. It was Lutz's best achievement as a pro. *Credit: Richard Evans*

Ion Tiriac, the man writer John McPhee once described as resembling "a triple agent from Alexandria—a used-car dealer from central Marrakesh," makes a point to some fellow players in the luncheon tent during Forest Hills 1972. Ismail El Shafei (back to camera) and Manuel Orantes listen, while in the background Tom Koch inspects the food. *Credit: Richard Evans*

Intense concentration is one of Stan Smith's greatest assets, as is evident here as Stan prepares to meet a return from Ilie Nastase in the 1972 Wimbledon final. One of the best finals ever seen on the famous Centre Court, Smith won in five sets. *Credit: Russ Adams*

Ilie Nastase, the lithe, mercurial Rumanian, roars in to reach a short ball from Arthur Ashe in the final of the U.S. Open at Forest Hills in September, 1972. After trailing by two sets to one and 2-4 in the fourth, Nastase turned the match around to win in five sets. *Credit: Richard Evans*

From the players' balcony two Queenslanders survey the scene at Forest Hills in September 1972. Mal Anderson, left, won the title there in 1957. Rod Laver won it in 1962 and 1969. Anderson's brother-in-law Roy Emerson, yet another Aussie from Queensland, was champion in 1961 and 1964. *Credit: Richard Evans*

Senator Edward Kennedy's lovely wife Joan was my partner in the Robert F. Kennedy Memorial Tournament at Forest Hills in August 1972. After losing a couple of matches in the round robin we finally seem to have done something right. *Credit: Richard Evans*

That ardent tennis enthusiast Charlton Heston watches partner Dennis Ralston deal with a forehand during the R.F.K. Memorial Pro Celebrity Tournament at Forest Hills. Herb Fitzgibbon is playing on the far court. *Credit: Richard Evans*

The legendary Pancho Gonzales turns to chase a lob on the Stadium Court at Forest Hills in 1972 during his match against the young Frenchman Patrice Dominguez. *Credit: Richard Evans*

After playing some of the best tennis of his career, Britain's Mark Cox arrived at Forest Hills in 1972 as the No. 3 man on the WCT tour. His good form continued as he beat Ken Rosewall in the second round of the U.S. Open, but this carefully watched backhand volley wasn't enough to get him past Dick Stockton, one of America's brightest hopes in round three. Stockton won in five sets. *Credit: Richard Evans*

If you ever need an example of how to watch the ball, this is it. Cliff Richey, pugnacious and determined as always, is pictured here on his way to the final of the NCNB tournament at Charlotte, North Carolina, in April 1972. It was Cliff's first appearance as a WCT pro. He eventually lost to Rosewall. *Credit: Russ Adams*

There goes a typical Okker top-spin forehand special—one of the most exciting shots in the game. Tom unleashed it against Bob Lutz in the final of the U.S. Pro Championships at the Longwood Cricket Club in Boston in August 1972. But Bob still won the title. *Credit: Richard Evans*

The glassware was for keeping, the silverware for show, but it all looked pretty good to Margaret Court and me in 1972 after we won the mixed doubles at Forest Hills for the third time. We beat Ilie Nastase and Rosie Casals in the final. *Credit: Richard Evans*

One of the girls we miss having around the circuit now that the segregation of the sexes has come to tennis—France's Francoise Durr. Here on the Grandstand Court at Forest Hills in 1972, Frankie displays that strange looking but very effective backhand. *Credit: Richard Evans*

Cliff Drysdale and Andres Gimeno, two of the keener and better golfers on the tour—Rod Laver is generally considered the best—enjoy a round on a misty morning at a course near Cologne during the WCT tournament there in 1971. *Credit: Arthur Ashe*

PART TWO

19

A FEW TIPS

The remaining chapters offer a few tips on how to play better doubles and mixed doubles. I do not feel that this is the place to give the reader the ABC's on the fundamentals of playing the game. There are many excellent instruction books available for the person taking up tennis for the first time. Rather, I have tried to give an insight into the strategy of match play by drawing from some of my own experiences on court which may be of use to the average player. I have also taken the opportunity, in the mixed doubles section, of discussing the sudden and rapid growth of the women's game.

20

DOUBLES

Whether your name is Tom Okker, Roy Emerson, or Joe Blow, the most important thing about doubles is your partner. Or, more specifically, your choice of partner. Don't team up with someone just because he or she has the best serve or a solid backhand or is generally considered to be the number one player at your club. All these things are important, but not nearly as important as whether your personalities are compatible. Your temperaments do not have to be the same but it is essential that they do not clash. Ideally, you should be friends on and off the court, but if that doesn't happen to be the case then you should at least respect each other as tennis players and enjoy each other's company while you are playing. The greatest potential partnership in the world will collapse at the first hint of trouble if mutual trust and confidence are lacking. And if you should happen to find yourself sharing a court with someone who is less than your ideal kind of person, never, never blame him for a lost point or even look as if you are blaming him. Unless he has a skin made out of rhinoceros hide, you will have achieved nothing other than to ensure that he misses the next point as well.

So, having observed this first golden rule, let us go through some of the fundamental aspects of doubles play.

Positioning Determine who is going to play the left-hand court on the basis of which partner has the stronger backhand. This tends to be the weaker stroke among beginners; as it is best to have your strength on the flanks, the player with the stronger

254

backhand should therefore play in the back-hand, or left, court. If a left-hander is partnering a right-hander, the southpaw should play the left-hand court, as you are thereby covering the flanks with two forehands.

Although the prime strategy of good doubles play is for both players to get to the net at the first available opportunity, one often sees all four contestants hugging the base line during long rallies in both social and competitive club tennis. But for beginners I don't think this is necessarily a bad thing. It gives a newcomer to the game more time to get the feel of the court and to understand his partner. But always remember that you will never make any real progress until you learn how to play the net. I know many players are afraid to get up there. My mother, for instance, is an enthusiastic social player who had played for years without ever venturing away from the base line until my father suggested she take the plunge. At first she was very reluctant to do so. "Oh, I'm afraid to go the net," I remember her saying. "The ball comes too fast up there." It was the sort of reaction I have heard from hundreds of people who play the game for fun, especially women. But it can be fun at the net, too, and unless you are playing out of your league, you won't find the ball coming too fast after a bit of practice. My mother didn't. Dad gave her a couple of lessons on how to volley and since then she has been fine.

Everybody has his own pet theory about where you should stand when you do decide to play net, but I would offer these suggestions: The server's partner should stand closer to the net than the receiver's partner. As your partner serves, you should be positioned two yards back from the net and one step away from being able to touch the outside line of the doubles alley with the tip of your racket head. In other words, if you are standing in the right-hand court, take up what you feel is the correct position, cross your left leg over your right as far as is comfortable without letting your right foot leave the ground and from there you should be able to touch the outside line with your racket.

The receiver's partner should stand the same distance from the outside line but three yards back from the net—or about a yard inside the service line. In this way he cuts down the angle at which his opponents can aim because his partner is unlikely to join him at the net immediately following a service return.

To receive serve, stand at the corner of the singles sideline and the base line, thus dividing the box into which your opponent is serving as evenly as possible. Obviously I am taking as a yardstick the average serve at whatever level of the game you happen to be playing. If your opponent has a weak serve and you are hitting the ball well, then move inside the base line a few feet and take it early.

Unlike in singles, when it is customary to serve from as near the center mark on the base line as possible, you should stand four or five feet to either side of it for the doubles serve. By doing so, you put yourself in a better position to cover the area of the court that your opponent will be forced to aim for with his return. For with your partner at the net, the ball is almost bound to come back cross-court, i.e. to the side of the court from which you are serving.

Strategy The first decision to be made is which partner should serve first. To obtain a quick breakthrough, which is always a good psychological boost, the player serving first should be either the better server or the one to warm up quicker. Or if one of you is a left-hander, then he should start, as most people find a left-hander's serve more difficult to handle.

Apart from the basic premise that you should serve mostly to the backhand, normally the weaker stroke, there are definite doubles serves that you should go for. One is a short serve sliced wide to your opponent's forehand when you are serving from the right-hand court. This draws him wide and opens up the court for the first volley. It should be kept as a surprise tactic and used no more than 20 percent of the time.

An important principle to be remembered about serving in doubles is to forget the power. Concentrate first and foremost on placement. The angles are far more important in doubles than in singles so use spin to help you put the ball precisely where you want it. In other words serve at three-quarters pace and use what would normally be your second serve in singles as your first serve. By doing so, you should be able to reduce drastically the number of second serves. This is vital because in doubles a receiver will take greater liberties with the basically defensive second delivery than he would in singles. Even in our league, where power servers abound, very few teams use the flat-hit first serve. Arthur Ashe and Bob Lutz tend to; so do John Alexander and Phil Dent, but it is not good percentage tennis, and in doubles percentage is the name of the game.

The principle of accuracy over power holds true for all shots, not just the serve. When a rally develops, don't be in a hurry to end it by looking for the big winner. Doubles is a game of tactical maneuver—a game of chess. Try to think one stroke ahead. Chip it there to pull your opponent in or draw his partner out wide; angle it that way to force him into going for an area of the court you know you have covered; lob to tire him or to give yourself time to get into position. The ability to think all this out and do it comes only with practice and experience over a long period of time, but in the end it is far more satisfying—and far more fruitful—than blazing away haphazardly in the hope that Ashe has suddenly loaned you his backhand for the afternoon.

Also don't be in too much of a hurry to get to the net. Although getting both of you to the net before your opponents attain the same position should be your ultimate objective, it is much better to rally from the base line until the time is ripe than to go charging in behind hurried or poorly directed shots. The decision of when you should both go up together comes only after you have established a complete understanding with your partner. But as a general rule you should both go in when you are given a short ball that enables you to take your time and place so as to put your opponents on the defensive.

Once you are at the net, the reverse problem may arise. When do you both go back? Obviously it is the lob that is going to present this question and the answer is fairly clear-cut. If one of you is quick enough to take it on the fly or hit an overhead off the bounce—in other words, make an aggressive return off it—then the other partner should remain at the net. If the lob is so deep that you are forced into a defensive return lob, then you should both retreat to the base line.

Of course the speed of the court plays a big part in determining to what extent you should play the match from the back court. The slower the surface, the more necessary it is to work from the base line, just as in singles. Tactical lobbing will be much more effective on really slow surfaces like European clay where the heavy balls become increasingly difficult to put away. Ion Tiriac and Ilie Nastase, one of the cleverest doubles teams in the world, reached the final of the French Championships in Paris one year by virtually lobbing their way through the tournament from the first round on. It takes patience and skill—and a certain sadistic delight in watching your opponents smash themselves into oblivion.

But at the club level, doubles should be primarily a source of enjoyment and fun. By all means try to improve your tennis by analyzing your opponents' strengths and weaknesses and putting some thought into your strategy and shot-making. However, if you are looking for nothing more than an hour or two of satisfying and stimulating exercise, then just remember these fundamental points: go for placement rather than power, especially on the first serve, the first volley, and the service return, keeping the latter as low as possible over the net. And always, in doubles as in singles, *keep your eye on the ball.*

Even a couple of tough old pros like Tom Okker and myself have fun playing doubles. Obviously our success has contributed to the enjoyment we get out of it. But equally I think part of the secret to our success lies in the fact that we do enjoy the game so much and look forward to the doubles eagerly every week. More than a lot of teams, we go on court in a very positive frame of mind, secure in the knowledge that if we are not absolutely the best doubles team in the world then we are fully capable of beating the best.

We consider that regular doubles play enables us to stay in good physical condition for the singles and there is the psychological aspect of it, too. On a tour as tough as the World Championship of Tennis, it is very important to develop a winning mentality. Even a player in the top half of the points table can go several weeks without winning more than one or two singles matches in each tournament. That sort of streak can begin to erode your confidence but it is much less likely to do so if you are winning doubles matches in the meantime.

I have explained elsewhere why I enjoy partnering Tom, and I think the sentiment is mutual. As Tom puts it: "One of the reasons I like playing with Marty is that he always tries hard. I've played with some guys who take it easy on some shots but I never have to worry about that with Marty. As I don't have a big serve, I couldn't really afford a partner who was not trying 100 percent all the time. His being so fast at the net compliments my game because it enables me to run round onto my forehand and try a big top spin. If they put the return too high, I know Marty will be there to knock it off."

Tom talks about my being quick at the net but, as he would agree, that is only part of it. Our whole style of play is based on speed, not just during rallies but throughout the entire match. We change ends quickly, walk back to serve quickly, and generally maintain a momentum of constant motion that can bother the hell out of our opponents when we are really in the groove. Although it is good tactics, it is not something we make a conscious effort to do; it is simply the way our style has evolved. With a guy like Tom there was no possibility of doing otherwise. He lives his whole life at breakneck speed, so he could hardly be expected to slow down on a tennis court. Sometimes, however, he is forced to because our opponents complain. Because he has this driving urgency to get on with whatever it is he's doing, he often comes very close to quick-serving opponents on court. It happened during our match against John Newcombe and Tony Roche in the 1972 Kemper International at McGaw Hall. Several times Newk held up his hand to make Tom wait a second before he served. Understandably, Newk wanted to get himself settled before receiving serve and he is experienced enough to know that you can always ask your opponent to wait for a moment if he is not giving you time.

We didn't give anyone much time that week. We hit one of

our brilliant streaks when everything jelled. It was one of those periods when we knew instinctively that we could dispense with percentage tennis and let everything flow in a flood of extravagance and daring. Our confidence was running so high that we felt sure no one could beat us, and no one did. Even Laver and Emerson, generally considered the top doubles team on the tour, were no match for us and we crushed them in the final. It was as if Tom and I were tied by an invisible string. Every move, every split-second reaction, every twist, every turn were executed in perfect harmony as if choreographed for the Broadway stage. But of course that kind of rhythmic perfection cannot be rehearsed. It is just something that develops naturally of its own accord as two players work week after week, year after year at the more mundane aspects of the game. But when it happens, it is a great feeling. In doubles play it is the ultimate sensation.

Even now, after five years of playing together, we don't reach those dizzy heights very often and the workaday realities of the game force us to pay greater heed to the rules of percentage tennis. This means that we take the minimum number of chances on our serve, concentrating solely on getting the first serve in and making the first volley. The carefully calculated risks are taken when we are receiving. Playing from the right-hand court, I try to get the ball back low over the net on the service return, and right from that stage Okker and Riessen are on the move. Tom's ready to cross, I'm ready to cover up behind him, and when we are beginning to play well, I'll sometimes follow my service return into the net so that we are challenging our opponents eyeball to eyeball in a volley duel at six yards' range. We are both quick enough with our hands to feel confident that we can take on anyone in this position and get the better of them.

But that, as I say, only happens when we are playing well. When things start to go wrong, I think we are more flexible than most teams—more willing to try something different. When we were in the process of losing the 1969 Wimbledon doubles final to Newcombe and Roche, I even suggested to Tom that we switch sides of the court—a virtually unheard-of move for an established doubles team. We didn't actually do it but I still be-

lieve that anything is worth trying if you are obviously heading
for defeat.

It had been a dramatic change of tactics that had enabled us
to reach the Wimbledon final that year. Facing Laver and Emerson in the semifinal, we had been having a lot of trouble with
Rod's cleverly chipped cross-court service returns off the backhand. So we switched to the Australian scissors formation—a
system that we seem to use more often than most teams. Basically,
it means that the net man moves across to the same side of the
court that his partner is serving from. In this particular instance
we employed it when I was serving to Laver from the backhand
court. With Tom now in front of me also on the left-hand side,
I moved my serving position in three yards to a point right next
to the center mark—the normal spot for the singles serve—and
then ran in behind my delivery to the right instead of the left.
This forced Laver to go down the line with his return because
Tom was blocking the path of the cross-court chip. As Rod
prefers to hit the ball rather than chip it when going down the
line, I was able to keep my first volley out of reach of the lethal
backhand volley with which Emerson had been killing us before.
It was easier for me to do this because it is much simpler to deal
with a ball that is hit at you than one that is chipped low, forcing
you to bend and volley up. Against a net man of Emerson's
caliber, that is suicide. Our change in tactics threw the Aussies
right out of their stride and we eventually beat them after four
exciting, close-fought sets.

In cases like this, it is usually the server who makes the decision to try something different, and the move is always made on
the spur of the moment. Neither of us considers himself the
leader of the team and I think this is true of most top doubles
partnership. With some teams it may not look that way from
the stands because one guy is always doing all the talking. Newcombe and Roche are a good example. Newk is a natural leader
and, just as some people rise to the occasion when responsibility
is thrust upon them, I think it helps Newk's game if he feels he
is directing the traffic over on his side of the net. But it is amusing to watch sometimes, because Newk can be having one of

those days when his game is off and Tony is quietly holding the partnership together with steady, error-free percentage tennis. Then suddenly Newk will turn round and start issuing orders. Tony will just plod, poker-faced back to the base line, letting it go in one ear and out the other, and continue doing precisely what he was doing before. It is a measure of the depth of their friendship and understanding that Tony never lets it bother him. He knows it is simply Newk's way of giving his own morale a lift, and as it often helps him play better, Roche is quite content to let him talk his head off.

That is why Newcombe and Roche are a great team and, conversely, why Ashe and Ralston were not. Dennis, who was often fraught with tension on court, used to get really hacked off when Arthur suggested he get his first serve in. Ralston felt he could do without that kind of advice, first because he had a much better doubles record than Arthur, and second because he *was* trying to get the damned thing in court anyway. "What do you think I'm trying to do—*not* get it in?" he'd snap back. Ralston's reaction was logical, but not particularly helpful to the harmony of the team.

I cannot stress too strongly how important compatibility of temperament and a totally understanding and unselfish attitude toward your partner's needs and idiosyncrasies are to the making of a successful doubles partnership. This goes for shot-making as well as personality traits. Never worry if your partner is hitting all the spectacular winners. Just be thankful that one of you is. With Okker and myself, it often looks as if Tom is hogging the limelight by poaching balls that appear to be mine. But that is the way we both want it because, with his deadly top-spin forehand, it is much better that he take anything that comes down the middle, even if it is obviously in my territory. This is balanced to an extent by the fact that I take most of the overheads, as I am better equipped to deal with this stroke even if it means moving into Tom's area of the court to reach it.

I will also take the responsibility of serving into the wind, which bothers me less than it does Tom. And even if it results in my dropping serve more often than he does, that is a calculated risk that we both understand and accept.

21

MIXED DOUBLES

When a nice, easy return comes looping off our opponent's racket in mixed doubles, what do I do? I go for the girl, that's what I do. I hit the ball just as hard and just as viciously as I would if it were Ashe and Lutz or Emerson and Laver on the other side of the net.

Ungentlemanly conduct? At the social level of the game, it would probably be considered worse than that—and rightly so. But I don't very often play social mixed, and at the professional level the woman is fair game. She is usually the weaker player of the two so it is logical to attack her. I literally try to scare her a little. I try to make her back up off the net so that she no longer has the confidence to play her natural game.

It took me several years to come to terms with these ruthless tactics. Instinctively I was reluctant to really hit out at the girl but Margaret Court, the great Australian champion who has been my most consistent partner over the last four or five years, soon talked me into it.

"Let them have it, Marty," she used to say. "They can take it. You're not going to hurt them anyway."

Of course, it is totally different if you are playing social mixed. There is absolutely no point in some great brute of a guy bashing aces and overheads past a poor, unfortunate lady who just wants a bit of gentle fun. However if you are playing in a proper tournament, I see no reason to pussyfoot around just because someone told you that hitting hard at the woman was not the nice thing to do. Tournaments are competitive. They are supposed to provide the opportunity for you to demonstrate how your game has improved and how well you stand up to pressure. Not everyone enjoys tough competition and there is no reason why they should. But people who enter serious tournaments must expect to come up against players who are out there to win. And under those circumstances, no one has the right to call "Foul play!" when a guy blasts one at his lady opponent. I am not, of course, talking about trying to literally hit someone in the stomach with the ball. Even in men's doubles on the pro tour we don't try to do that, although there have been occasional instances of it in grudge matches on the International circuit. But you can still unnerve an opponent by drumming shots past either side of him or smashing down hard at his feet.

The same applies to the social etiquette of letting the woman serve first. In tournaments, the player with the best serve should serve first. Equally, the stronger player should play in the backhand court and, more often than not, this will be the man. There can be exceptions to this—even at the top level. Ilie Nastase and Rosie Casals, two extremely quick, agile players, won the Wimbledon mixed doubles title in 1970 with Rosie playing in the backhand court.

I found this worked very well when I partnered Stephanie DeFina Johnson on the South African Sugar Circuit one year. Stephanie is a left-hander and was therefore quite happy playing in what, for her, was the forehand court. She was steady on that side, always getting the ball back in play on the big points, either with good lobs or careful returns, and we were pretty successful.

I have been very lucky with my mixed doubles partners. Because I feel there is no point in entering the competition unless you intend to win it, I have always sought out the very best women players. I like aggressive, competitive partners who are not afraid to volley and attack in tight situations and who, above all, really enjoy the game.

The pretty Australian blonde Helen Gourlay was my first regular mixed partner in the mid-sixties and we had a very successful tour in Italy. Shortly afterwards I teamed up with Pat Walkden—

now Pat Pretorius—to win the South African Championships over Margaret Court and Bob Hewitt in 1968. I found Pat another very competitive player who was fun to have alongside on the court.

Clark Graebner's wife Carole—one of the best singles players in the world before becoming a mother—was another mixed doubles player who did not let her desire to win detract from the fun and enjoyment she got out of the game. Carole and I didn't play together very often but we did manage to win the Pacific Southwest title in Los Angeles one year.

My partnership with Margaret Court began in Rome in 1968. I didn't have a partner for the Italian Championships and although I was sure Margaret would already be fixed up I felt there would be no harm in asking. As it happened, Ken Fletcher, her mixed partner of long standing, was off on one of his jaunts to the Far East or somewhere—one was never quite sure where the nomadic Fletch was in those days—and Margaret was looking for someone to play with.

We developed an immediate understanding and I helped her retire the Italian title, as she had won it the previous two years as well. Although Fletch reappeared to resume his partnership with "Big Marge" at Wimbledon that year, Margaret and I started playing together pretty much full-time in 1969, 1970, and 1971, and as far as I can remember we lost only three matches in all the time we were together: Virginia Wade and Tom Okker beat us in Berlin in 1968; Billie Jean King and Bob Hewitt got the better of us in Durban the following year; and in 1971, in our most disappointing loss, we went down to Billie Jean and Owen Davidson 13-15 in the third set of the Wimbledon final. I was disappointed for myself because it was the nearest I had ever gotten to winning a Wimbledon title; but I was equally disappointed for Margaret who had already been beaten in two finals, losing in the singles to Evonne Goolagong—the sensation of Wimbledon that year—and, with Evonne as her partner in the doubles, to Billie Jean and Rosie Casals. It was really tough getting to all three finals of a major championship and not winning any of them.

But, that disappointment apart, we have had plenty of success together. We won Forest Hills in 1969, 1970, and 1972, the French Championships in 1970, and we shared the Australian title in 1969 with Fred Stolle and Ann Jones because the final somehow never got to be played.

As in men's doubles, mixed partners tend to be good friends off court as well, and Margaret and her husband Barry spend a lot of time with Sally and me at tournaments. Of course, we have not played together so much recently, partly because Margaret has been busy producing a baby and partly because the men's and women's circuits have started to go their own separate ways since the advent of the WCT tour and the Virginia Slims women's pro circuit.

I miss having the girls around at tournaments. Some of us have traveled the world together for years and obviously many of us have developed strong and lasting friendships during that time. I always used to enjoy the company of that charming Parisienne Françoise Durr for dinner or a drink after the day's play, and it seems strange not to find Ingrid Bentzer, Val Ziegenfuss, Judy Dalton, Pam Austin, or the vivacious Gail Chanfreau livening up the scene in the clubhouse. But I, for one, can't complain. When the girls used to complain about the huge difference in prize money between the men's and women's events, I was one of several male pros who used to say, "Go off on your own and prove you are as big a drawing card as we are." The Women's Lib movement would call that a typically male chauvinist attitude, but at the time there was no indication that the spectators were coming specifically to see the women play.

Well, the girls took our advice. Joe Cullman of Philip Morris, one of the game's most generous benefactors and ardent enthusiasts, provided the sponsorship through Virginia Slims; *World Tennis* publisher Gladys Heldman provided her own dazzling brand of energetic leadership; and the tireless Billie Jean King, a dedicated and courageous person, worked her tail off to provide the necessary headline-grabbing quotes and interviews. The net result was that the women's pro tour caught the public imagination and interest continues to grow week by week.

Obviously the arrival of Chris Evert and Evonne Goolagong offered a brilliantly timed piece of star-struck rivalry, injecting exciting new blood into the women's game just as it was daring to strike out on its own. Now, of course, they are on their way. Billie Jean has become the first woman athlete ever to win more than $100,000 in a single year and the Virginia Slims circuit has tournaments offering fifty and one hundred thousand dollars in prize money. I think their emergence as a big crowd-pulling force in their own right is great for the game but, having opened my big mouth, I must admit it would be nice if we got back together once in a while so we could play mixed doubles again.

22

A MATCH

In the third round of the Spanish International Championships in Barcelona in October 1971 I played Andres Gimeno. In the course of describing this match in detail I hope to be able to pass on to the reader some valuable tips and insights into how a match of this type should be played. I have chosen this particular match for several reasons. It was played on European clay, which requires greater thought and tactical ability than any other surface. I was up against a highly experienced and talented player who would feel, quite literally, at home on these courts. This, for Andres, was where it had all begun. The first time he ever saw a tennis ball bounce, it had bounced on the powdery red clay right there at the Real Club of Barcelona where his father was the club professional. That made it all the more of a challenge for me. So, too, did the fact that Gimeno had beaten me the week before in Cologne on a fast indoor carpet that should have been ideally suited to my serve-and-volley game. So the match provides an indication of how a player should set about trying to overcome certain tactical and psychological disadvantages.

Also, I have deliberately chosen a match that I won. Not to show how clever I am, for even in winning it I made mistakes that would rightly mortify the average club player. But rather because I think it best that the story be told from the winner's side of the net. I am a firm believer in a positive approach to any tennis match, no matter what the level of play. Even if the odds are stacked heavily against you, never anticipate defeat before you go on court. Even if the person you are about to play is obviously more experienced, more powerful, and more talented than you, he is also human and therefore susceptible to the "off" day. Why shouldn't it be today? Always think positively. Always give yourself a chance.

So although the odds were definitely with the Spaniard on this occasion, I did my best to minimize them in my own mind. Granted he was better equipped for the clay-court game; but, I quickly reminded myself, I was no stranger to the stuff either. The only WCT title I had won at that point had, after all, been on clay in Tehran. And although he would have the crowd's vociferous support, he would be nervous; and nerves have always been one of Andres' greatest handicaps. Yes, I told myself, the pressure in many ways would be on him.

Tactically, of course, I approached the match very differently from the one in Cologne a week earlier. On the fast carpet I had only one thought—aggression. I went to the net behind both my first and second serve and when Gimeno was serving I tried to return the ball as low as possible over the net. In this way I limited the chance of his being able to make a decisive first volley and thus gave myself the one opportunity I was likely to get of making a passing shot. Although I did not play well enough to make them work in Cologne, these are sound tactics for anybody playing on a fast surface where the rallies are short and the chances to break service rare.

On clay, it would be another story. Here it is necessary to prepare mentally for the fact that most of the tennis is played from the back-court. The rallies would be long—sometimes interminably long—and they would require enormous patience and concentration. The reasons for this revolve around the very basic fact that on clay it is extremely difficult to hit a winner. It is not only the lack of speed of the ball off the court which makes this so, but also the slowness of the ball through the air because the balls fluff up and become very heavy. So even if you do manage to hit a good hard shot to the corner, the chances are that your opponent will be able to run it down. And even the strongest server can forget about hitting a significant number of aces.

All this was going through my mind as we warmed up on the

outside court nearest the clubhouse where a large and eager crowd had already gathered. The warm-up itself deserves attention for it is a vital part of any preparation for a match. First of all, avoid the mistake of trying to hit the ball too hard. This is not the moment to show off all your best shots. Keep your knees bent, watch the ball right on to your racket, and stroke it. In other words work yourself into the groove you would like your game to be in throughout the match. Get the basics working fluently; ease your swing into its natural rhythm; loosen up. If you feel you want to work a little on one particular stroke, then ask your opponent to give you some balls on your forehand or whatever, and of course be prepared to do the same for him. Among the pros, it is routine for us to give each other all the shots to hit, but I remember warming up against guys who insisted on hitting winners all the time. Don't let them get away with it. Remind them, if necessary, that the warm-up is for both of you and that you would appreciate a little cooperation. Remember, especially, to hit a lot of serves—at least twenty—so that you can start serving flat out with all your muscles properly warmed up. The best way to pull a muscle is to try to unleash an ace in the first game when you are still cold.

Some players take a great deal more time to get grooved than others, and if you are still a slow starter after all this preparation in the warm-up, don't get discouraged. John Newcombe is a slow starter and Rod Laver notoriously so. And most people who play on a varied assortment of surfaces find it takes longer to get into the rhythm of a clay-court match.

Gimeno, winning the toss and electing to serve, held for fifteen in the opening game and then I won my own serve also to fifteen. It was 1-1 in the first set.

I was coming in behind my first serve, looking for the telling first volley that, on clay, really has to be thumped or acutely angled if it is to make any impression. My tactics at the outset were based on cautious aggression. When playing on an alien surface, ideally one should try to marry the demands of that surface with one's own natural style. In other words a serve-and-volley player competing on clay should never come charging blindly into the net as a matter of routine nor should he retire into an unfamiliar pattern of defensive play and remain rooted to the base line. Unless his ground strokes are uncommonly sound, the serve and volleyer will find himself outrallied by the clay-courter in the end, even if it takes all afternoon.

So it is really a matter of judgment. Choosing the right moment to go into the net is the all-important factor. The natural serve-and-volley player should always be pressing to get up there, but it is essential that he prepare his path with careful approach shots or deep, punishing serves. If he has his opponent stretching, retreating, or off balance, then—and only then—should he go to the net. Under any other circumstances a good clay-courter will take cool, deliberate aim and pass him any way he pleases.

As far as specific tactics relating to this match were concerned, I was also concentrating on Gimeno's backhand. Obviously I had the advantage of knowing my opponent's game intimately—and he mine—and I knew that, whereas he could hurt me on the forehand, he could do little more than place, or occasionally lob, off the backhand flank. If you are playing someone you have never seen before, as often happens in interclub matches, try to get a quick feel of his strengths and weaknesses and remember them. In the later stages of the match this knowledge could prove vital.

However "playing to the backhand" doesn't necessarily mean hitting every single shot to that side. Once you become accustomed to playing on clay, you develop patterns for the rallies. Against Gimeno, I was hitting two consecutive strokes to his backhand and then sliding one away to his forehand to make him run. Then I reverted to the backhand for two more strokes. So I developed a two, one, two pattern with the accent on the backhand. It can, of course, be reversed if it is the forehand you wish to pressure. This pattern play also tests your opponent's stamina and patience. It's hard work running from side to side under a hot sun and if your opponent is not sure of his ability to last the duration, he may be tempted into rash strokes in an effort to break up the pattern.

The same, of course, is true when the man on the other side

of the net is directing the traffic and forcing you to do the running. If you are fully confident of both your own fitness and ability to hit ground strokes ad nauseam, stick with it until his length and accuracy falter. Only then should you attempt to break up the pattern and attack. When you get that short ball which permits an approach to the net, come in fast; hit deep for the corner and cover the line. As a straight line is the shortest distance between two points, the chances are that your opponent will go down the line rather than cross-court, so you will be playing the percentages by anticipating that type of return.

But on clay, in particular, there is something else to watch for: the lob. Gimeno soon started throwing up some good lobs, encouraged, no doubt, by the fact that I like to play very close to the net when I do come in. As soon as your opponent starts to get into the groove with his lobs there is no alternative but to back off the net a little so that you are better prepared to run back and retrieve them.

There was one other noteworthy incident during these opening exchanges. During the second point of the match Gimeno served wide to my backhand and, as I reached for it, the force of the ball knocked the racket from my hand. However, I still managed to get the ball back over the net. I tried to recover my racket in time to stay in the point, but he volleyed away a simple winner at the net. If this happens to you, always make an attempt to get hold of your racket again no matter how hopeless the situation may seem. I have been involved in many instances like this when the player who dropped his racket has won the point, mainly because his opponent has been distracted. The sight of you floundering around trying to find your racket may well tempt him to take his eye off the ball and as soon as he does that, you are back in the point with a chance.

In the third game I held break point on Gimeno's service at 30-40, lost it when he drew me wide on the backhand, moved to ad point with a short cross-court pass off the backhand, and clinched the break for 2-1 when he put a backhand out.

The short cross-court backhand pass was crucial in that game and it was a shot I played with increasing effect throughout the

match. It was a stroke I had only recently added to my repertoire
—out of necessity, really, because my natural instinct had always been to go down the line with my backhand passing shot.
Players on the tour had become so accustomed to this that they
had started playing the odds and simply sat on the line waiting
for it.

The short cross-court ball was, strangely, one that I had
worked on developing in matches rather than on the practice
court and it had changed my thinking on how to hit a passing
shot. Instead of belting the ball as hard and as close to the line
as possible, I just let it roll, short and easy, a foot or two inside
the line. By not pushing for the very edge of the line nor worrying about trying to hit the ball really hard, I was giving myself
a much better chance of making the shot. And even if it also
gave my opponent a greater chance of reaching the ball, the odds
were against his being able to hit a winner off it. In case he did,
I would be well placed to put away the return. These tactics are
just another aspect of percentage tennis, and unless your opponent is as fast as Laver or Nastase, you should find the percentages working for you.

*In the fourth game I led 40-love on my service, got passed
and lobbed three times coming into the net, held one more ad
point, and then lost the game on forcing forehand errors. It was
now 2-2.*

It was a stupid game on my part. I was starting to be too aggressive. At a break and 40-love up, I should have taken my
time and let him do the worrying. Instead I came storming in
behind my serve and watched the balls go by.

*In the next game I grabbed another break, aided once again
by a short cross-court backhand pass; I held my own serve in
the sixth game, throwing in an ace for good measure, and then
Gimeno held service to take the score to 4-3 in my favor.*

Technically I was in good shape but I still wasn't very happy
with my game. Even though I held serve in the sixth game, I
allowed Andres to take it to deuce after I had led 30-love. The
ace I served a few points later was the only easy point I won,
and too often I wasn't taking advantage of simple opportunities

to establish a commanding lead. I had him 15-30 on his serve
in the seventh game and let the chance slip. "Concentrate!" I
told myself furiously. During one of the long rallies that developed I even committed the sin of trying to break up the pattern with a drop shot. I'm not a drop shot expert—few players
brought up on fast surfaces are—and when I netted it I paid
the price for not obeying the rule which says, "Don't try to win
crucial points with shots you don't have." I think I tried four
drop shots in all during the match and only made one of them.
That's not very good percentage tennis.

*A total of four forehand errors on my part helped Gimeno
break back for 4-all. He held serve with a great lob at 40-30
in the ninth game, and then broke me again—this time to love—
to take the set 6-4.*

I had led 40-30 when he broke me the first time and again
I blew it by going for an aggressive forehand down the line and
missing. I was still trying to be too aggressive. That unnecessary
error let him into the game and into the set. Another piece of
bad thinking let him hold serve for 5-4 when I misjudged that
lob on game point at 40-30. I thought it was going long and
started chasing it far too late. I should have realized that the
balls were fluffing up and getting heavier. A little extra weight
makes all the difference between a lob floating out or dropping
in. "Think, Marty, think." I was really mad at myself by that
time, for I knew I should have covered that lob whether I
thought it was going out or not. *Always* run back to cover a
lob unless you are desperately trying to conserve energy at the
end of a long match. I had been having trouble timing my forehand for most of the set but now, as I chose another ill-judged
moment to attack, my backhand slipped out of its groove, too.
By trying too hard, by rushing my shots, I handed the set to
Andres in deplorable fashion.

*Gimeno held service in the opening game of the second set to
love and then broke immediately as I made further errors on the
forehand. Gimeno led 2-0 in the second set.*

The match was suddenly swinging away from me, and at this
stage the battle I was fighting was as much mental as it was phys-

ical. Confidence is everything in this sort of crisis and I kept telling myself that no match is lost just because you are a set and a break down. I was fit enough to last as long as was necessary, and that was what mattered. Tennis isn't just a question of being able to hit a ball well and play classy strokes. Proper physical conditioning is vital, too, not simply because it enables you to run more quickly for longer periods but because the very fact of knowing you are fit gives you the will and the determination to keep on fighting.

But that alone is not enough. There is another rule to be observed. Always change a losing game. Despite my private prematch pep talk about the patience required to win on clay, I had been too aggressive. I had been giving too much free rein to my natural style and paying too little attention to the rigorous demands of that clinging red clay. So I had another severe talk with myself and set about climbing back into the match.

At 30-40 in the third game Gimeno put a backhand out to give me the break back, and after that games went with serve until 3-all, second set.

The first order of business as far as I was concerned was to get my forehand working. So although it meant playing to his strength, I started hitting my forehand cross-court to his forehand corner instead of going down the line onto his backhand. Almost immediately I regained my rhythm and found a good length. The break-back in the third game lifted my spirits and although he tried to tire me in the fourth game with a series of well-judged lobs, I dealt with the overheads confidently and felt better for it. Many players have difficulty in deciding whether or not to take a lob on the full. I follow this rule: If the lob is going to fall nearer the base line than the service line or if I find I am badly positioned to get the angle I want, I let the ball bounce. Otherwise I take it on the full. Also when you are on the receiving end of an overhead, watch which way your opponent hits his smash. Many players tend to hit their overheads always the same way and if you note this, you will have a better chance of knowing which area of the court to cover.

I broke Gimeno's service on my third break point of a tough

game to lead 4-3 and then dropped my own serve to love. The
score was 4-4.

Once again I worked hard for a breakthrough, got it, and then
chucked it away through a maddening impulse to rush into the
attack. Three hurried, careless forehand errors offered Andres
just the kind of present he was looking for and I could hardly
believe my own stupidity. "You've been telling yourself to stay
calm, to stay in the back-court, and to take your time, and you
do exactly the opposite," I told myself in the course of another
long self-lecture. "You've really got to stop it. If you can't control your mind better than that, you've got no chance."

We both held serve for 5-all and then I forced Gimeno into
errors with some good overheads as he threw up several more
lobs and I broke to lead 6-5. Still using the overhead to good
effect, I served out for the set 7-5.

It had become obvious by this time that Gimeno wasn't hurting me. I was simply hurting myself by being too impetuous.
Having finally convinced myself of this fact after dropping service
in that eighth game, I was free at last of any inner conflict. I had
made up my mind to stay back and only work my way into the
net slowly and calmly as the situation allowed. This, of course,
was what I had set out to do at the beginning, but it is amazing
how difficult it is to curb years of conditioning that have taught
you to go for the jugular when you have your man down. But
now, at long last, I had myself on a leash and when I served in
the tenth game I stayed in the back-court, swinging freely through
my shots now that I had found my length and touch, and I scored
with some apparently casual passers. Andres thought I had
"gone," as we say. He thought I looked so relaxed that I had
virtually given up. The change in tactic and the peace of mind
that had come from having made a final and irrevocable decision as to how to play him had, in fact, relaxed me—but not to
the point of carelessness or defeatism. On the contrary, I was
relaxed because I felt confident that the pendulum was swinging
for the last time in this strange, fluctuating encounter and that
it was swinging my way. When, at 6-5 and 40-30 on my serve
—the second set point in my favor—I maneuvered him out of

position at the climax of a long rally and put away a sound smash, I knew the momentum had really changed.

I broke Gimeno in the opening game of the third set and again in the third to lead 3-0 with a leaping backhand volley. He double-faulted to go 5-0 down in the fifth game and I completed the sudden headlong rush to victory by serving out in the next game to take the set 6-0.

Luck and a little piece of good judgment on my part helped turn my intuition into reality in the opening game of the third set. A blocked half volley which sent the ball leaping back over the net for a spectacular winner on the third point was definitely a case of a lot of luck aiding a little skill, and it put Gimeno love-40 down on his serve. He fought back to deuce and I felt it was important not to let him escape. A service break so soon after losing the second set would be a big psychological blow and I thought the situation called for a surprise tactic—something to catch him off balance. So I let rip with a forehand service return down the line off a second serve—a shot I had not tried since switching to the cross-court stroke on my forehand a set earlier. I hit it well and it was a winner all the way, primarily because Gimeno was not expecting it. It gave me break point and when a let ball bounced back into his court to give me that vital 1-0 lead, Andres' luck seemed to have run dry.

Gimeno seemed to lose heart after that, and in the third game he put up an aimless lob—a strange thing for Andres to do, for this vastly experienced and canny player rarely hits a shot that has no purpose. I knew then that I had him in my clutches and this time I didn't let go. I maintained the pressure without doing anything reckless and found games coming my way thick and fast.

It was odd to be sweeping through the deciding set with such comparative ease after all that had gone before. But it offered a fine example of how a match—and, in particular, a clay-court match—can be turned around with careful thought and disciplined application of the correct tactics. It is a demanding, frustrating surface but no victory tastes quite as sweet as one on clay.

23

WHAT TO WATCH

How do you watch a tennis match? Do you just sit back and take in the overall scene, waiting to be entertained by a spectacular shot on a crucial point? Well, that's okay. We are there to entertain you, and like any spectator sport, pro tennis is trying to offer excitement and diversion for the fan who just wants to go out and enjoy himself.

But the spectator's role doesn't have to be that passive. Instead of merely watching, you can study a tennis match. That takes almost as much concentration as playing in it. But if you are interested in improving your own game, it can be worth the exercise, for there are many things to be learned by zeroing in on a particular stroke and trying to analyze how the player hits it and why. Apart from helping you when you next get the chance to play, an analytical approach to tennis watching can also make the pastime much more enjoyable and fulfilling.

To give the spectator some idea of what to watch, I will cover each basic stroke in the game and discuss the players who, in my opinion, execute those strokes in the classical manner—players, in fact, whose strokes deserve to be imitated.

The Serve   For pure classical economy of motion, no one in the game can match the serve of Pancho Gonzales. There is nothing forced or hurried about it—just a smooth, easy coordination of effort that almost inevitably produces devastating results.

To my mind, the secret of Pancho's serving success stems from

278

his toss. Many players vary the position or height of their toss either by accident or in a deliberate attempt to avoid throwing the ball up into the sun or against the wind. But not Gonzales. He places the ball up there in exactly the same position each time. By doing so, he is far less likely to lose the smoothness of rhythm that all good players work on in practice. Great serving is mainly a question of rhythm and timing, and the toss is the starting point of that flowing synchronized cycle. If you vary the first note, the result is a jangling mass of discord all the way through the set piece.

Watch how Gonzales comes through the backswing very slowly. That, too, never changes. The speed and power that he puts onto the serve will vary only at the last moment as the arm comes up over the shoulder. Most of the time he will serve at three-quarters pace, allowing the entire movement of his perfectly coordinated action to give his delivery extra pace. A final thrust of speed with the racket and a snap in the wrist are the factors that create the blockbuster Gonzales ace.

As he demonstrated when he reached the final of the Pacific Southwest Championships in Los Angeles in September 1972, Roscoe Tanner now possesses one of the most dangerous serves in pro tennis. But I would not recommend that anyone try to copy it. In marked contrast to Gonzales, Tanner has a very quick action and a very low toss. I didn't have the chance to study his serve at great length in Los Angeles, but from what I could see, he may even hit the ball before it reaches the full height of the toss. To do this and still keep the ball inside the service line requires absolutely perfect timing because the server is hitting forward instead of down. Nikki Pilic, another left-hander, also has a very low toss, and while this makes it easier to serve in the wind—and more difficult for the receiver to "pick" its direction—it leaves far less margin for error.

Charlie Pasarell provides the opposite example to Tanner in that he throws the ball high and twists his whole body back and around in a corkscrew motion before swooping down on the ball. It is a classical service action because he is really getting his shoulder moving into the stroke. This enables him to serve very hard; there are days when I find Charlie's service the toughest of all to handle. Although it is well worth imitating, I would hesitate to recommend your doing so unless you have very strong back muscles, for Charlie's action puts a tremendous strain on the lower back.

No one would recommend copying the ugly-looking windup that is the most catching feature of Roy Emerson's service, but then I doubt if anyone could if they tried! There are, however, some good features about Emmo's service—there have to be, otherwise he wouldn't have won all those grass-court titles. Notice how he drops the racket head all the way down his back at the start of his swing. As he brings the racket up and over from this position he gets a lot of shoulder twist into his action, which is a vital ingredient of a good serve.

And what about the famous Arthur Ashe service? Frankly I don't think it is quite as good as it used to be. Arthur has never totally regained the beautiful fluidity of rhythm that enabled him to wreak such havoc with his serve before he suffered a shoulder injury in 1969. He does hit streaks when his serve can be as effective as ever; however there now seems to be a subconscious check in the movement at the last moment so that he almost seems to be pushing the ball instead of letting the swing flow right through. The difference is minuscule and often Arthur himself is not even aware of it. But it provides a clue, I think, as to why he has not been as consistent as he was during the period leading up to his victory in the U.S. Open in 1968.

The Forehand Quite rightly, everyone raves about Rod Laver's backhand, but I feel that it is the power and consistency of his forehand which provides the sheet anchor to his game. Certainly I find Rod's forehand the toughest shot to handle. His backhand is predictable in that he will go cross-court with it if he can, but I am rarely able to pick the passing shot off his forehand.

Watching Laver hit a forehand, you will notice how he comes into the ball very low, knees bent, perfectly positioned. Then, just as he makes contact he will straigthen slightly, coming over the ball to load it with top spin. The discouraging thing about

playing Rocket is that even when you do get him out of position
and force him wide, the incredible strength of his wrist enables
him to hit the ball with equal power and accuracy on the run.

A good forehand is also one of Ilie Nastase's greatest assets.
Another peculiarity of Nastase's game is that he chips the ball
off his forehand. That makes him unique among modern-day
players. I have often read about the forehand "chop" that was
so favored by the great players of the twenties and thirties, but
apart from Manuel Santana, who also used it on clay, the
chipped forehand—as we call it now—is practically extinct.
Nastase may well put it back in fashion.

Although it is unlikely that you will get many more opportunities to watch Santana now that he has practically retired
from the game, his forehand will be remembered by all who saw
the great Spaniard in his prime—and certainly by those of us
who played against him! It was one of the outstanding shots of
the modern era and it had one particularly devastating quality
that can best be described as a curved ball. By some magical
use of spin, Manolo could make the ball curve back into play
when he went for a down-the-line passing shot. I hate to think
of the number of times I let balls go because they were actually
outside the court area as they passed me, only to turn and see
the curve bring the ball back and drop it on the line. Santana
was an artist, all right.

The Backhand   No one hits the backhand as consistently well
as Ken Rosewall. Laver may hit it harder and sometimes he has
streaks when he is more dangerous with the stroke. But day in
and day out, the Rosewall backhand has to be one of the greatest
shots in the game. Off the return of serve, both Rosewall and
Laver like to chip—thus forcing the server to volley up—but
on the next stroke of the rally they differ in that Rod opts for
aggression with top spin while Kenny prefers solid placement
with a shot that is hit almost flat.

If you are looking for perfection in tennis, watch how many
times Rosewall clears the net by no more than an inch off his
backhand. He keeps the ball lower and hits closer to the line
on a higher percentage of shots than any other player I have

seen, and that is as near perfection as one is going to get on a tennis court.

The secret to Rosewall's success lies in his footwork. Try to forget everything else that is happening in a match for five minutes and keep your eyes riveted on Kenny's feet. Then you might begin to understand why this is so. Watch how rarely he is off balance; watch how nine balls out of every ten are hit as if he were giving a demonstration of perfect positioning for a photographer on a practice court. Most of us on the pro tour hit a tennis ball as well as Rosewall—many of us can certainly hit it harder—but there is one vital difference: Ken's anticipation and speed enable him to get into position before the ball arrives, whereas most of us are still running, stretching, and struggling to adjust to that textbook position when we have to make the stroke. There are, of course, occasions when Rosewall is *not* stepping into the ball, taking it on the rise out in front of him, shoulder turned into the line of flight, knees bent and racket swinging through a smooth, precise arc. But compared to most players, those occasions seem to be very rare.

The Lob   Again, watch Rosewall. I have found no one who lobs more often or more accurately than Ken. If I win the toss and begin serving against him, I know that I will have to handle two or three lobs in the first game. There are sound tactical reasons why he lobs so much right at the start of a match. He does it to make me stretch and bend before I am thoroughly loose; he does it to keep me away from my favorite volleying position close to the net, thus preventing me from getting into the groove on my volley and, by forcing me to watch and cover for the possibility of a lob, he gives himself more room to make passing shots down the line.

He will lob an opponent down the line off his forehand which—if you start looking for it—will give him a setup for a forehand cross-court pass, and then, on another point, he'll lob cross-court off the backhand and so open the gap for the backhand pass down the line. The tactics are fundamental but few players can execute them with such pinpoint accuracy as this mesmerizing little Australian.

Unlike other expert exponents of the lob—Nastase, for instance—Rosewall is not looking to win the point outright with this shot. Nastase uses the aggressive top-spin lob with the intention of winning the point then and there. Rosewall, who hits most of his lobs with underspin, is merely trying to force an opponent into the back-court so that he can move to the net and take charge of the rally. Nastase produces one of his spiraling top-spin winners as a spectacular surprise tactic on a crucial break point. But Rosewall employs the lob more or less continuously throughout the match, moving his opponent up to the net and back again as if he had him on a string. The result is, of course, frustratingly predictable for the man on the other side of that net who suddenly discovers that it is he and not his 37-year-old opponent who is getting worn out.

The Volley Before his arm injury started to plague his career, Tony Roche's backhand volley was as confident and as solid a stroke as one could see on the tour. At the peak of his form, Tony was practically infallible with it. He never seemed to lose control of it and even when he was fully extended, covering a wide return, he still had the strength to punch it away with power and precision.

Roy Emerson's backhand volley is just as good. Like Roche, Emmo can hit hard and true for the corners with great power. John Newcombe stands out as a player with an especially effective forehand volley, as he is always decisive with it. He knows precisely where he wants to hit the ball long before it reaches his racket and it doesn't really matter where his opponent happens to be at the time. Great volleyers tend to play their favorite shot, knowing that if they connect properly, it will be a winner no matter where the other guy is standing.

Bob Lutz is also a fine volleyer although somewhat different in style to these three Australians. You will notice how Bob uses more touch and finesse on the volley, preferring to use acute angles and deflections rather than sheer power—although he has plenty of that, too.

The Drop Shot Most top-class European clay-court players have a good drop shot but few were quite as expert at it as

Manolo Santana. When he felt like entertaining the crowd he would underslice a drop shot so that the ball would spin back into the net. Nastase is just as effective with the stroke now, but you will notice that even he does not use the stroke very often.

The drop shot requires touch, but more than that it requires tactical judgment if it is to be truly effective. No one playing percentage tennis tries to drop shot from the back-court. The odds of a player winning the point by doing so are just not good enough. Like the drop volley, which requires perfect timing and a loose wrist, the drop shot can be used most effectively as you approach the net, having driven your opponent deep and wide on the previous stroke.

The Overhead   There are a lot of players with exceptionally good overheads in the game today. Pierre Barthes, the acrobatic Frenchman, is one and Rob Maud is particularly solid when the ball is high in the air, Stan Smith, of course, uses his great height to get up there and put away anything but the most perfect lob, but height is not essential. Once again Rosewall provides an example. Ken has one of the best overheads in the game, but more often than not he will let the ball bounce so that he can get himself perfectly positioned to choose his spot for the put-away.

If you watch carefully, you will notice that many players prefer to smash in one direction, and that is why you will often see a player racing full tilt to one side of the court as his opponent prepares to hit the overhead. The man on the receiving end is gambling that, by covering the court his opponent prefers to smash into, he will force him to switch direction and miss. And there is always the chance that he will take his eye off the ball for a fraction of a second as his opponent makes a sudden dash in one direction or the other. Most times it is a hopeless gesture, but it is still better than just standing still.

The Half Volley   Bob Hewitt's great feel for the ball makes him one of the best half volleyers in the game at the moment. Bob's burly build gives him a deceptive appearance on court. In reality, he is one of the finest touch players of his era and often it is his temper that beats him—not his opponent.

Certainly the half volley is not a good shot to try when you are tense. It requires a relaxed arm and perfect judgment—not only of timing but of where the racket should be in relation to the bounce of the ball. Hewitt is particularly good at getting his racket firmly behind the ball as it comes up off the court, and his touch is such that he can control the stroke beautifully.

Depending on the speed of the court, the racket should be between half a foot and a foot behind the ball as it bounces. It will rise about a half foot off the court before it meets the racket, and this combination of angles should produce the desired result—providing you have sufficient feel for the shot, which is something that only comes with considerable practice.

I find that most players reared on cement have a good half volley; cement is a surface with a generally true bounce—a factor that encourages use of the stroke. Dennis Ralston, who learned much of his tennis at the University of Southern California, has a good half volley and the legendary Whitney Reed, who is still active in local Northern California tennis, seemed to spend much of his time in mid-court when he was on the circuit—scooping all sorts of unlikely shots off his toes.

These, then, are the basic strokes of tennis and the players who, in my opinion, play them best. If you really study how they hit the ball, you won't do your own game any harm at all.